Photo essay

1 Toronto skyline
2 St Joseph's Oratory, Montreal
3 Québec old town

6

8

9

6 Bow lake at Banff National Park
7 Boat garage
8 Canada geese

9 Polar bears
10 Snowy owl

15 Parliament buildings, Ottawa

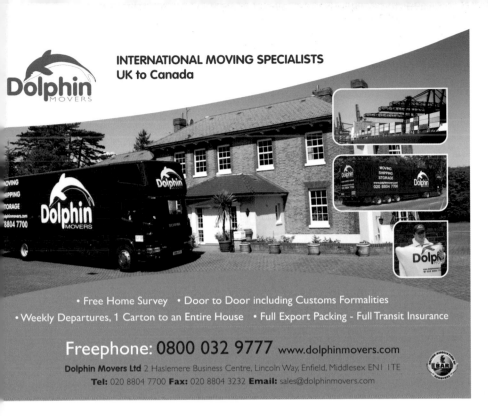

INTERNATIONAL MOVING SPECIALISTS
UK to Canada

- Free Home Survey • Door to Door including Customs Formalities
- Weekly Departures, 1 Carton to an Entire House • Full Export Packing - Full Transit Insurance

Freephone: 0800 032 9777 www.dolphinmovers.com

Dolphin Movers Ltd 2 Haslemere Business Centre, Lincoln Way, Enfield, Middlesex EN1 1TE
Tel: 020 8804 7700 **Fax:** 020 8804 3232 **Email:** sales@dolphinmovers.com

Dolphin Movers provides a professional portfolio of relocation services that are reliable, prompt, cost-effective and responsive to the requirements of each individual.

Our services include international and national removals, shipping and storage solutions throughout the UK.

. Overseas Removals to any destination in the world. We provide fully export-packed, door-to-door removal services, not only from but also into the UK. We offer frequent services to Australia, New Zealand, USA & Canada.

. Excess Baggage & Small Consignments can be moved by air, sea or road, in the least possible time or cost.

Storage is available either for the short or long term prior to your move. We can store anything from a single box through to the complete contents of your home.

FOR FURTHER INFORMATION & TO BOOK YOUR FREE HOME SURVEY
PLEASE CONTACT US ON
Freephone **0800 032 9777**, email **sales@dolphinmovers.com**
or visit us on **www.dolphinmovers.com**

Canada offers an exciting range of opportunities for many prospective migrants, including those who do not currently fit the Federal Skilled Worker Program. Immigration Unit specialise in helping prospective migrants in all walks of life to fast track through this often lengthy process (currently processing times exceed 5 years through this route!).

With a shortage of skilled professionals and tradespeople in Canada, student courses have become a desirable route to permanent residency. You can retrain at an accredited institution in many occupations in trades and the hospitality industry, either in Canada or whilst still living and working in your current country of residence. Most courses begin with the equivalent of 9 to 12 weeks of full-time study then move on to the more practical aspects of your chosen occupation whilst you still attend college on a part-time basis.

A number of Canadian provinces now have "Occupations Under Pressure" lists. Our job placement services in Canada can arrange work for you in a wide range of occupations, particularly within the trade and hospitality industries. You can live, work, and lodge permanent residence applications after your arrival. You won't have to wait years outside Canada whilst your application is being processed.

When you arrive in Canada, you are greeted by a Relocation Unit who are there to provide practical support to help you settle into your new home. They will arrange accommodation and a rental vehicle ready for when you arrive in Canada and will make you feel at home when you get there, even providing you with a mobile phone so you can contact family and friends.

We have many years' experience in helping people with training, education and relocation. We can help you realise your dream of a new life in Canada.

Horizon Properties is a <u>free</u> service designed to match you with your ideal real estate agent !

In today's fast-paced property market, having the right agent on your side can make a tremendous difference. Horizon Properties understands this.

That is why our goal is to match you with your ideal Canada real estate agent based on your unique needs and criteria. Using our extensive network of top-notch agents from across the country, Horizon Properties will help put you in touch with the Canada real estate broker who is willing and able to make your property dreams come true. Our free service was designed specifically to facilitate our clients' experience **selling homes with a real estate agent in Canada**, **buying a house in Canada**, and **relocating to Canada**. We guarantee our service through our post-sell/buy survey to ensure that our standards always meet yours.

Visit our website today!!

www.horizonproperties.ca

Patrick Twomey

Working and Living
CANADA

CADOGANguides

Contents

07

Working in Canada 217

08

References 243

Author's acknowledgements

Writing both editions of *Working and Living Canada* has been an interesting project to undertake and would not have come to fruition without the help and support of numerous people. First I would like to offer a warm thank you to my friend **John Watson**, who connected me with this work and offered excellent advice throughout. John is busy with his own writing endeavours in London, but we certainly hope to see him back in Canada one day soon.

I would like to extend my gratitude to everyone I interviewed, with questions ranging from welfare to personal case studies. Specifically, I would like to recognise **Rod Faulkner** (the computer guru), **Murray Hainer** (teacher, climber, skier and enthusiastic Canadian), my brother **Graham** and **Dr Alan Finkel** who has helped to reveal difficult aspects of Canada's social history. I would also like to remember **Jose Rodrigo**, who lived a fascinating life and chose British Columbia for his final quarter-century, and **Sue Yates** who shared his vision and has long been a wonderful friend to my family and me.

I would like to extend a loving thank you to my wife, **Sarah**, for her continuous support. As an immigrant to Canada, Sarah has had to navigate many of the often-unclear steps involved in making a new home in this beautiful country. Lastly, since the first edition we have been joined by our beautiful son, **Finn** – the joy he brings is infectious and as an enthusiastic young Canadian he already expresses himself in both official languages!

About the author

Patrick Twomey was born in Vancouver and grew up in western Canada. His father is from an Irish back-ground, and immigrated to Canada from Britain in the 1960s. With duel nationality Patrick has worked, travelled and studied in over 25 countries and of course across Canada. He completed a university degree in history followed by Latin American studies at graduate level. As a life-long student, he is now pursuing further graduate studies. He speaks fluent French, Spanish and English.

Patrick has been guiding tours through over 25 countries on and off for 13 years and has led over 100 trips in Canada. In addition to another guide book, Patrick developed a tourism training manual for the Chilean Park service and is currently pursuing various other writing projects. When he is not on the road exploring or guiding, Patrick is at home with his wife, Sarah, and their son Finn. They have spent the last four years living in Edmonton's beautiful river valley, but are in the process of planning a new adventure!

Cadogan Guides is an imprint of
New Holland Publishers (UK) Ltd
London • Cape Town • Sydney • Auckland

New Holland Publishers (UK) Ltd	80 McKenzie Street	Unit 1, 66 Gibbes Street	218 Lake Road
Garfield House,	Cape Town 8001	Chatswood, NSW 2067	Northcote
86–88 Edgware Road	South Africa	Australia	Auckland
London W2 2EA			New Zealand

www.cadoganguides.com
t 44 (0)20 7724 7773

Distributed in the United States by Globe Pequot, Connecticut

Cover photographs: Back cover © Natalia Bratslavsky/SHUTTERSTOCK; front cover all SHUTTERSTOCK, © Hannamariah, © Elena Elisseeva, © Volodymyr Kyrylyuk, © robcocquyt, © Chris Howey, © Mayskyphoto
Photo essay photographs all from Fotolia.com: © Viktor Gmyria, © outdoorsman, © Bernt-Inge.com, © Howard Sandler, © Andrew Breeden, © Amma, © Theresa Martinez, © rrruss, © RFphoto, © Sharon Day, © Sam Spiro, © GJ Thomson, © Ulrike Hammerich, © glen gaffney, © Jodie Johnson, © Paul Lechevallier
Maps © Cadogan Guides, drawn by Maidenhead Cartographic Services Ltd
Cover design: Sarah Rianhard-Gardner
Layout and editing: Linda McQueen
Proofreading: Dominique Shead
Indexing: Isobel McLean

Produced by **Navigator Guides**
www.navigatorguides.com

Printed in Finland by WS Bookwell
A catalogue record for this book is available from the British Library

ISBN: 978-1-86011-404-5

The author and publishers have made every effort to ensure the accuracy of the information in this book at the time of going to press. However, they cannot accept any responsibility for any loss, injury or inconvenience resulting from the use of information contained in this guide.

Please help us to keep this guide up to date. We have done our best to ensure that the information in this guide is correct at the time of going to press. But laws and regulations are constantly changing, and standards and prices fluctuate. We would be delighted to receive any comments.

Introduction

People from Britain and Ireland have been going to work and live in Canada for a very long time, and Canada now stands as the number one choice for people emigrating from the UK. Canada's two official languages – English and French – mark the country's colonial past, but do not reveal the whole story. Aboriginal people have lived in North America for thousands of years and Europeans have been crossing the Atlantic ever since a group of Vikings built a village in Newfoundland 1,000 years ago.

As is expressed throughout this book, Canada is as much a concept, or geographical area, as it is one unified nation. Relatively safe, prosperous and infinitely diverse, Canada is a confederation of ten provinces and three territories spread between three oceans. Most Canadians see themselves as just that – Canadian – but a move to the Great White North means choosing a region and lifestyle. From big city sophistication to tiny villages in the high Arctic, the Canadian experience is driven by climate, culture and economy. Understanding what part of Canada best suits your lifestyle choices will determine many other factors.

Chapter 01 gives a broad historical overview of Canada as well as discussing climate, language and food – all of which are extremely varied in a country larger in territory than Europe. Chapter 02 continues by looking at Canada in terms of its regions, including localised culture and economy. Chapter 03 explores social and political aspects including religion, government, economics, culture and sports. Chapters 04 and 05 begin to examine your move to Canada. Having helped you get there in Chapter 04, in Chapter 05 we launch into the red tape, offering a solid overview of the rather complicated bureaucratic process of moving to Canada.

Chapter 06 is dedicated to the basics of living in Canada, discussing everything from finding a home to taking your pets. Some aspects of daily life will be very familiar to you, whereas others are quite distinct. Chapter 07 then looks at working in Canada. In a young country with a disparate population, the working environment is in many ways less structured than in Europe. As a result of the country's size, raw statistics about Canada's economy offer little real economic advice. Included in this chapter are some interesting work ideas, particularly for working holidays, as well as information about taxation, the labour market and the initial steps of starting a business. Chapter 08 concludes the guide with a helpful Reference section.

Throughout *Working and Living Canada* you will enjoy a variety of information boxes and personal case studies that discuss everything from 'The Greatest Canadian' to the national anthem. In order to help you with your move, many links to appropriate websites are listed. When applicable, telephone numbers are also included, but, embracing the new economy, much business in Canada is now conducted online rather than by phone.

Canada is a beautiful land, full of energy and opportunity. It is the aim of this guide to make your transition as smooth as possible.

Getting to Know Canada

01

The world's second largest country seems made for superlatives: vast, extreme, beautiful, diverse, sparse, cold, staid and unique. From its almost-infinite north, gleaming white for much of the year, to the countless clogged lanes of traffic circling the dense population corridor around Toronto, Canada as an entity encompasses a peculiar world that is defined more often by what it is not than by what it is. With barely over 30 million inhabitants, the Great White North is a series of diverse communities loosely tied together across a continent. Inhabited for possibly over 50,000 years, 'Canada' means simply 'village' in the words of the Iroquois. Alternatively, the name may have come from the Spanish, who found nothing of value here – *aca nada* – or, to the French ear, 'Canada'. Any understanding of the country that spans the width of North America and extends from the Great Lakes to well above the Arctic Circle will depend a great deal on which part is being discussed.

The First Nations or aboriginal people of the west coast were somewhat sedentary and are known for their evocative totem poles. The Plains natives, on the other hand, who knew little of the temperate coast, hunted buffalo by following the herds and engaged in trading. Further east, the Mohawks, Iroquois and Huron peoples had more defined borders and were some of the first to encounter Europeans. To the north, the Cree and Inuit (Eskimo) people have survived and even flourished in a world of utter extremes.

Even in the modern Canada of today, people in the prairies encounter snow as early as October, whereas golfers can tee off on Vancouver Island on Christmas Day. In autumn much of eastern Canada erupts in a spectacular array of colours just as ice starts to float into the bays of Newfoundland. Canada is diverse, and that diversity represents the essence of the country.

Climate and Geography

Canada encompasses nearly 10 million square km, which makes it nearly 40 times larger than the entire United Kingdom. Consequently both the general climate and topography understood by Canadians depend greatly on which part of the country they live in. As a general outline, Canada is divided into six regions; the **Western Cordilleran** (mountain) region, the **Interior Plains** (prairies), the **Canadian Shield** (the largest region, and barely inhabited), the **St Lawrence Lowlands**, the **Atlantic (Appalachian) Region** and the **Arctic**. The west of Canada is slanted eastward by the Pacific plate, which, pushing under the North American plate, causes waters east of the mountains to drain into the Great Lakes, the Arctic, Hudson Bay or all the way south to the Gulf of Mexico. The massive wall of mountains in the west and the lower hills of the east isolate much of the Canadian interior and create a truly continental climate. Smack in the middle of the country, Winnipeg, Manitoba, with over 600,000 people, is the coldest city in the world, yet can easily break 30°C in summer.

Generally speaking, the Pacific and Atlantic coasts are the mildest and wettest parts of the country, with southern Vancouver Island experiencing the fewest days of snow. For Canadians living inland, snow is a reality of daily life during four to eight months of the year. Humidity varies greatly across the regions – from thick and wet in the central Great Lakes/St Lawrence basin to irritatingly dry in Alberta and the Rockies. While the western prairie provinces often experience, technically, the coldest weather of the populated regions, the humidity of the east exaggerates the temperature extremes: minus 20°C in Calgary is much less cutting than minus 10°C ripping off Lake Ontario into Toronto. Rain on the west coast rarely turns to snow, whereas the eastern Maritime provinces can experience massive snowfalls, measured in metres. The north, which includes the three territories and the top half of all but the four eastern provinces, is sub-Arctic to Arctic with much of the coastline permanently frozen, though thawing as the planet warms. Winters are long, dark and cold, whereas summers are bright and surprisingly warm. Wind, a factor throughout the country, exaggerates the effects of cold, and winter temperatures must be understood in terms of wind-chill.

Summer can be as beautiful as all the tourism propaganda suggests. Visitors are surprised by the truly hot weather in the world's coldest country, and air-conditioning is welcome in central regions. Both Toronto and Montreal can be steamy, reaching and even surpassing 40°C. Lake swimming is popular at these times and windows are often sealed shut to keep the heat out. The mountain areas are cooler and drier during the summer, with even the hottest days giving back at least 10 degrees in the evening. The west coast is milder all around – similar to the climate in southern England – while temperatures on the east coast match more closely those found in Ireland or Scotland.

Geographically the majority of Canada's territory consists of low plains, although images of the mountains are ubiquitous. The Canadian Shield is the largest single geographical region. The Shield, dominated by rock and lakes left over from the last Ice Age, forms a band from the northwest down through the three prairie provinces and into Ontario and Quebec. Much of the Shield is barren land or tundra, while the remainder is boreal forest. The entire Shield area is extremely sparsely populated, with large sections of the Northwest Territories and Nunavut remaining uninhabited. Despite the lack of population, the Shield and Arctic regions have not escaped the modern world. With huge reserves of fresh water, many of the lakes and much of the pack ice are being affected by global pollution. Underground, minerals remain an important, but only partially explored, contributor to the economy.

The bulk of Canada's population lives along the banks of the St Lawrence River and the Great Lakes. The area around Lake Ontario is now highly industrialised, whereas the traditional Habitant farming of French Canada can still be seen downriver. The eastern provinces have rough, rainy coasts, famous for legendary yet dwindling fish stocks, and the dry plains of the prairies will forever evoke images of cowboys and fields of wheat. The western mountains are nearly a thousand kilometres wide and result in a staggering variety of climatic systems affected by precipitation, soil and temperature. Generally the country is geologically stable; however, the far west experiences earthquakes, and active volcanoes exist in Alaska and just south of the British Columbia border. Droughts are common on the prairies, and ice storms have wreaked havoc in central and eastern Canada. New Brunswick's Bay of Fundy has the world's largest tides, and almost all areas of the country without light pollution can view the evocative northern lights, which increase in clarity northwards.

Although Canada is cold, the climate varies a great deal across the country and the cool environment has kept many warm-weather irritants away. Canada has no malaria, killer snakes or deadly spiders, although global warming and trade have led to the arrival of some viruses and the spread of foreign insects. Although well equipped for the weather, Canadians both embrace and complain about their environment and, much like the British, many escape south to the sun during the long winter months and spend as much time as possible out of doors during the summer.

Historical Overview

Prehistory

It has long been accepted that the first Canadians arrived from Siberia towards the end of the last Ice Age, between 10,000 and 25,000 years ago. With much of the Earth's water held up in glacial ice, a natural land bridge across the Bering Sea became exposed. Linking modern-day Russia to Alaska, it provided a passage for migrants coming to the New World in pursuit of game. This land bridge is named Beringia and, while heated debate surrounds the date of migration(s), their route of arrival is generally accepted. Archaeological evidence throughout the Americas strongly suggests that humans were well established as far south as modern-day Chile at the same time as traditional dating has the first immigrants wandering into Alaska. Consequently, the dates of initial migration are under intense scrutiny and it is now thought that humans may have crossed from Asia in several migrations any time during the last hundred thousand years.

The first Canadians of whom there is hard evidence are loosely referred to as Paleoindians; they were hunter-gatherers who followed herds of mammoths, bison, mastodons, deer and caribou to almost all corners of the continent. Archaeological sites along the Porcupine River in the northern Yukon suggest an ice-free northern region with some evidence of settlement dating back at least 20,000 years. Other migrations may have occurred along the coast of British Columbia and perhaps north from South America.

However the first Canadians arrived, several large linguistic groups exist. The native languages of the Americas fall into three broad categories. Eskimo-Aleut, as the name suggests, comprises the language group in the far north and around the coast of Alaska; the Na-Dene group exists down through the northwest and in isolated southern areas, and includes, along the west coast, familiar totem-building peoples such as the Haida and Tlingit; and all others, including Aztecs, Iroquois and Incas, are broadly grouped into the Amerind language grouping, to the dismay of some linguists. Before contact with Europeans, over 60 languages divided into 11 general categories would have been spoken in Canada.

Prehistoric North America was a cultural and linguistic mosaic tied together through common tools, trade and conflict; for example, the Clovis culture is identified with the stone tools and arrowheads that were used widely throughout the continent between 9,000 and 10,000 years ago. As groups adapted to their particular environments, technologies also developed and led to various forms of agriculture through Central and South America, to the development of the bow for hunting in central North America, to advanced fishing techniques on both coasts, and to unique means of transportation such as canoes on rivers and kayaks in the Arctic. Trade was important, and products such as tobacco are known to have been consumed even in northern Canada, although produced thousands of kilometres to the south.

The First Europeans

Columbus may have lost his way but he certainly wasn't the first European to set eyes on the New World. Scandinavians and particularly Icelanders continue to celebrate Leif Ericsson's journey to Vinland (probably Newfoundland) around AD 1000 – nearly half a century before Columbus. A Norse settlement at L'Anse aux Meadows on the northern tip of Newfoundland, unearthed in the 1960s, provides concrete proof of Vikings in North America. The Vikings didn't stay at L'Anse aux Meadows very long and even their colonies in Greenland vanished, probably as a result of climatic changes, but it can be assumed that Scandinavians and the First Nations made contact with each other. It is interesting to note that, while even the hardy Vikings found settlement in Greenland and Canada unsustainable, the Inuit people managed to survive and even thrive in the harsh northern conditions.

Finding a New Land

When Columbus and crew set off, hoping the world was round, they were not looking for new lands to settle; rather they left in search of a quick route to the Far East by sailing west. When they landed on Hispaniola, Columbus thought he had encountered islands off the coast of India. The explorer credited with finding the new land was another Italian. In 1496 Britain's Henry VII financed Giovanni Caboto – John Cabot – to investigate 'whatsoever islands, countries, regions or provinces of heathens and infidels, in whatsoever part of the world placed, which before this time were unknown to all Christians'. John Cabot planted the British flag on North American soil in 1497 and declared it a new-found-land. Although others may have preceded that journey, Cabot is recognised as the first to lay claim to the territory.

Unfortunately for Cabot, and many subsequent explorers, the new continent proved massive and the only obvious routes in filled with ice. While the Spaniards were finding great wealth in Mexico and the mountain of silver at Potosí, Bolivia, British and French explorers continued to look for a quick route to Asia. In 1534 the French king dispatched Jacques Cartier from St-Malo. Armed with good charts of the east coast of Canada, Cartier sailed beyond Prince Edward Island into the Gulf of St Lawrence and landed on the continent itself, where he fished and traded with the Mi'kmaq people. Further upriver he made contact with the Iroquois, two of whom were abducted and taken back to France with the expedition. The following year Cartier returned to the St Lawrence with his Iroquois guides and travelled to the current site of Quebec City and on to an island when rapids prevented further travel west. Nearly 120 years later, Paul Chomedey de Maisonneuve would found Montreal on the island and the rapids would retain the name Cartier gave them – La Chine, or China Rapids. Those early explorers still believed there was a water route to the Orient.

Settlement

Throughout the 16th and 17th centuries explorers continued to search for the Northwest Passage to Asia, but, while Spanish and Portuguese holdings to the south grew rapidly on the backs of mining and slavery, the British and French holdings in North America remained small and distant. The greatest interest in Canada was associated with the incredible fish stocks off the east coast that drew vessels from across western Europe. As a by-product of the fishing expeditions, some limited trade developed with the indigenous people and popular furs, such as beaver, were introduced to the European markets.

Settlements were attempted in various locations in order to secure the new territory and exploit its furs. Harsh winters and scurvy devastated the early villages and numerous British and French settlers perished. Eventually in 1608 Samuel de Champlain sailed up the St Lawrence and established a colony at the site of the Indian settlement of Stadacona. The indigenous name of Quebec, meaning 'strait', or 'narrowing of the river', was given to the community. New France took on a decidedly religious–feudal tone, with only Catholics permitted to settle. The seigneurial system was based on that in France, albeit requiring the *seigneuries* or landholders to live on their land. Colonists, known as Habitants, worked long strips of farmland along the banks of the St Lawrence, and early life in the colony was regimented and hard. As New France was being established along the St Lawrence, British settlers were building a fort and community further south at the site of Jamestown in present-day Virginia. Subsequent French and British colonies, along with Dutch and even Swedish communities, sprang up along North America's east coast. The colonies in Canada remained small, but grew in strategic importance because of trade and the geopolitical situation in Europe. While populations along the St Lawrence expanded slowly, another French settlement was established near the Bay of Fundy in what is now New Brunswick. These settlers named the region L'Acadie or Acadia and developed a distinct culture. Focused on fishing and trade with the local First Nations communities, the French Acadians became political pawns in the conflicts between Britain and France. Acadia's other name, Nova Scotia, was bestowed in 1621 after a British adventurer chased out most of the settlers. In 1629 the British made their first attempt at permanent settlement when Scottish Sir William Alexander sent a group of settlers to Canada. Although a short-lived experiment, it set an important precedent – migration by Scots to Canada.

Newfoundland's development was distinct from other parts of British and French North America, as the Island and principal port of Saint John's remained isolated and focused specifically on the region's important fishery. As early as 1555 Basque and French forces fought for control of the port. Permanent settlers arrived in the early 1600s, but control of Newfoundland continued to shift between different European powers.

The Fur Trade

No other economic activity has defined Canada to such an extent as the fur trade. From the great homes of Montreal to the forts that gave birth to the western cities, the fur trade opened and exploited the North American hinterland. To this day, Canada earns much of its wealth from these resources, and, though trapping has lost favour as a result of depleting stocks, protests and improved synthetic fibres, the northern tradition of wealth extraction and exploration lives on. Synonymous with the fur trade are the noble Canadian beaver and the Hudson's Bay Company (HBC) – the oldest corporation in North America. Moreover the two founding nations of Canada fought over the fur trade for nearly a hundred years but, as a by-product, fostered aspects of a Canadian identity that persist. From the lone *voyageur* in his canoe to empire and bureaucracy, the fur trade and its forts and traders ruled the centre, west and north of Canada up to, and even beyond, Confederation in 1867.

Long before the HBC and its truly Canadian rival, the Northwest Company, the fur trade was alive and well, bringing explorers to the Canadian interior and greatly increasing trade with the First Nations. It is very possible that, because of trade, many indigenous groups in Canada were using European goods before they ever set eyes on a European. The spread of unfamiliar introduced diseases such as smallpox and influenza devastated some populations. The Spanish reintroduced the horse, which had disappeared from the Americas, and it quickly gained importance among both the indigenous and non-indigenous populations, as the increased mobility provided by the animal supported trade. Guns obviously changed warfare and hunting techniques, and the axe proved to be a useful addition for both nomadic and sedentary peoples.

Europeans were drawn by beaver pelts. The Russians, with their great holdings in Siberia, were the principal furriers of Europe, but increased demand combined with severely depleted Russian stocks made North America all the more attractive to the early explorers. Henry Hudson's doomed journey in 1611 (into the Bay that now bears his name) charted a route into the continent, while explorers such as Etienne Brûlé ventured overland to the Great Lakes and discovered aboriginal meeting and trade sites such as the Huron 'Toronto Trail'.

The French settlers of Quebec allied themselves with the Huron for trade and as defence against the Iroquois, who eventually defeated and disbanded the Huron nation. Notwithstanding the current realities of First Nation society, the fur trade may be seen as advantageous to native Canadians as well as Europeans. The Huron, for example, refused to speak French and expected trade to be conducted in their language. As commerce expanded through the continent, the Cree very successfully played a middle role between the Plains peoples and the HBC and Northwest Company. Over time, however, depleted fur stocks and an increasingly manipulative credit policy indebted many First Nations and led to greater market (and government) dependency and a functional end to traditional economic structures.

In a twist of irony, the HBC owes its charter to two French Canadian *coureurs de bois* fur-traders. Médard Chouart des Groseilliers and Pierre Radisson travelled far inland and become aware of huge beaver stocks. Returning to Quebec with canoes laden with pelts, they were severely fined for trading without a permit. In response they travelled to Boston and eventually on to England, where they regaled the court with stories of great wealth in the interior of the continent. After the British erected a fort in James Bay in 1668 and traded successfully with the local Cree, King Charles II granted the company a charter in 1670. The extent of the charter is almost unbelievable. It bestowed on the king's cousin, Prince Rupert and his 17 associates, the right to 'sole trade and commerce' in all the lands draining into Hudson Bay. The 18 associates were to be 'the true and absolute Lordes and Proprietors of the territory'. The area of drainage includes much of modern Ontario and Quebec, the three prairie provinces, Nunavut and the Northwest Territories and a large area of the United States.

Needless to say, the French and other Canadian merchants did not accept the legality of the charter. Nevertheless, the HBC's dominance was reaffirmed several times and it remained the most important administrative presence in much of Canada until, with the rescinding of the charter in 1870, Rupert's Land was absorbed into the newly independent country of Canada.

Conflict and Trade

The HBC began trading at a series of forts along the shores of Hudson Bay almost immediately after the granting of the charter. The French, too, had pushed into the interior and, as was also the case with coastal settlements in Nova Scotia, Cape Breton (Ile Royale) and Newfoundland, forts regularly changed hands. The War of Spanish Succession (1702–13) spilled over to Canada, with the French taking control of many HBC posts. Finally, the 1713 Treaty of Utrecht managed to settle some of the territorial claim and resulted in significant French concessions. Specifically, the French returned the captured forts along Hudson Bay and ceded claims to Newfoundland and Nova Scotia, but not Ile Royale (Cape Breton) or Quebec.

The mid-18th century witnessed the gradual development of a Canadian identity, particularly among French settlers who began to see themselves as *Canadien*, an ethnic group distinct from those of their native lands. The Acadian society also developed along the east coast in the area defended by the impressive fortifications at Louisburg on Cape Breton Island. Although the British colonies to the south were growing, the British population remained small in Canada. Settlers were moved to Halifax and Newfoundland for strategic reasons, while the French continued to control the all-important waterway up the St Lawrence.

The Seven Years War (1756–63) between Britain, France and most other European powers really began in 1754 in the Americas, and American historians remember it as the French and Indian Wars. In 1755 Governor Charles Lawrence of Nova Scotia summoned representatives of the neutral Acadian community to Halifax. Fearing they would join the French ranks in Louisburg or Quebec, he carried out a longstanding threat and expelled all those who would not swear allegiance to the British king. The Acadians were rounded up and dispersed to the southern colonies, where they formed what would later become the Cajun population of Louisiana.

In 1758 the British overran Fort Louisburg on Cape Breton and then continued on to Quebec City. Perhaps the most famous battle in Canadian history, the Battle of the Plains of Abraham, pitted British General Wolfe against his French rival Louis-Joseph de Montcalm. Unable to break through the fortifications of Quebec City, the British sailed at night past the fortified community and scaled the cliffs to the south. On 13 September 1759, 4,500 British regular troops lined up against roughly 4,500 irregular French troops. The battle lasted 15 minutes. Montcalm and Wolfe were fatally wounded and, although several more battles took place later, French control of the New World was essentially surrendered.

War raged on in Europe until 1763, when, in the Treaty of Paris, France ceded almost all of its American holdings except for two tiny islands, St Pierre and Miquelon, in the Gulf of St Lawrence, and several islands in the Caribbean. This historically interesting fact puts Canada at that time into a humbling perspective: in the 18th century France considered the sugar-cane fields of Haiti and Martinique more important to it than the vast territories of Canada. Britain viewed Canada's relevance in terms of the HBC and resources such as lumber; its interests lay in the growing colonies to the south.

The Quebec Act and Revolution

The taking of New France presented Britain with a series of new challenges. Suddenly British holdings included 70,000 French subjects, a very light military presence and aggression from First Nations. In 1774 the British parliament passed the Quebec Act, a first in terms of ethnic rights, acknowledging the supremacy of the French language, the Catholic Church and the French legal *Code Civil* in Quebec. The protection of French in Canada has contributed significantly to the country's character, but the independence granted to the province (and by virtue the Church) has significantly limited Canada's ability to develop and mandate national policy on health, education and a variety of other social issues. When, in 1776, the 13 American colonies revolted against British taxation and rule, the French-Canadian militias remained loyal to their British rulers and resisted the American assault on Quebec. Benedict Arnold's attempt to take the '14th Colony' was the only battle on Canadian soil during the American Revolution.

Empire Loyalists

The American War of Independence changed the face of the Americas by setting off a chain of events that encouraged revolutions throughout the region, and even in France. Canada, on the other hand, became a bastion of loyalty and doubled its English-speaking population by receiving thousands of British subjects loyal to the king. While the seeds of French Canada were truly sown by 1763, English-speaking Canada was confined to HBC trading posts, several military garrisons and the coastal populations in Nova Scotia, Newfoundland and Prince Edward Island.

After the peace treaty of 1783 some 40,000 to 50,000 loyalists or Tories moved north. The majority ended up in the Maritimes, populating Nova Scotia and leading to the creation of New Brunswick in the former Acadian territory. Those settlers who moved further west to the province of Quebec were not satisfied with French-Catholic laws and the colony split into Upper and Lower Canada. The upper reaches of the St Lawrence later became Ontario, while Lower Canada became Quebec.

The Canadian West

At a time when the eastern colonies were growing and the United States of America was emerging, much of the Canadian and American West remained

The War of 1812 and the Canadian–US Border

In the shadows of the Napoleonic Wars in France, the United States declared war on Britain, which meant Canada. Despite superior numbers, the war was a stalemate, with the USA burning Canadian towns and in turn British forces burning Washington; the fire damage to the president's residence in Washington resulted in its being painted white.

The war ended with France's defeat in Europe and clarified the Canadian (British)–US border. The western frontier was agreed to be the 49th parallel from the Lake of the Woods (Ontario) to the mountains and was extended to the Pacific coast in 1849, with only the small outpost of Victoria on Vancouver Island dipping south of the arbitrary line. The other international frontier was with Russia, vaguely defined along the mountains of the northwest.

relatively unknown. Explorers had made it as far as the foothills of the Rocky Mountains, but exploration took place with furs in mind, not settlement. It wasn't until 1793 that Alexander Mackenzie managed to cross the western mountains to reach the Pacific. In that same year Captain James Cook sailed past Vancouver Island and charted the west coast.

The Northwest Company was formed in 1783 by a group of Montreal merchants. The Nor'Westers brought stiff competition to the HBC's stranglehold on the fur trade by opening up greater areas in the Canadian centre and west. As a direct consequence of this exploration, a new population arose on the Canadian prairies – the Métis. As the overwhelming majority of traders were males it was only a matter of time before mixing occurred with aboriginal women. The Métis culture born of this mixing expressed itself as a fusion of many cultures. The largest groups spoke French but added in words from English and native languages. Trade jargons, such as Chinook and Michif, grew out of this linguistic fusion. The Métis people were most populous in the area that is now Manitoba. Their trade with and supplying of the Northwest Company virtually helped to exterminate the buffalo from the Canadian prairies; the buffalo populations never recovered from the slaughter of herds that at one time numbered in the hundreds of thousands.

The first serious attempt at a permanent European settlement in the west occurred between 1812 and 1814 when Thomas Douglas, fifth Earl of Selkirk, purchased from the HBC for 10 shillings an area around the Red River that was five times the size of Scotland. In the face of serious opposition from many quarters, Douglas managed to convince a few displaced Highland families to relocate to the centre of the New World. Life was extremely hard for these new colonists and their settlement was vigorously opposed by the Métis and the Northwest Company. Many of the first settlers died and those who survived did so because of the help they received from the First Nations peoples. Nevertheless, the Red River settlement became the genesis for Winnipeg and the first step in the colonisation of western Canada.

Growth and Confederation

Canada and the Atlantic provinces grew throughout the 19th century. The birth rate in French-Catholic Canada was high, and Upper Canada, coming under increasing influence from the Orange Order, was also growing. Expansion to the canals through the Great Lakes brought commerce to York, which gained its charter as a city in 1834 and was renamed Toronto.

The first serious challenge to British governance occurred in 1837, when rebellions broke out in Upper and Lower Canada. The two principal leaders, William Lyon Mackenzie (mayor of Toronto) and Louis-Joseph Papineau (leader of the Lower Canada Patriot Party), wanted greater representation and accountability in the colonies. Although the uprising ended quickly, it set in motion the process of unifying the two Canadas and eventually led to a more representative government. The small community that administered the construction of the Rideau Canal was incorporated as Bytown in 1850 and renamed Ottawa in 1855. Ottawa became the logical capital city as it straddled the Ottawa River and, therefore, Upper and Lower Canada.

The Move to Confederation

The American Civil War and a series of Fenian raids hastened the move to unite the provinces of British North America. The Fathers of Confederation met in Charlottetown, Prince Edward Island (PEI), in September 1864 and agreed on the details for unification. In 1867 the Dominion of Canada became the first independent country within the Commonwealth, with four provinces – Ontario, Quebec, Nova Scotia and New Brunswick. The first prime minister was Conservative Sir John A. Macdonald. Unification did not so much usurp the roles of provincial governments as create a new level of administration. Each province maintained its own assembly and even senate, although the upper chambers were later eliminated. The new provinces that were created later developed their own provincial legislatures and maintained a significant portion of political management.

The first serious test for the new country came from the Métis lands along the Red River in modern-day Manitoba. The Dominion government purchased Rupert's Land from the HBC in 1869 and the Métis people of the area, fearing economic and cultural loss, rose up against Fort Garry (Winnipeg). Government forces quelled the uprising led by the charismatic, self-acclaimed prophet and leader Louis Riel; after a second revolt in the 1880s Riel was hanged. His memory continues to elicit strong emotions among many Métis to this day.

On the west coast, staunchly British Victoria was growing and, despite American interests in the area including the 1867 purchase of Alaska, the new colony wanted to retain its British heritage and merge with the Dominion of Canada. The deal struck with British Columbia included a rail line that would link the country from coast to coast. Way over budget and late, the Canadian Pacific Railway fulfilled the promise and a transcontinental Dominion became a reality. PEI joined a few years later, but Newfoundland, the site of the first British claim to North America, remained a colony for 82 more years.

During the later part of the 19th century there was significant immigration to parts of Canada, but settlement in the prairies did not really take off until the completion of the railway. While the new country wanted solid, British immigrants, many of the migrants were Chinese rail workers, Eastern European Anabaptists, poor Irish and the like. In 1867 Canada had a population of roughly 3.5 million spread across the four provinces and the territories. By 1914 the population had reached almost 8 million and the country was divided into nine provinces and two territories. Other major events of the 19th century included the formation of the Northwest Mounted Police, 'the Mounties' (1873), Alexander Graham Bell's invention of the telephone (1874), an economic depression that resulted in migration to the south, composition of the song 'O Canada' (see p.34), the Klondike Gold Rush, the first basketball game, a warming of relations with the USA, the creation in Banff of the world's second national park, the Boer War and a gradual dismantling of the gender barrier as women entered professions such as medicine and law.

The 20th Century

Canada's first Francophone prime minister, Wilfred Laurier, presided over the country's transition into the 20th century and declared that the century would belong to Canada. While grandiose pronouncements are always political, the statement proved not entirely untrue. While early Canada can be described as a regressive, uncompassionate and conservative colonial backwater, it transformed, in a little over 100 years, into one of the most prosperous nations on earth, combining diversity, human rights, healthcare and a strong economy. Women fought for and won the vote – and the country was the first in the Commonwealth to elect women to public office. First Nations people, on the other hand, watched the devastation of their ancient cultures and enjoyed fewer rights than any other inhabitants of the land. While tragic inequity still exists, aboriginal issues slowly increased in importance and the end of the century saw the formation of a new territory, Nunavut, run essentially by the Inuit. Soon, all services in the territory will be obliged to be offered in Inuktitut.

In the early 1900s the majority of Canadians saw themselves clearly as British overseas citizens, playing a proud role in a great empire. When Britain declared war on Germany and Austria in 1914 Canada automatically joined in the fight. Thousands of young Canadians enlisted and, with a national population of only 8 million, over 60,000 were killed and thousands more wounded.

The Great War had a profound effect on Canada and changed the country forever. Income tax, introduced during the war, has increased at regular intervals ever since. The political rift between English and French Canada began to take shape at that time and focused around the issue of conscription. Women's role in the economy increased greatly and they attained the vote federally in 1918. Despite huge war costs, Canada became an even more significant food and resource exporter. Returned servicemen who lacked both adequate housing and employment opportunities led the 1919 Winnipeg General Strike. This important event set the stage for prairie politics and is seen as creating the roots of Canadian socialism.

As a result of a strong economy and significant immigration Canada boomed in the 1920s. Changes to society were generally positive in light of the good times; however, the stock market crash of 1929, combined with drought on the prairies, devastated the economy. Economic depression was not new, even in the young country, but the depth of hardship overwhelmed many – including the politicians. In the wake of the economic downturn, the newly elected government proved ineffectual despite spending millions on relief. The western provinces, the most affected region, began to express a distinct political outlook during the 1930s. Three different political philosophies emerged in Alberta, Saskatchewan and Manitoba on the back of the Progressive movement of the 1920s.

The western farming tradition in Canada differed from that of the United States, as settlement in Canada was a planned, structured affair. Furthermore, the farmers themselves came from different cultural and political traditions. Unlike those in eastern Canada, westerners felt less loyalty to traditional political divisions such as the Tory/Grit divide. In Alberta the United Farmers government gave way to Social Credit, born from a peculiar mix of creative banking ideas and religious conservatism. The most significant change took place in Saskatchewan, where the Cooperative Commonwealth Federation, a true socialist political movement, gained political importance. Although the party did not govern the province until 1944, this shift to the political left started a trend that would help define modern Canada.

When war broke out in Europe in 1939, Canada once again enthusiastically answered the call, however as a slightly more sovereign country. Prime minister William Lyon Mackenzie King waited two days after Britain's declaration of war before throwing in Canada's hat. While two days had little effect on the conflict, it did signify a new independence in Canadian foreign policy.

As in the First World War, Canada's contribution in the Second World War far outstripped the country's actual economic size. During the six years of conflict thousands of lives were lost. Canadian soldiers gained respect in Europe and at home and the country was transformed into a major industrial power. In fact by the end of the war Canada, now with just over 10 million inhabitants, had the world's third largest navy. Throughout the war the economy was almost completely managed by the central government, something that would never work in peacetime.

The war years revealed deep-seated racism in Canadian society. While First Nations soldiers proved to be outstanding snipers and soldiers, their people were still not legally recognised as citizens in their own country. Japanese Canadians with generations of tradition on the west coast were rounded up and interned and their land and fishing vessels confiscated, acts for which the government did not officially apologise until the mid-1980s. While it is true that there were a few collaborators, the rights of German and Italian Canadians were not stripped to nearly the same extent.

Post-war Canada boomed. Women were finally granted the vote provincially in Quebec in the 1940s, although the state of politics in *la belle province* remained a parochial, religious affair. Newfoundland rounded out the Union by joining in 1949. The mass immigration of the 1950s began to transform Canada into the multicultural, North American country it is today. Toronto 'the Good' was diversifying, while Montreal remained the economic centre of the country. Vancouver and Victoria's growth owed much to the value of British Columbia's resources and the high quality of life afforded by a much gentler climate. The staunch British culture of the west coast gradually began to give way to the more diverse, relaxed culture that is now associated with the area. In 1947 oil was discovered just south of Edmonton, Alberta. While not considered of great significance at the time, the discovery would prove extremely important after the oil crisis of the 1970s.

For Canadian social development, the Depression and Second World War greatly increased the role of the central government. The British North America Act (BNA), that was the essence of confederation, placed social policy and services almost completely under provincial jurisdiction. The military and veterans however were federal (as were some First Nations issues) and the national government was able to circumvent provincial governments (and churches) in instituting an unemployment insurance and housing policy.

By the 1960s Canada's view was shifting away from Britain and more towards the United States and the United Nations. It played a peacekeeping role during the Suez conflict and, under the diplomatic guidance of Lester B. Pearson, Canada introduced the peacekeeper's 'Blue Beret' to the United Nations. During the 1960s there were many major shifts, including the establishment of public healthcare, first in Saskatchewan, then countrywide. Prime minister Pearson dumped the Red Ensign in favour of the distinctive maple leaf as the national flag and forced the issue of bilingual services within the government.

By defeating the ultra-conservative Union Nationale in Quebec, French-Canadian society dragged itself into the 20th century in what has come to be known as the Quiet Revolution. Almost totally non-violent, it resulted in Quebecers en masse leaving the church and demanding higher education and greater opportunities. The birth rate in the province fell from one of the highest in the world to among the very lowest. An articulate nationalist voice formed in the political vacuum and continues to be a major theme in Canadian politics.

Quotations About Canada

Having hit a wall, the next logical step is not to bang our heads against it.
Stephen Harper (Prime Minister)

There are no limits to the majestic future which lies before the mighty expanse of Canada with its versatile, aspiring, cultured, and generous-hearted people.
Sir Winston Churchill

The great themes of Canadian history are as follows: Keeping the Americans out, keeping the French in, and trying to get the Natives to somehow disappear.
Will Ferguson

In Canada we have enough to do keeping up with two spoken languages without trying to invent slang, so we just go right ahead and use English for literature, Scotch for sermons and American for conversation.
Stephen Leacock

We Canadians live in a blind spot about our identity. We have very strong feelings about who we aren't but only weak ones about who we are. We're passionate about what we don't want to become but oddly passive about what we should be.
John Cruickshank (*McLean's Magazine*)

The die is cast in Canada: there are two ethnic and linguistic groups; each is too strong and too deeply rooted in the past, too firmly bound to a mother culture, to be able to swamp the other. But if the two will collaborate inside of a truly pluralist state, Canada could become a privileged place where the federalist form of government, which is the government of tomorrow's world, will be perfected.
Pierre Elliot Trudeau

...whether we live together in confidence and cohesion; with more faith and pride in ourselves and less self-doubt and hesitation; strong in the conviction that the destiny of Canada is to unite, not divide; sharing in cooperation, not in separation or in conflict; respecting our past and welcoming our future.
Prime Minister Lester B. Pearson

In a world darkened by ethnic conflicts that tear nations apart, Canada stands as a model of how people of different cultures can live and work together in peace, prosperity, and mutual respect.
US President Bill Clinton

I want to thank all the Canadians who came out today to wave to me – with all five fingers!
President George W. Bush (during his first visit to Ottawa, 30 Nov 2004)

The beaver, which has come to represent Canada as the eagle does the United States and the lion Britain, is a flat-tailed, slow-witted, toothy rodent known to bite off its own testicles or to stand under its own falling trees.
June Callwood

Pierre Trudeau's controversial governance from 1968 through to 1984 transferred the constitution from Britain to Canada and enshrined bilingualism and multiculturalism as national institutions. In opposing US actions in Vietnam, Canada continued to maintain an independent foreign policy within organisations such as NATO. Trudeau's government, pushed by the leftist New Democratic Party, greatly increased social spending and programmes and encouraged diverse immigration. Support for Trudeau evaporated in much of western Canada as a result of the government's partial nationalisation of oil, while in Quebec the election of a separatist government in 1976 solidified a profound political divide. The aftermath of the Trudeau era saw a return to more fiscally conservative governance. Government involvement in the economy, in conjunction with macroeconomic issues of the 1970s, left Canada with huge public debts both federally and provincially. Governments throughout the 1980s and 1990s cut spending in many fields and Canada has retreated from some of its international roles. With the signing of a free-trade agreement with the United States, followed by the North American Free Trade Agreement (NAFTA), along with its membership in the Organisation of American States (OAS), Canada finally confirmed its location in the Americas. Also confirmed was the country's economic dependence on the United States, which purchases over 80 per cent of Canada's exports.

Events such as the 1976 Olympic Games in Montreal and the very successful 1988 Winter Olympics in Calgary, as well as the huge flow of capital from Hong Kong to Greater Vancouver, have shaped this diverse modern country through the final decades of the 20th century. Provinces from Newfoundland to British Columbia confirm Canada's diversity, yet, despite ongoing efforts from leaders such as Pearson, Trudeau and Mulroney, a single Canadian identity remains elusive. The Canadian experience has always been shaped by region and personal history. The role of France, Britain and the Commonwealth has faded and, although some notes and coins bear the Queen's portrait, the predominant influence comes from the neighbour to the south.

Food and Drink

It would be misleading to suggest that Canada is known for its gastronomic contribution to the world. In a country where the British and even Americans can find the food a bit tasteless, it is worrying to think the French have left so little of their influence. Nonetheless Canada has a limited but unique culinary tradition, as well as offering a varied and affordable restaurant environment (*see* **Living in Canada**, pp.185–8). The broadly based diet reflects the country's diversity and regionalism. American-style fast food is ubiquitous, but losing ground to sushi, and Canadians are increasingly health-conscious, with notably lower rates of obesity than in the USA or Britain. Maritimers, and particularly

Newfoundlanders, have lived off the sea and its cod stocks for a long time. The prairies are beef country and wild game remains fundamental to northern peoples. Giant salmon runs continue on the west coast, and French Canada has its own unique interpretation of new-world cuisine.

Canadian portions are enormous, and fried food is common, yet it remains easy to maintain a healthy diet. While much fruit is imported, Canada produces great quantities of apples, pears and other temperate produce. Canadians do not cook their vegetables for as long as the British do, and salads are commonly found on all menus. Eating well is easy and affordable, and there are some fantastic restaurants and thousands of mid-range eating establishments. Coffee shops are everywhere and many pedestrians carry coffee-filled cups as they walk along the street. The entire country has essentially gone smoke-free; holdouts in Quebec and Alberta have succumbed to public pressure, finally banning cigarettes in restaurants and bars. Toronto has moved to further limit smoking in public places and Nova Scotia town has even made smoking in a vehicle with children an offence. Less than 15 per cent of super-healthy British Columbians use tobacco, although a distinct cannabis odour is not uncommon.

Quintessentially Canadian, maple syrup is harvested in central and eastern Canada and is enjoyed poured over pancakes, spilling gently on to the eggs and back bacon at many a Canadian breakfast table. Indeed, Europeans are often surprised by the plethora of breakfast restaurants found throughout the country. On the prairies, *perogies*, boiled or fried filled dumplings, came with the Ukrainian and Russian settlers and are common at breakfast and even at other meals. While a classic breakfast will always be important to the northern psyche, healthier options such as yogurt and muffins also form part of the national diet.

Perhaps the vilest contribution to the Canadian table has come from French Canada as an assault on the heart – *poutine*; these are French fried potatoes, covered in cheese curds (the fatty bit) and smothered in onion gravy. Especially popular in Quebec, this delicacy will also be encountered in other parts of the country. The *voyageurs* (fur traders) sustained themselves with stew and particularly pea soup, just as easily eaten with a fork as a spoon. On the upside, Jewish immigrants from Romania brought smoked meat to Montreal. This corned beef, sliced thinly and piled high on rye bread, is a mainstay in the city and popular across the country. Cheese, which is almost always served on burgers, is not available with the smoked meat, as Jewish dietary law forbids dairy products from being served with meat.

It is difficult to describe 'normal' dinner-table fare in Canada as ethnicity plays such a big role in household eating patterns. Canadians will frequently dine out – even three or four times a week. Chinese food has developed regional variations and is so integrated that it is no more 'ethnic' than American food. Pizza is everywhere and pub grub consists of fried chicken wings (prepared in many different ways), ribs, hamburgers and nacho corn chips. In fact, while

Mexicans may find 'hot' Canadian salsa no spicier than a glass of milk, Canadians have incorporated Mexican-style food firmly into their diet. Corn chips or crisps have as large a market share as their potato cousins, and corn (maize) is grown throughout the country.

Meat

The first Canadian hunter-gatherers were not vegetarians; although they ate plentiful berries and some roots, meat or fish formed the staple part of their diet. Buffalo is a delicious, healthy meat which is gradually regaining some of its historic popularity, and salmon has always been a key element in the coastal diet. It is said that the early settlers of French Canada did not bring a rich dining tradition and, indeed, barely survived their first years on the new continent. Early migrants across Canada lived marginally and depended on good stores of food to get them through the winter. To this day beef jerky (dried salted beef) is sold all over North America and harkens back to the days before refrigeration.

Natural berries spring up across the country and traditions have grown around picking and preserving them. One of the most popular berries, found throughout the prairies, is the Saskatoon. Despite being used fresh or in jams and syrups for centuries, this little blue berry was blocked from import into Britain, and therefore Europe, because the British Food Standards Agency considers them to be 'novel' and not proven fit for human consumption. Fortunately, as no Canadians seem to have dropped dead from ingesting the berries, pressure from the EU led to the ban being lifted.

Canadians eat far more beef than mutton or lamb, and the rangeland of the west produces high-quality stock. Alberta beef is known throughout the country and, despite the severe repercussions from a few isolated cases of BSE, the industry remains important to the prairies. Beef is generally excellent and available in all types of restaurants. Steak sandwiches, seen everywhere, consist of a cut of steak on top of garlic bread. In general, Canadians eat their beef a little less well cooked than the British do. Pork is also common, but does not hold the same stature in the culinary hierarchy as beef. Chicken is served frequently, but turkey tends to be reserved for special occasions such as Thanksgiving and Christmas, although current health trends have increased the large bird's popularity.

Bread and Dairy Food

Despite its great farming tradition, Canada has not managed to produce a national bread. Nevertheless, Canadian wheat is considered by some to be the world's best and, even though carbohydrates are currently under attack, supermarkets and bakeries offer a wide selection of loaves. Restaurants commonly serve bread with meals.

The situation regarding dairy products is considerably more complicated. Roughly 70 per cent of all dairy items produced in Canada come from Quebec and Ontario, and internal quotas protect manufacturers. For Europeans, particularly the French and even the Dutch, Canadian cheeses and yogurt are very expensive and the selection is limited. Cheese is heaped on to pizzas, nachos and burgers, but it is expensive when compared with other products. Furthermore, much of the commonly consumed cheese is the orange processed cheese popular in the United States and easily recognisable on American burgers.

Filling the niche between processed cheese and the expensive imported options is an equally high-priced yet popular organic cheese market, which is particularly thriving in British Columbia. The variety of these cheeses is growing quickly and establishing cheese as a delicacy. Yogurt, too, while popular and commonly consumed, is no bargain, and foreign brands are relatively expensive. Luckily, milk is affordable and excellent.

Fresh juices are also pricey, but the condensed, frozen varieties are very affordable. Climate, and the need to import fresh juice, has historically affected its availability, but prices are falling and juice bars, catering to the trend towards a healthier diet, are now common across the country.

The Influence of Immigrants on Canadian Cuisine

As the country grew, its culinary diversity expanded and waves of immigrants brought their traditional foods and introduced them to the regional diets. Many of those settlers were poor farmers who toiled to break in their land, so their diet, reflecting this background and the harsh environment, required many calories. Northern explorers finally learned to survive the cold by copying the Inuit diet, which consisted of huge quantities of fat.

Fishing has always been important on both coasts as well as throughout internal waterways. It is quite possible that European ships harvested cod off the east coast even before John Cabot's claim to the territory. The east coast also has great stocks of lobster and other shellfish. The west coast's salmon and other Pacific fish stocks sustained important native populations up and down the coast for centuries and attracted migrants from Asia. Although internment during the Second World War dispersed the coastal Japanese population inland, aspects of Japanese cooking, such as teriyaki sauce, have been incorporated into the national diet.

Vancouver's Granville Island Market is perhaps the best place in Canada for speciality and ethnic foods. The mild coastal climate allows this market to be predominantly held outdoors and it sells a wide variety of west coast products, as well as specialities from around the world. Toronto's St Lawrence Market, although not quite as diverse, has almost everything under one roof, and exhibits that city's unique ethnic mix. Winnipeg's The Forks acts as a good source for fresh local products, and Edmonton has a popular farmers' market. In addition to such markets, the ethnic quarters of most cities have speciality food stores where one can find French pâtés, Mexican salsa, Portuguese baked goods, Ukrainian sausage and all the Chinese chicken feet one could desire. General supermarkets are gradually giving way to even larger superstores with generic everything, but these across-the-country retailers attempt to reflect local tastes and gastronomic trends.

Fast Food

Food is everywhere and fast food is no exception. Hamburgers are eaten across the country and almost all the US-based chains, such as McDonald's, Burger King and Wendy's, are widespread, but are by no means the only fast food establishments. Whereas Canada does not have the same sort of sandwich culture as in the UK, the Subway chain and many similar products are everywhere. Most shopping centres have a food court with a wide selection of fare that includes Chinese and Japanese food, as well as a 'health food' option such as a fresh sandwich bar. Greek, Italian, Thai and entirely mixed or original cuisine might also be found among the outlets. Eating quickly *and* well is not impossible, and food courts are popular among the lunch crowd.

Coffee and Tea

Despite its strong British roots, Canada has a coffee culture, and, while a few tea houses have either survived or developed, coffee is everywhere. Coffee shops exist in many different forms in every corner of the country and Canadians drink huge quantities of lattes, cappuccinos, espressos and even cups of reasonably strong black coffee. 'Going for coffee' is gradually replacing a 'quick drink at the pub', and competition is fierce. The giant, Seattle-based Starbucks is ubiquitous, but so is the very blue-collar Canadian institution Tim Horton's, where doughnuts remain high on the menu and locals gather to discuss the day's events. Several other coffee-based chains exist, either regionally or nationally, and all appear to be profitable.

Even before the influx and growth of a coffee-house culture, coffee was widely consumed. Canadians, like Americans, will drink coffee with their meals, and refills are usually free. Coffee has traditionally been served stronger than in the USA, although it is still weak by French or Italian standards. The newer, more expensive blends served in all the fashionable outlets certainly have a stronger taste. The lingo takes some getting used to, as the order is rarely 'a small coffee, please'. The consumer is more likely to ask for a 'tall medium blend with space for milk' – Canadians do not use the term 'white coffee'.

Newcomers will also quickly note that locals have taken to walking the streets with large plastic or metal coffee cups in hand. Not only may coffee-drinkers get a small discount for bringing a personal container, this is one environmental initiative that seems to have really caught on. Rather than throwing away two or even three disposable cups each day, people simply rinse out their own insulated cup. The coffee even stays warm longer.

Alcohol

Oscar Wilde decided to move to Canada after reputedly seeing a sign in Dublin encouraging him to 'drink Canada Dry'. He may even have tried, unsuccessfully. Canada's relationship with booze is a mixed one, combining hard northern living with commerce, temperance and bureaucracy. Some of the world's most important names in liquor, such as Seagram, Bronfman and Molson, come from the Great White North, and drinking is popular. Several provinces have attempted to introduce prohibition, but with much less fanfare than south of the border, and Canadian whiskey, along with Canadian-trafficked rum, generated significant wealth during that period. Politically, alcohol is a provincial matter, with each province maintaining a liquor (and gaming) control board or corporation. Consequently, the importation, production and, most importantly, the distribution of alcohol remains strictly controlled. Only in Quebec can you purchase beer and wine in a grocery store. In all other provinces, separate liquor or beer and wine stores are the only outlets. As a result, by international standards alcohol is expensive and pricing not very competitive. The Ontario Liquor Control Board (OLCB) is the single largest purchaser of liquor in the world as it controls almost every drop consumed in Canada's biggest province. Alberta, the one jurisdiction that has genuinely privatised the sale of alcohol, has by far the lowest prices and the greatest level of convenience, with the market dictating pricing and availability.

As for actual consumption, Alberta, Manitoba and Quebec allow people to imbibe at age 18, whereas the rest of the country makes teenagers wait one more year. Perhaps because of the long, dark winters and/or the frontier culture, Yukoners are by far the biggest per capita drinkers in Canada, consuming over 175 litres of alcohol annually. The Canadian average is 104 litres per year, with over 80 of those litres being beer.

Beer

The best-known beer producers are Molson and Labatt, although their name brands represent only a fraction of the varieties available across the country. Smaller regional breweries are popular and foreign beers are very common in bars and restaurants. Beer in Canada is quite strong, with an average alcohol volume of 5 per cent. So-called light beer usually comes in at around 4 per cent.

For the most part, beer is served cold, with little distinction made between ales and lagers. Darker beers are common, particularly in the west, and, although available, American beer does have a presence in the market and the vast majority of Canadian brewing is now owned outside the country. As distribution is controlled provincially, beers vary between regions, as do tastes.

Litre-sized cans are sold in Quebec and less commonly throughout the rest of the country. Generally, beer is purchased in 360ml bottles or cans. The most common packaging takes the form of packs of six (six-packs) or twelve (a case). Bars usually have draught beer on tap, which is consumed by the pint in the British way or in a shared jug or pitcher – often the most economical option.

Wine

Canada has a vibrant and growing wine industry, and vineyards in Ontario and Quebec have long produced reasonable quantities of average wines. More recently, British Columbia has entered the market in earnest, making wines that rank competitively on a world scale for quality. The dry, warm valleys of the Okanagan in central British Columbia have proven excellent for grapes. On a smaller scale, wine production is growing on Vancouver Island and in other temperate areas such as Nova Scotia. 'Drinking locally' has become a reality for Canadians. Although wine continues to increase in popularity, it remains a luxury item and is priced accordingly in restaurants.

The Niagara peninsula in southern Ontario produces the bulk of Canadian ice wine. Made by pressing frozen grapes, in a process that originated in Germany, this late-harvest wine is promoted as a luxury item; consequently it is extremely expensive and considered a posh accompaniment to dessert. Reasonably popular in Canada, Canadian ice wines have done very well internationally, particularly in Japan. As more competition enters the market from countries such as Chile, prices may begin to fall.

Spirits

The true Canadian booze, rye whiskey, has become quite popular internationally. Sweeter than the Scottish and Irish firewater, rye is often mixed with ginger ale or cola and will be drunk any time during a meal. There are several different brands of rye, with Canadian Club and Crown Royal probably being the most recognisable. Other spirits such as vodka are also produced, as well as Yukon Jack – the self-professed 'Black Sheep of Canadian Whiskey'. Surprisingly, given its 50 per cent alcohol content, it is so sweet that it can, and probably should, be drunk straight from the bottle. Water is recommended the next day.

Dining and Holiday Celebrations

Dining is rarely a formal affair in Canada. Meals at Thanksgiving (early October) and Christmas usually involve a turkey and perhaps a ham, although ethnicity governs the various customs. Christmas is a big event everywhere, despite a relatively low church attendance. As December is the darkest month of the year, the lights on houses and the festive environment of the holiday season help to break the monotony of winter. Mandarin oranges imported from Japan and China also appear around December, as does (non-alcoholic) eggnog. Pumpkins and pumpkin pie are as popular as in the USA, while Thanksgiving is celebrated early because of the earlier Canadian harvest. The end of October sees a spike in sugar consumption and cavities as children circulate their neighbourhoods 'begging' for Halloween candy.

Festivals are common in most cities, but food rarely forms the centrepiece unless the festival is ethnic in origin. The Calgary Stampede, the world's largest rodeo, is celebrated each July and free breakfasts of flapjacks (pancakes) and sausages are offered across the city.

Although guests invited to a home usually bring a bottle of wine, it is not necessarily ordered in restaurants as costs are prohibitive. And because dining out is so extremely common, people do not bother with much ceremony. Except in upmarket restaurants, servers are relaxed and friendly and water is a perfectly acceptable accompaniment to a meal. Formality varies throughout the country, with the larger urban areas being predictably more stylish, yet not always more formal. Rarely will a restaurant have an enforced dress code, but patrons usually prefer to wear a jacket or suit at nicer establishments. Private clubs have codes, but their importance in Canadian society is marginal.

Generally Canadians use their cutlery in the same manner as the British, but the American style of eating almost exclusively with the fork does occur. Such social mores vary throughout the country because of the immigrant culture. Ethnic districts of the bigger cities really do mimic their cultural heritage, both in food and style. Virtually all Canadians know how to eat with chopsticks, for example, and wouldn't think it odd to have sushi one day, followed by pizza delivered to the home and then Mexican, with a more formal French or Italian meal at the weekend; Sunday might mean meatloaf or roast beef.

Language

Language is important in Canada and forms a common theme in both politics and daily life in many regions. French Quebec represents only one example of the diversity, as both urban and rural communities across the country retain some of their linguistic characteristics.

People basically fall into three linguistic groups: **Anglophone** (English-speaking), **Francophone** (French-speaking) and **allophone** (neither English nor French). At a federal level Canada has been officially bilingual since the 1960s, and enshrined multiculturalism helps protect other minority languages. While threatened, many aboriginal languages are still spoken and Inuit even employs a different alphabet for the language's difficult phonics.

Bilingualism and the Government

Since the 1960s Canada has had an official policy of bilingualism, which in theory means that all residents may be helped in either English or French. New Brunswick is the only province that is officially fully bilingual, but the federal government displays both languages across the country. All young Canadians are required to study the other language for at least a few years, although only a small number of them achieve proficiency. It would seem logical that Quebecers would have a particular focus on English as a firm second language, given the minority status of French in North America; however, nationalists have resisted bilingual education and all things English. Nonetheless, Montreal is very multilingual and, as in Ottawa, both official languages plus a host of others are frequently heard and intermixed.

The introduction or imposition of national bilingualism was a contentious process. French Canadians had historically been under-represented and some in English-speaking Canada were opposed to what they saw as an imposition. One story that circulates is of an Albertan who apparently declared, 'God meant us to speak English, that's why He wrote the Bible in it.'

Overall, French was embraced, and English Canadians have long been studying French with varying degrees of success. It is common for all teaching in schools to be in French and, although graduates do not come out perfectly bilingual, their comprehension is usually excellent. There are also programmes to teach ethnic communities solely in French. Spanish schools are on the rise; although Canada will remain an English–French–Aboriginal country, parents may decide that Spanish is a more relevant second language in the Americas.

As many government departments require bilingual proficiency, and as a result of Ottawa's geographic location, a disproportionate number of French Canadians are present within the national bureaucracy: many of the federal government's employees come from Hull, Quebec, across from Ottawa. Bilingual training is paid for and increasing numbers of Anglophones are gaining a working proficiency of French, but western Canadians will not be employed by the federal government because of the travelling distance.

Canadian English

Frequently mistaken for the American or Yankee variety, Canadian English has some unique features and Canadians take great exception to being mistaken for their southern neighbours. Many Brits will say they cannot differentiate between the two voices, but with a little effort it can be done. What is often taken to be American may well be Canadian, as Canadians do not have a Southern drawl, nor do they use the tough, mid-mouth New England pronunciation. The mid-west USA uses much harder vowel sounds while the west coast of the USA is somewhat closer to the Canadian voice, although those speakers still draw out their vowels.

Canadian spoken English is relatively free of slang, which renders it quite understandable. The most distinct expression employed throughout the country is the national plea for affirmation – 'eh?'. The origin of 'eh?' as a termination to a sentence is not clear, but it may have come from the French, who tend to increase the pitch of a sentence, particularly a question: 'How's it going, eh?' Whatever the root, 'eh?' is heard frequently, and the general pitch of Canadian phrases increases through the statement, whereas Americans tend to emphasise the beginning of a sentence. The other easily identifiable element of speech is the tight pronunciation of 'ou' in words such as 'out' and 'about'. This probably came from the Scots and is an easy way to identify Canadian English.

Enunciation does change from west to east, although not nearly as dramatically as in the UK. The most distinct accents are found in Newfoundland and Cape Breton Island (above Nova Scotia) with some carry-over into the other Atlantic provinces. While the post-revolutionary loyalist influx from the USA greatly influenced Canadian English, both Newfoundland and Cape Breton already had well-established populations before that time. Many visitors will take the regional lilt as Irish and this influence has spread to different parts of the country. In rural Ontario and in the west a particularly nasal form of English can be heard. It has a western twang, but is unique to the region.

Canadian English is polite and straightforward. 'You're welcome' is almost always used in response to a 'thank you'. 'Please' is important. While 'Zee' is on its way in, 'Zed' remains the last letter of the alphabet. Canadian spelling, although distinct, is closer to British spelling than American and was introduced by the first prime minister, Sir John A. Macdonald, to stem the tide of American influence. Because of television and the Internet, American spelling and styles of speech are always present, but new influences in the American voice, such as Ebonics, do not appear to be crossing the border. In a trend that flows in the other direction, Canadians have long been hired to anchor news and talk shows in the United States, at least partly for their clear spoken language.

French Canadian

Just short of one in four Canadians speaks French as a first language and, in stark contrast to the crisp English of the country, Canada's French is unique and can be difficult to understand. That noted, it is important to understand that French Canadian is not a *patois* or Creole, in fact it is perhaps the oldest French still spoken on the planet, predating the French Revolution and even a unified language in France. Immigrants to the New World spoke and retained royal French. In France this gave way to Parisian French after the Revolution, while the many English words incorporated into the language in both Canada and France have been absorbed differently. Despite the obvious differences, it is a myth that French-speaking Canadians are not understood in France.

Canada contains many French-speaking communities and two general Franco-linguistic groups – Québécois and Acadian. Acadian French is found in the Atlantic provinces, particularly New Brunswick, as well as in the small surviving community in Louisiana in the southern USA. Québécois French is spoken, with different accents, throughout Quebec and in parts of all the provinces west of Quebec. Some communities roll their Rs and a Z sound is everpresent, particularly in Montreal where working-class communities speak with an accent that has come to be called *joual*.

Visitors with an average command of French will be able to make themselves understood, but it takes time to pick up all the idiosyncrasies of French Canadian speech. Although more and more educated and well-travelled people do not use older French Canadian forms, you may still hear pronouns placed on both sides of a verb: *t'en veux-tu?* (Would you like some?) and the basic *Je suis* (I am) manifested as *Chu* (don't attempt this yourself; stick to formal French). Unlike in France, there is no weekend in Canada, rather a *fin de semaine* (end of the week) while a hot dog is not *un ôtdog*, but is translated directly and becomes a *chien-chaud*. This is a common coping tool within French Canadian. In the face of so many English and American expressions and products, rather than always inventing entirely new words, they are simply translated. When English expressions are incorporated into speech, they are often pronounced with an exaggerated American accent – *le GANGster*.

Radio-Canada, the French arm of the Canadian Broadcasting Corporation, generally uses a more standard type of French in its news and current affairs programmes, and most print materials also match the rules of standard French. The use of French varies across the country and ranges from a small percentage of the population in BC to an overwhelming majority in Quebec. It is wrong to assume that all French-speakers know English or that all Anglophone Canadians are unilingual. Schooling and the reality of geography have meant that most French Canadians have at least a minimal exposure to English. On the other side of the divide, thousands of Anglophone children are schooled in French, so many English Canadians do have some facility in that language.

Allophones

As many as 18 per cent of Canadians, over six million people, grow up speaking a language at home that is neither English or French, although most will have some facility in at least one of the national languages. Aboriginal languages should understandably be seen apart as they are not immigrant tongues per se. The largest aboriginal linguistic group is the Cree, with around 80,000 speakers, the majority of whom live across the central north. The second largest group, the Inuit, constitute a majority of Nunavut's population. Many other languages exist and, while some are tiny and threatened, they manage to survive due to isolation and a strong cultural heritage.

The First Nations

Canada's aboriginal people are now generally referred to as First Nations, a term dating back to the 1970s. First Nations, Inuit and Métis peoples in Canada are collectively categorised as aboriginal or native, but are never called Indians. The term 'Indian' continues to be used legally for the Parliamentary Indian Act and hence Status Indians – those who qualify under Canadian law as First Nations. In common vernacular, 'Indian' is used with decreasing frequency and has negative connotations. The First Nations do not include the Inuit people, who have historically been called Eskimo – or Cree, for 'eaters of raw meat'. The Métis or mixed-blood aboriginal–European people, are not included as a First Nation, but their unique cultural heritage has gained some legal representation.

The third most commonly spoken language in Canada is Chinese, which overtook Italian a number of years ago. The bulk of the Canadian Chinese community is centred in the major cities and speaks Cantonese. The handover of Hong Kong to China had a major effect on Canada's Chinese community and particularly that on the west coast. Although Toronto is home to the largest Chinese community in Canada in percentage terms, Chinese form the largest visible and linguistic minority in Greater Vancouver and British Columbia. Italian is the fourth most commonly spoken language and German the fifth, but these groups are diminishing because of reduced immigration and greater assimilation. Punjabi will likely replace German in fifth place and Spanish will continue to grow in importance with the increase in new Canadians from Mexico and elsewhere in Latin America.

The language mosaic in Canada is even more complicated than the sheer numbers suggest. Toronto receives by far the greatest influx of immigrants, where 44 per cent of the population now qualifies as allophone, yet languages are more likely to survive several generations in isolated environments. German, for example, remains an important language on the prairies and in rural Ontario, particularly among Mennonites, Hutterites and other similar groups. Equally, Icelandic, barely statistically relevant, survives in a few communities in Manitoba, much as Ukrainian does in other communities. In Montreal, a sizeable Haitian community adheres to the language and the political reality of that country.

Visitors to Canada are often surprised to encounter Canadians, born and raised in the country, who have either a very limited or an accented use of the majority language. Through a national policy of multiculturalism, the government supports education in different languages, but the reality of the modern economy and Canada's location next to the monolithic United States means smaller language groups will be gradually enveloped, yet individual traditions will carry on.

Architecture

Almost invariably, Canada's architectural styles reflect the country's climate, diversity and youth. With an interpretative eye, visitors may distinguish and enjoy influences from Canada's many immigrant groups as well as the economic realities of the different regions.

Scottish brick, once used to ballast ships coming from the Old World, stands proudly mixed with French and modern building styles in the large cities of central Canada. French regions are dotted by Catholic churches (often nearly empty, even on a Sunday) with Montreal's Notre Dame Cathedral competing in grandeur with European edifices.

Where several variances of faith settled the construction reflected that history. There are Protestant churches – some very modern, with an American style of evangelism – throughout Canada. Southern Alberta has the first Mormon temple built outside the United States. Looking back to earlier migrations, some prairie cities and towns exhibit beautiful orthodox cathedrals where services continue to be held in Ukrainian.

The Atlantic provinces combine stone with wood construction. Clapboard houses perched on rocks in tiny fishing villages are reminiscent of the fishing out-ports that protected the distinct Newfoundland accent and folk music. Saint John's, Newfoundland, has narrow, hilly streets that become so clogged with snow that trucks must dump it in the harbour.

Fredericton, New Brunswick's capital, is defined by impressive loyalist construction. After the American Revolution, Canada's population virtually doubled and the new settlers brought their style of living with them from New England. Houses once adapted from Britain again complied with their new environment, developing more insulation and eventually shrinking from two or more storeys to one when migrants settled the prairies. Large wooden homes with wide verandas adapted well to New Brunswick and Ontario, but did not survive long in the dry, windy west. Indeed it is only in modern times that homes in western Canada have grown in response to wealth, insulation and excellent central heating. Modern Calgary, home to Canada's oil wealth, is an impressive, if excessively spread out city, where three- and four-car garages are not uncommon.

The 'downtown' sections of Canadian cities also reflect wealth and climate. Tall towers appear almost glued together – a fact that proves alluringly warm in February. Montreal has gone a step further, building a city, or more specifically a network of tunnels, underneath the older one. While the lack of sunlight is unappealing, the underground city keeps everything going until spring, when the inhabitants emerge from hibernation.

Vancouver is Canada's great experiment – high-density living among raw nature. By building up rather than out, Vancouverites have little space, but a dense urban environment with access to mountains and ocean. Everything on the west coast is constructed with earthquakes in mind. The glass towers of Vancouver have been greatly financed with money from Hong Kong and purchased from people from around the world. The success of the Vancouver construction market has begun to spread, with Toronto's new waterfront developments taking on a distinctly west coast feel.

Victoria has responded to this boom by imposing a height restriction, protecting its colonial atmosphere. Between Victoria and the mainland, the islands, which enjoy Canada's warmest climate, are dotted with beautiful cottages and impressive west coast houses. Inland in British Columbia, some towns are immaculate whereas others maintain a rough mining or lumber feel – some residents, rather than gardening, choose to decorate their gardens with old cars.

The one quintessential style of Canadian architecture derives its roots from the country's unification. As the Canadian Pacific Railway was laid out across the continent, a series of dramatic château-style hotels was built. Large stone structures, often with copper roofs, are found in large cities and the dramatic western parks. The Banff Springs Hotel is testament to Canada's grandeur, and the Château Frontenac in Quebec's French colonial old town stands as an image of Canada and Quebec's uniqueness within North America. The Canadian parliament in Ottawa also reflects this style and offers a degree of stability and history to a very young country.

British migrants will perhaps feel most at home in central Canada, where brick remains the dominant building tool (excluding some Québécois wood construction), whereas further west and on the east coast wood dominates. While wood construction may not last hundreds of years, it is a fantastic tool for experimenting with styles. Sandstone, used for larger buildings through the mid-20th century, has since given way to steel, cement and glass as witnessed in modern towers throughout the country. All the glass helps to maximise light during the short winter days.

To enjoy Canada's architecture it is important to understand how the different regions and the climate influence it. Although gradually changing, Canadians are primarily a suburban people, generally opting for private homes with gardens and basements over apartments. Large roads are not beautiful, but they are functional during winter and a result of urban sprawl. Houses that are plain on the outside may be truly unique on the inside, and, slowly, interesting art is decorating the ultra-modern city centres. Where older buildings exist they have been protected, providing a sense of history.

One of the enduring British legacies within Canadian cities is the abundance of park space. Even in Montreal, the second-largest French city in the world, the British were able to designate green spaces, leaving the city with a legacy of over a thousand parks. In Toronto, Canada's oft polluted mega-city, a view from the CN Tower reveals thousands of acres of green space.

Profiles of the Regions

'O Canada'

The Canadian national anthem is heard quite frequently (mainly during sports events) and is sung in both official languages. Although the tune is the same, some of the words have different meanings in English and French. 'O Canada' was declared the national anthem 100 years after it was first sung, and there is no copyright on either the lyrics or music.

O Canada, our home and native land.	*O Canada, terre de nos aïeux,*
True patriot love in all thy sons command.	*Ton front est ceint de fleurons glorieux.*
With glowing hearts we see thee rise,	*Car ton bras sait porter l'épée,*
The True North strong and free.	*Il sait porter la croix.*
From far and wide,	*Ton histoire est une épopée*
O Canada, we stand on guard for thee.	*Des plus brillants exploits.*
God keep our land glorious and free.	*Et ta valeur, de foi trempée.*
O Canada, we stand on guard for thee.	*Protègera nos foyers et nos droits.*
O Canada, we stand on guard for thee.	*Protègera nos foyers et nos droits.*

It is easy to understand how a country stretching 5,000 kilometres from east to west, and as much again from north to south, could be particularly regional in its make-up. The trip from Victoria, British Columbia's capital, to Ottawa, the national capital, involves nearly a full day of travel – flying – and Saint John's, Newfoundland on the far east coast is not much closer! Canada's geographic diversity is legendary, and its people reflect that reality. Historic immigration patterns are regionally biased, as is language. Even economies vary, and provincial governments control major social services such as education and the bulk of healthcare.

Our image of Canada often focuses on the French–English duality, but this is only part of the equation. Frequently, without even knowing it, Canadians will generalise about their country from their local perspective, and assume food, drink and climate are the same everywhere. Many Canadians will never visit their capital city, national art gallery or even one of the three bordering oceans. With great distances between cities, communities are geographically isolated and, although the vast majority of Canadians live in urban areas, big city life in Toronto differs substantially from that of St John's or Whitehorse. Pierre Berton, one of Canada's great popular historians, once defined a Canadian as 'someone who can make love in a canoe without tipping it'. Canada's political balance is just as precarious, resembling perhaps that of the European Union. In many ways Canada is as much an idea as it is a nation in the traditional ethnic and geographic sense.

There are ten provinces and three territories. Canadian bureaucracy is not simple, and each provincial jurisdiction has its own rules and even professional organisations. Qualifying as a medical professional in one province, for example, does not necessarily facilitate working elsewhere in the country. Quebec, like Scotland, maintains a different legal code, and each province and territory manages details such as insurance and vehicle registration. When choosing to live in Canada, it is vital to understand which Canada. The Maple Leaf flies quite proudly in most parts of the country, but lifestyle is driven by topography, economics and climate. Immigrants to the country are particularly proud of their new home and are, perhaps, the least regional in their outlook, while some Quebecers, Westerners and Maritimers long for greater autonomy – or even outright independence. Despite constant denials, Canadians *are* nationalists, but they have trouble articulating what that nation is. In understanding the whole, Canada must be seen as the sum of its parts, united by basic concepts of human rights, social services, individual freedoms and the cold realities of winter.

British Columbia

Indisputably Canada's most beautiful province, British Columbia has towering mountains, a spectacular coastline, salmon runs, giant cedars and Vancouver, the country's most glamorous city. Despite fantastic natural wealth, British Columbia's economy is often in flux due to a shaky resource sector, powerful trade unions and a sometimes-frenetic housing market. Increased demand from Asia helps to offset the weakening US market to the south, and the construction boom associated with the 2010 Winter Olympics has resulted in labour shortages in the Vancouver area.

Quick Facts: British Columbia

Population: Over 4 million.

Largest cities: Greater Vancouver (2.2 million), Victoria, Kelowna and Okanagan Valley.

Major ethnic groups: British/Western European, Chinese (particularly Cantonese-speaking), South Asian (with a strong Sikh influence), First Nations (many different groups), increasing Latino population.

Physical highlights: Mountains, ocean, islands; the country's mildest climate; and the threat of earthquakes.

Major events: World Exposition 1986; planning for 2010 Vancouver/Whistler Winter Olympics; Indy race now gone from Vancouver after local opposition.

Economic highlights: Regionally low unemployment. The resource-driven economy suffers many challenges: lumber and fishing are in decline, mining is strong, and oil and gas are booming in the northeast. Filming and information technology are in flux; tourism and other services; many retirees.

Issues if moving to British Columbia: Many others have the same idea; most expensive housing in Canada; bureaucratic and heavily unionised.

Attractive to immigrants, the Lower Mainland area around greater Vancouver receives the second highest number of non-Canadian migrants after Ontario. An impressive flow of capital from Hong Kong has poured into real estate, and the pejorative nickname 'Hong-couver' is bantered about.

There are many reasons to choose British Columbia as a place to live: a mild climate, healthy lifestyle and physical beauty. These factors have also had a great impact on prices and have led to Vancouver's housing being the most expensive in all Canada. The apartment that rents for C$700 a month in other parts of the country can cost C$1,200 in Vancouver, especially if located near the water. On Vancouver Island, greater Victoria has also seen a significant rise in housing prices, driven by retirees and those who embrace that city's drier microclimate. Communities further up Vancouver Island are considerably more affordable, as are those well outside the greater Vancouver area.

Culturally, the west coast has its own relaxed approach to life, with a little image-consciousness thrown in. Vancouver is one of the healthiest cities on earth and people engage in active pursuits such as biking, walking and enjoying Stanley Park, one of the world's great urban parks. The area is one of those rare places where one can ski and sail on the same day. Vancouver Island's west coast even has a good surfing beach (wetsuit recommended), and sea kayaks are seen all over the coast.

A frequent complaint among newcomers concerns the difficulty of the job market. Even though the province is young, the economic élite are well established and their community reasonably closed. Ethnic groups have become more ghettoised in British Columbia than in other parts of the country (except for Montreal) and it can be a long process to be recognised. For climatic reasons, many immigrants choose British Columbia in the hope of enjoying the benefits of Canada without experiencing the extremes of climate. Internally, Canadians have long migrated to the west coast to retire, driving up house prices, but introducing no new industries beyond construction. Many, many British Columbians try to build a consulting clientele, but competition is fierce. More traditional employers such as the government have implemented mass layoffs, and tariff disputes with the United States have hurt a lumber industry so aptly endorsed by Monty Python's 'Lumberjack song'.

Vancouver

With more apartments than houses, Vancouver almost strikes a balance between dense urban living and accessible raw nature – bears and racoons are not too clear on boundaries. Two hours north of Vancouver 'as the BMW flies', in the words of Canadian journalist Allan Fotheringham, is the resort town of **Whistler**, the country's largest ski resort, which will host the alpine events during the 2010 Vancouver/Whistler Winter Olympics. In an ironic twist, British Columbia has all but banned cigarette smoking while tacitly tolerating cannabis (this may not last). Depending on political winds, one Vancouver café sometimes encourages its patrons to smoke pot openly. Smoke-ins (pro-marijuana rallies) take place fairly frequently in both Vancouver and Victoria and police just let the offending material burn off.

Greenpeace was born in Vancouver in the 1960s and David Suzuki and his environmental foundation are based in the city. The Green movement, important in British Columbia, often pits traditional blue-collar workers against middle-class, urban youth. The biggest conflict in recent years revolved around the old-growth forests of Clayoquot Sound along Vancouver Island's west coast. The lumber industry, still a principal employer, intended to harvest the giant old-growth trees while environmentalists, scientists and First Nations actively opposed any such move. The economics were obvious as the huge trees are extremely valuable, but in the end protection prevailed for much of the area. Support for conservation runs high across the country and big business was presented as the enemy. Nevertheless, few alternative industries exist for many of the workers, and timber, in and of itself, is a renewable resource.

Vancouver Island's communities are eclectic. It seems as though half the homes on the island are works in progress, with cottage industries, tourism and organic farming slowly replacing lumber and fishing. Burdened by fewer snow and frost days than the rest of the country, the Island and the Lower Mainland are attractive places for migrants. Trees stay in leaf much longer than elsewhere and the snow generally remains up in the mountains – good news for both skiers and drivers. Precipitation nevertheless hits the coast eventually, and Vancouver's rainy skies are similar to those in Britain. Areas further up the coast and the Queen Charlotte Islands (Haida Gwaii) often experience torrential rains. Prince Rupert, a small port city located just south of Alaska, is the rainiest community in the country.

The economy of the Lower Mainland, like other urban areas in Canada, is service-driven and the IT sector has done well. Beyond the political boundaries of Canada, British Columbia belongs to another important economic zone

Stanley Park

Vancouver's heart and soul suffered a major loss during the 2006–7 winter when hundreds of majestic old-growth trees were lost to powerful wind storms. With sustained winds over 160kph (over 100mph), ancient trees were uprooted and a landslide caused a partial closure of the seawall – the paved trail around the park. Even the air-supported roof on BC Place Stadium (where the Olympic opening ceremonies will be held) deflated. Wind storms are certainly not unknown to the Pacific coast, but their frequency and sustained ferocity may be attributed to increased climate change. Again in the 2007–8 winter, major storms caused power cuts throughout the Lower Mainland and Vancouver Island. Stanley Park itself remains wonderfully green, however, and much more open in areas due to the massive loss of trees.

Housing in Whistler

The accommodation situation in Whistler remains in a state of crisis that will only be exacerbated by the Olympics. It is not uncommon to find four young people sharing one or at best two rooms and paying prices unheard of in the rest of Canada. Housing costs are astronomical in the resort and even with thousands of hotel rooms competition has not driven prices down. In addition to outstanding skiing and outdoor activities, service jobs are abundant and wages (with tips) are relatively high, but finding accommodation can be such a challenge as to make the option unappealing. As the Olympics approach, the community is scrambling to develop lower-cost housing for workers; one idea being discussed is to adapt cargo containers into modular apartments!

called Cascadia. Taking its name from the Cascade Mountains, the region is loosely defined as British Columbia and Washington State but it sometimes stretches to include Oregon and Alaska. Regardless, the region's economy was bolstered by Microsoft and the new economy that came to life in Seattle. Vancouver did not experience the boom that Seattle went through in the 1990s, but by virtue of its proximity, education and lifestyle it benefited from significant spill-over effects. With Vancouver as Canada's largest port, the Asia-Pacific economic environment has become extremely important to British Columbia, with Cascadia's view focusing perhaps even more towards the Pacific than the traditional east.

Another noticeable addition to British Columbia's and Vancouver's economy involves the film industry. Competing with Toronto and Montreal for the title of 'Hollywood North', Vancouver has the largest film industry in Canada. Originally American productions were drawn north by a favourable exchange rate and a diverse environment. Gradually the market responded and a billion-dollar industry emerged. As a result of a stronger currency, greater competition and a political shift in California, filming in BC and across Canada has experienced a few difficult years: before becoming governor and championing the return of filming to Los Angeles, Arnold Schwarzenegger actually filmed in Vancouver! Current productions appear to be on the rise in Vancouver and across Canada, although the industry will certainly remain fickle. Among many well-known productions that were filmed in Vancouver were: *The X Files*, *Catwoman*, *The Butterfly Effect*, *The Core*, *Fantastic Four* and three of the 'Scary Movie' series. In 1981 Stallone swam in the Frazer River for *Rambo, First Blood* – and fought his way back in 1985 for *Rocky 4*!

Driving the current economy in the Lower Mainland is an unprecedented construction boom linked to the 2010 Winter Olympics, housing speculation and a labour shortage (partly due to similar booms in neighbouring provinces). Many construction projects have been put on hold because costs have risen so dramatically, and cost overruns associated with the Olympics may even double the projected costs of the event.

The west coast's artistic community is vibrant and a regional style of fine art has appeared. Artists are everywhere. Vancouver has a film festival and several theatre companies, but native art is most distinctively British Columbian. BC's most celebrated artist, Emily Carr (1871–1945), was born in Victoria and after studying in the USA, England and France returned home to discover the beauty of her own land and to capture the indigenous world. There is now an Emily Carr School of Art and exhibits of her work take place frequently. Images of evocative skies setting over the islands and interpretative paintings of animals, particularly whales, salmon and ravens, are common themes in west-coast art. The artists use curved, clean lines and versions of such works turn up everywhere. While the customs and immigration experience is never enjoyable, a beautiful customs hall, framed by totems and a waterfall, greets those arriving at Vancouver's airport after an international flight. A recently released C$10 note captures British Columbia with the Queen on one side and an image of a First Nations jade sculpture on the other. The actual work, one of the finest of its kind, can be seen in the departures terminal at Vancouver airport.

The Great Outdoors

Beyond the Lower Mainland and southern Vancouver Island, the rest of British Columbia is a vast territory and home to about 1.2 million of the province's 4.2 million inhabitants. 'Up Island', referring to everywhere north of Victoria on Vancouver Island, is lumber, fishing, retirement and holiday country, with a strong dose of environmentally conscious, alternative lifestyle hippies – the Green Party may win its first seat in the area.

The Great Outdoors can be found everywhere, with skiing, kayaking and just about any other activity easily available. There is a rougher edge to British Columbia in its frontier roots. Beyond flashy, modern Vancouver and class-conscious **Victoria**, many British Columbians are straight-talking, beer-drinking working folk who support conservative politics, play hockey and who may even go to church. Residents of larger cities view these many smaller communities as redneck or hick, and rural British Columbian culture can differ markedly from that of the Lower Mainland. In a heavily unionised environment, BC's labour organisations are militant and often at odds with the provincial government. Cutbacks in government services have caused much consternation in interior parts of the province, but a beautiful environment and a controversial resolution to international lumber disputes continue to keep hopes alive.

Further inland, the other reasonably populated area of the province embraces the **Okanagan Valley**, which stretches from the city of Kamloops in south-central British Columbia, down through Vernon, Kelowna and Penticton to the border with Washington State. Whereas the American Okanagan region is seen, at best, as a hinterland, the British Columbia valley is a holiday destination for western Canadians. Long, warm lakes, attractive, service-driven cities and a

Case Study: Sarah Wright, Physiotherapist

Sarah, an English physiotherapist in her 40s, moved with her Canadian husband Peter and three children to British Columbia from Dorset in 2000. Currently they live in the community of Tsawwassen, just south of Vancouver. This is Sarah's second time living in Canada, as she worked for three years in Toronto in the late 1980s.

Was it difficult for you to practise as a medical professional in Canada?

It was quite easy for me to get my physiotherapy licence, but only as a result of being grandfathered in, as I had worked in Toronto from 1988 to 1990. Had I not worked in Canada prior to 1993 it would have been a lengthy and costly business and involved a lot of studying for the national exam.

As a physiotherapist in England, I found the profession was more highly regarded and we had greater latitude in treating patients according to our judgement. I also believe we were called on for our opinion far more as equals by the physicians than we are here in British Columbia.

It is a great shame that families without cover have to struggle to find payment for certain medications and end up hitting hard times and sometimes bankruptcy. Also, the fact that we do not wear uniforms is disgusting when you think what lands on you day in, day out while treating patients.

On a positive note, the Canadian work day starts earlier, leaving more time at the end of the day to pursue leisure activities. Leisure is a much bigger deal here, with a more relaxed way of life and far more opportunities.

How do you find the general quality of life for your family?

I find the people much friendlier than in England – they don't have to have known you a lifetime to welcome you into their social group, and our social life is very active, with gatherings in people's houses, kids included. This has been very important to me, as we left a great group of friends in the UK.

vibrant wine and produce industry define the dry valley. The Okanagan produces great quantities of apples, pears and stone fruits. An important highway (British Columbia's only toll road) cuts across the mountains and has made the Okanagan or 'interior' accessible by car from Greater Vancouver in only four hours. Lower house prices and more sun have drawn people to the interior from other parts of the province and from the east.

Physically, British Columbia is like an accordion, with range on range of mountains pressed together, with the Pacific to the west and the rest of Canada to the east. Resources drove settlement of the different valleys, and each area has a distinct feel. Only four main routes cross the province from east to west and populations are scattered up and down the valleys. Lumber remains vital, as does mining and tourism, with the latter driven by lakes, golf and mountain recreation in the summer and skiing and snowmobiling in the winter. Northeastern British Columbia, which flattens out into range and oil country, has a culture closer to

The kids absolutely love it out here. They were 8, 6 and 3 when we moved; the older ones had their reservations, but camping holidays, seeing bears, whale watching and all the sports they partake in have definitely made living in British Columbia their preference. The boys play hockey three-quarters of the year and they also play baseball and dabble in other sports. My daughter plays soccer and is trying out softball this year. On that same note, Peter and I also play baseball, not very well but it doesn't seem to matter; we are part of a beer league and there is always a party at one of the team players' houses after the game.

With regard to schooling, the environment is far more relaxed. There is no pressure to conform to the dreaded SATs, and far more emphasis on play and co-operation between classmates than reading, writing and maths. Canadian children have caught up to the English kids by the time they reach high school. I wonder what all the fuss is about educating kids as they turn 4 – this may work for a few, but here they are of the opinion that it is worth letting kids be kids for a little longer and tackling reading age 6. The boys were definitely a year ahead academically when they arrived and the older boy is a year ahead at school. English teachers told us to keep them challenged and ahead, whereas the Canadian teachers said let them be with age-equivalent kids. Now the older one is a year ahead of his age and the middle one with his peers.

The fact that children do not wear uniforms is difficult as a parent but the kids are thrilled. I have to say it is shocking to see adolescents coming out of school dressed as if they could go straight to a bar.

Generally I feel that the Canadian way of life offers more opportunities; my children definitely would not have been able to partake in as many activities back in England as the local communities simply do not have the same parent-organised programmes. Moreover, the costs of leisure activities are prohibitively high for middle-class families in the UK.

that of neighbouring Alberta. Dawson Creek in the province's northeast marks the official start of the Alaska Highway and is a long way, physically and figuratively, from the liberal, urban southwest.

The entire west coast is unstable geologically. Little yellow triangles posted along arterial roads designate disaster response routes. Everyone is waiting for a *big* earthquake. Some time, somewhere in the future, the Lower Mainland, Vancouver Island, the west coast and Seattle to the south fully expect a major shake – perhaps measuring over nine on the Richter scale. Preparations for such an event have been under way for years, and although it is impossible to predict magnitude or timing, British Columbia remains fully aware of the threat and has factored plate tectonics into construction, health and emergency response plans. Living along the coast means feeling the odd tremor and having earthquake insurance. Perhaps because of the decriminalisation of marijuana, residents appear quite relaxed about the whole thing.

Case Study: Eric Hall, Computer Systems Consultant

Eric is in his early 60s and has lived in Canada since 1974. Although work has taken him across the country, he has lived only in the province of British Columbia. Originally from Nottingham, Eric and his wife Marion settled in Surrey, British Columbia, a booming, multi-ethnic city located south of Vancouver, just north of the US border. In 2001, Eric and Marion sold their Surrey home and moved to the Okanagan Valley in the province's interior.

In his 30-plus years working and living in Canada, Eric has had a good quality of life and has enjoyed various professional successes. Interestingly, while Eric still feels very much like a British person living in Canada, his children see themselves as entirely Canadian. Having worked with computer systems in the lumber industry, Eric moved on to private consulting in addition to leading British visitors on tours around Canada.

How has British Columbia's Lower Mainland changed during your time there?

British Columbia has very polarised politics and a variety of views and people, but has always been a beautiful place to live. Surrey reflects Canada's policy of multiculturalism. Unlike in the United States, where everyone is encouraged to become 'American', in Canada people are encouraged to maintain and celebrate their ethnic background. Living in British Columbia's Lower Mainland, different ethnic groups dominate particular areas. Whereas Vancouver proper is fairly mixed, central Surrey has become a centre for the south Asian and particularly the Punjabi community from northwest India. Overall the ethnic diversification has been smooth, but the modern face of the Lower Mainland has changed quite dramatically.

European Settlement in British Columbia

European settlement in British Columbia dates back only to the mid-1800s when, in 1843, Fort Victoria was established as a distant post of the Hudson's Bay Company. Soon afterwards, the Colony of Vancouver Island came into being in order to fortify the area against American claims and the Oregon Treaty, which was to establish the 49th parallel as the western US–British North America border – Vancouver Island reaches below the imaginary line. In 1858 gold was discovered in the British Columbia interior and soon 20,000 prospectors arrived in sleepy Victoria. According to one theory, the town of Hope to the east of Vancouver, now known for spectacular wood carvings, was originally a supply centre for miners and was named Fort Hope in 1848 in the 'hope' that it was north of the 49th parallel. As miners rushed inland, a separate colony, British Columbia, was formed with its capital in New Westminster, a city that now makes up part of Greater Vancouver. In 1866, one year before Canada was born, the British government combined the two colonies and the capital moved to Victoria in 1868. After the rough early days of the gold rush, British Columbia took on and mostly retained a staunchly British outlook. Thousands

In addition to significant immigration from Hong Kong, India and elsewhere, the population has boomed as a result of internal migration. Through the 1990s Surrey was one of Canada's fastest-growing cities, more than doubling its population in a short period to its present 400,000. Such growth has resulted in obvious problems with crowding, traffic and housing prices. The climate remains attractive, when compared with more eastern points, but the winter rain can take a toll.

Why did you move to the province's interior?

As has been the case with many people from the greater Vancouver area, we found that by moving to the Okanagan we could build or purchase a similar house to what we had in Surrey much more reasonably. In the interior we live in a community of around 5,500 people, but are not far from larger centres with all the necessary services. The dry Okanagan climate may be slightly colder than we like in the winter and a little hotter than ideal in summer, but overall, when compared to Surrey, we are happy to leave the rain behind.

What recommendations would you have for someone considering a move to Canada?

After our first year in Canada, we returned to Britain in order to confirm that the move was the right one for us. For people currently considering a move, they should at the very least come for an extended holiday – or perhaps consider a house exchange. Unlike most European countries, there is no 'Canadian' climate or economic circumstance; each province and city is different. Different parts of Canada offer different lifestyles. Although we have been happy living in Canada, life is what you make of it, wherever you live.

of Chinese arrived to help construct the railway but they were clearly second-class citizens and not welcome once the work was finished. British Columbia spearheaded the 'Keep Canada White' laws, which were aimed at removing the Chinese and preventing migration from India. While passage throughout the Empire was meant to be unrestricted, Canadian law limited it by passing a 'continuous journey' regulation, which required uninterrupted transit from foreign ports to those in Canada. This law stopped ships from India, as British vessels could easily cross the Atlantic. In 1914 a Japanese ship, the *Komagata Maru*, loaded with would-be migrants from the Punjab, docked in Vancouver, only to be detained and eventually turned back.

The First Nations of the west coast and British Columbia are distinct from other Canadian groups and remain in a different legal position. Unlike the situation with tribal nations of the east and the prairies, treaties are still being negotiated with some British Columbia groups. The traditional European claim that the land was not permanently inhabited is particularly weak in British Columbia as coastal nations built houses and villages, had governments, boats and the enigmatic totems. While many of the challenges facing aboriginal peoples throughout Canada are relevant in British Columbia, some groups have

Case Study: Shirley Whyte, Restaurant Manager

Shirley is in her mid-30s and from Cork, Ireland. She first came to Canada on a one-year work visa. After arriving in Toronto she was quickly offered a job as a restaurant supervisor by Intrawest's Panorama Resort in the British Columbia Mountains. Although a teacher by profession, Shirley did not give teaching in Canada much serious thought, as that would have required medical examinations, which can take up to six months.

How did you organise your work permit from Ireland?

USIT organises the Canadian work visas for Canada and I believe when I applied they had 500 of the one-year visas I received. The Cork office only had 50 available visas so my friend and I camped out in line all night long. The entire process cost around C$1,300, including the visa, flight and insurance.

Why did you choose to fly to Toronto?

Although I am not particularly a city person, I wanted to see Toronto and eastern Canada, before going west. USIT is partnered with SWAP in Canada and therefore we needed to fly to Toronto, Montreal or Vancouver. Coming from Ireland, I had heard about the winter rain in Vancouver so decided to go to central Canada instead. My original plan was to work through the winter in Toronto and then make my way out to the mountains in the summer. As it worked out, I was almost immediately offered a job at Panorama, so made the move faster than at first planned.

What have been your impressions of Canada and Canadians so far?

Despite not being a great fan of cities, I was extremely impressed by Toronto. For such a large city it is clean, friendly, well lit and very diverse. The people are friendly and there was a great deal to do. I would also like to mention just how fantastically helpful the staff were at the SWAP office in Toronto. They were kind and offered many work ideas, eventually putting me in touch with Intrawest, the company that runs Panorama Resort.

One impression of Canadians is that they are very polite and not nearly as sarcastic as we are in Ireland. They respond politely to even the stupidest of questions, something that would surely elicit a snide comment back home.

The country is beautiful and Christmas in the mountains was lovely, despite having less snow here than they did at home in Ireland. While I have no concerns driving on the right, I would not consider driving in Canada during winter; the mountain roads can be treacherous and terrifying.

Economically, wages are higher in Ireland. Even as a supervisor I only earn slightly more than the Irish minimum wage and my employees earn less than the Irish minimum wage. The basic cost of living in Canada is probably lower than in Ireland and staff earning tips make much more than they do officially, but currently in Ireland wages are generally higher and there is just more opportunity.

maintained a vibrant cultural life and identity. With new, progressive treaties and an aggressive political stance, First Nations have won several land claims and have seriously disrupted the development of two ski resorts in the interior. Many of these issues are not likely to be fully resolved in the near future.

Modern British Columbia has shed most of its colonial roots. Elements of society in Victoria still maintain a 'last outpost' attitude where high tea can cost over C$30, but they are progressively drowned out by hippies, environmentalists, immigrants and people who just don't care. British Columbia has a conservative vein to its society, but this is now more manifest in free-market economics, as opposed to social issues. A so-called bible belt inland from Vancouver spills over into the interior, but Greater Vancouver, with half the province's population, is vibrant and mixed. Coined *The Crystal City* by local author Douglas Coupland (known for *Generation X*), because of its ultra-modern, glass skyline, Vancouver is not one city, but a conglomeration of several. The three dominant ethnic groups represented in the area are British/Europeans, Chinese and South Asians, with many other cultures rounding out the mosaic. The principal ethnic groups remain concentrated in certain areas but mixing is increasing as second and third generations become incorporated into the broader British Columbian society. Vancouver also has a vibrant and openly gay community, as well as Canada's roughest area in the 'downtown east side' – an area with serious drug problems.

Summary

Getting to know British Columbia takes time. Already a huge area, its mountains affect travel and define its regions. Many newcomers successfully settle around the bigger cities, but others find the Canada of their imagination in smaller communities buried under snow and sheltered by mountains. As an example, the small city of Nelson in the West Kootenay region is an architectural gem. With its mixed forestry-hippy culture, it became home to many US draft-dodgers during the Vietnam War. Deep snow creates excellent skiing conditions while the rest of the year favours fishing, hiking and hunting. These activities, only hours from a big city, typify British Columbia.

Geographically, British Columbia is very distant from the rest of Canada and could probably survive on its own. Few nations are as blessed with natural wealth and beauty and British Columbians, while being proud Canadians, are very loyal to their province. The west coast is a world unto itself and the interior is wild, beautiful and certainly much more conservative. Climate and geography will always attract other Canadians to British Columbia and, despite Vancouver's faults, it is often rated first or second as the best city in the world in which to live. For those interested in an environment that is a little less modern or refined, British Columbia has hundreds of beautiful valleys, with the more populated having good services that support forestry, mining, farming and ranching activities. Every licence plate states it: 'Beautiful British Columbia'.

Alberta

With its western border defined by the Rocky Mountains and the continental divide, 'Wild Rose Country' has historically been included with the other two prairie provinces. Politically very conservative, Alberta is no longer the lone right-wing province. Rural Alberta is not dissimilar to either Saskatchewan or Manitoba, but the reality of modern Alberta is that the province is one of Canada's most vibrant regions. Calgary has become the country's second most important business city, despite being half the size of Greater Vancouver and one-third the size of Montreal. For numerous reasons those contemplating a move to Canada need to consider Alberta seriously. The strongest economy, low taxes (including no provincial sales tax), a friendly environment and, of course, the Rocky Mountains make Alberta a frequent destination of choice for Canadians migrating within the country.

Alberta is often the butt of jokes in other parts of the country. The question was once asked, 'What is the difference between Calgary and yogurt?' Answer: 'Yogurt has culture.' Albertans are sometimes presented as rural right-wingers who oppose all things Canadian. Alberta was the last province to legalise gay marriage and may be the first to partially privatise healthcare. With huge oil revenues and a booming economy, present-day Albertans pay far more to the federal government than they take out, and the image of former prime minister Pierre Trudeau saluting them with his middle finger sums up the province's feeling of alienation from the rest of the country. Alberta responded by rejecting the eastern political establishment it had never really embraced.

Despite being the most conservative province politically, Alberta is anything but staid. Tourists flock to the Rocky Mountains, and even though Calgarians are friendly, asking for directions can present problems because so many people are newcomers. From the oilfields north of Edmonton, the province's capital, south

---

Quick Facts: Alberta

Population: Over 3.3 million, and growing.

Largest cities: Calgary, Edmonton – over 1 million each and experiencing massive growth.

Major ethnic groups: British/Western European, Ukrainian, Vietnamese, First Nations; many internal Canadian migrants.

Physical highlights: Rocky Mountains, very dry, high desert, prairies.

Economic highlights: Some of the biggest oil and natural gas reserves on earth; educated workforce; booming economy; low taxes; strained public services.

Major events: The Calgary Stampede; the 1988 Winter Olympics and continued sporting events; hosts over 30 festivals annually.

Issues if moving to Alberta: Rising house prices and housing shortages in some communities; oil accounts for nearly one-quarter of the economy; mountain parks are wonderful, but seasonal in terms of employment opportunities.

along Highway 2 to Red Deer through Calgary and south to Lethbridge, the province's main corridor is a booming economic zone that is speckled with oil pumps and surrounded by vast wheat fields and ranch land. Over three million Canadians call Alberta home and, with the highest levels of growth and internal migration, it is expected to have four million inhabitants by 2028. As much as eastern politicians rail against Alberta, Canadians are pouring into the province and its economic contribution is extremely important. For many reasons, businesses from other major centres are relocating to Alberta, bringing in a specialised workforce and over 90 billion dollars in capital investments. Oil and gas have made Alberta rich and continue to represent around 23 per cent of the province's economy. Although significant, a more diverse economy has reduced this percentage from a high of 37 per cent.

Alberta is young. 2005 was the province's 100th birthday and anyone old enough to remember the early days must be amazed by the changes. The 1947 discovery of the Leduc oil field just south of Edmonton led to a boom in the 1970s that doubled the province's population. Workers from across Canada flooded into the cities and turned them from small agricultural centres into important business hubs, with skyscrapers and housing developments as far as the eye could see. In 1971 Peter Lougheed brought the Progressive Conservative Party (yes, an oxymoron) to power by replacing, and all but wiping out, the religious, right-wing Social Credit Party that had ruled since 1935. The Tories have been in power ever since with very little opposition – early in 2008 Albertans again handed the Tories a powerful mandate of 73 out of 82 seats in the provincial legislature. Under the new leader, Ed Stelmach, the Conservatives actually campaigned on a platform of change, but really counted on low voter turnout and an organised political base.

The lack of political diversity in Alberta remains a source of great debate, but Alberta maintains a reasonably clear image of where it is going and who is in charge. The individual is important to Albertans and an incredible sense of community bonds people. The 1988 Winter Olympics in Calgary were widely seen as a great success because of effective management and, in particular, the huge numbers of volunteers. Thousands of Calgarians gave their time to make sure the city welcomed the world. Even today, volunteers wearing cowboy hats greet visitors at the province's two main airports.

Edmonton and Calgary

This tradition of 'boosterism' or support for the local community dates back to the early days of western Canada when new communities desperately sought immigrants to develop the economy. As an obvious result, communities also competed with each other and those rivalries continue to be expressed in sports. Edmonton and Calgary are very similar, both with around one million inhabitants, but they are inveterate rivals. In the days when the two cities'

Case Study: Dave Horan

David Horan is from Shildon, in northeast England, approximately 30 miles from Newcastle. An electrical engineer by trade and now in his late 30s, David was in the process of moving to Canada for several years and only became fully established in his new country in 2005.

What spurred the desire to emigrate to Canada?

I decided several years ago that I was stuck in a rut and fancied a total change in lifestyle. I had always wanted to visit Canada and decided that I would visit for a holiday.

On returning home I decided that I had enjoyed the experience so much that I was prepared to start pursuing the possibility of moving there. I returned to Canada and visited the eastern side in 2003 (staying in Toronto, Kitchener and Belleville) and last year visited the western side (staying in Calgary). Overall the three visits I made were fantastic and the country just got better and better. The standard of living is so much higher than in England; the overall cost of living is greatly reduced compared to our country; the way of life appears to be much more relaxed and the opportunities to experience the great outdoors are vast. Overall the country, I feel, has so much more to offer me than England and I intend to enjoy and reap the benefits the Canadian way of life has to offer.

To make matters even better I have the found the people so friendly and hospitable towards the English. I was quite taken by the level of hospitality the Canadians show. There is so much more to see and do in Canada, and I decided that Calgary was the place for me.

Why have you chosen Calgary?

This part of the country seems so right for me, being an outdoors person. The province has a low taxation bracket, which did help in my decision, and it is a mere one-hour drive to the most beautiful scenery in the world – the Rockies.

professional hockey teams were among the best in the league, stickers on cars stated: 'My two favourite hockey teams are Edmonton and whoever is playing Calgary.' And vice versa. Edmonton is blue- to grey-collar, whereas Calgary is a more white-collar city. In other words, Calgary owns the oil and Edmonton digs it out of the ground. Of course the divides are not that simple and, with the provincial government in Edmonton, a fairly important professional community exists in both cities.

When the oil boom of the 1970s came screeching to a halt with lower prices and an extremely unpopular federal policy, two more bumper stickers came along: 'Please Lord, grant me another oil boom and I promise not to p*** it away this time' and 'Let the eastern bastards freeze in the dark'. Oil costs more to produce in Alberta so lower prices closed down much of the industry, but before prices fell Pierre Trudeau's Liberal government imposed the National Energy Programme, which capped internal prices and nationalised some of the industry. The NEP continues to rankle among Albertans and forms a rallying cry

Cleanliness and standard of living appear so high. The people are fantastic; when I was there in October 2004 the people were so helpful, so much so as to offer me help with job-searching and cheap accommodation in the area, should I not obtain accommodation of my own immediately...something you would not find in England.

How was the immigration process?

The process was very arduous and slow. I registered with a company called 4 Corners Emigration in April 2002 after a seminar and points evaluation appraisal. I began the application process on 15 April 2002 and it was still under way in 2004; however, the bulk of this time was taken up compiling and collating the required information requested by 4 Corners. This included: secondary school and college qualifications, proof of financial funds (required for self-sufficiency if work was not obtained immediately in Canada), proof of not having a criminal record (payment required to obtain certificate from police crime computer showing no criminal activities), a quantity of identical photographs (specific size for future ID card system in Canada).

I had to obtain certification from Canada with regard to my trade qualifications, which were accepted and approved. An employment reference was required from my previous and then-current employer. A birth certificate was also required. I also, on top of the fees required by 4 Corners (almost £5,000), had to pay C$1,525 for a landing fee (this was refundable if I had not been accepted) and C$175 to the Canadian Council of Technicians and Technologist to obtain my certification for my trade qualifications. The information took a substantial amount of time and effort and it was not until January 2004 that the Canadian High Commission started processing my information. 4 Corners quoted an approximate time scale of around 18 months...and that, in the end, was roughly how long it took.

for provincial rights and outright western and Alberta separatism. Resources are a provincial matter in Canada and, along with healthcare, can be a source of friction between the levels of government.

The majority of Alberta's population lives in and around the two main cities. Albertans, unlike Vancouverites, are not apartment-dwellers, and a private home with a garage and a garden is by far the most popular form of housing. The consequence of single-family dwellings is mass urban sprawl. Driving from one side of Edmonton to the other can take up to an hour – not because of traffic, but size. Albertan and prairie cities are very spread out and resemble conglomerate country towns. Each neighbourhood or community has shops, services, parkland and schools. By UK standards, houses are large and still affordable, particularly when compared with southern England. This emphasis on suburbia means that Alberta's and Canada's cities do not have a high-street culture and shopping malls dominate. Edmonton has West Edmonton Mall, the largest shopping/entertainment centre in the world; although Europeans will at first scoff at the apparently false environment, the mall is enjoyable when the outside temperature drops to minus 40 (Celsius and Fahrenheit are equal at that point). Edmonton's mall includes an indoor amusement park, a skating rink and a giant indoor water park that even makes waves.

The 'downtown' cores of the cities are modern and impressive. Extremely compact, the banking and oil towers are linked together with walkways and underground passages. When the towers were being built in the 1970s it was easy to know when the work day was over because hardly a soul could be found on the streets. Apartment construction and festival activities have brought some life to city centres, but they remain a workday world, with the working population driving out to the suburbs in the evenings. The cities do have tourist attractions but were never really designed for show. With ample resources, services and infrastructure have developed around needs; roughly one fifth of these urban populations are immigrant.

Other Cities

The cities of western Canada are clean and modern. British visitors frequently comment on the pride people appear to take in their communities. Graffiti is rare, as is litter, and excellent walking and cycling trails run through the communities and are actively used year-round. It takes a certain kind of person to spend a lunch hour jogging in weather that is minus 20°C. Alberta is at its least attractive in spring when the coat of white melts to reveal brown, dead grass and the wind kicks up the dust. Roads are heavily gravelled when snow falls and the gravel frequently damages car windscreens. Several times each winter Chinook winds blow off the mountains, with cold air compressing warm air, and embrace southern Alberta. During these times Calgary and its surrounding area can climb from deep sub-zero temperatures to well above freezing. Although it is not clearly proven, some people associate migraine headaches and joint pain with this weather phenomenon. If a Chinook persists, trees can begin to emerge from their slumber as if it were spring, only to die as sap freezes when the Chinook lifts. As a preventative measure, locals will sometimes pour water around the base of trees early in the winter, to create an ice barrier that maintains a constant ground temperature.

Mountains and Parks

Alberta is sometimes referred to as Texas North, but a more apt comparison may be Alaska South. The province is big, rich and confident, but locals love their environment and enjoy the mountains and the many parks as much as possible. Some of the best skiing in Canada is found in Alberta as well as one of the country's most recognisable resort towns – **Banff**. Only 1½ hours by car from Calgary, Banff is a world-class resort that hasn't completely lost its community feel. Nestled in the mighty Rockies, Banff National Park is the second oldest national park in the world. Despite having only around 7,000 inhabitants, Banff is still worthy of discussion as it is such an important destination for British tourists and working holidaymakers.

Much of the Alberta Rockies is protected as parkland, with a few small communities dotted through and around the parks both in Alberta and British Columbia. Banff is by far the principal community within the park boundaries, although **Jasper** too is a living town with over 4,000 inhabitants. **Lake Louise** also has a permanent village but is officially considered a service centre. Located just east of the Banff park gates, the former mining town of **Canmore** has grown quickly and could even qualify as a city. Because it is outside the park boundaries, and therefore park regulations, Canmore has evolved into the largest community in the Canadian Rockies and is very popular with migrants from across Canada and abroad. Favoured by a strong pound, the British have become an important part of Canmore's booming housing market, but as a result many homes sit empty for much of the year. Owning a home inside the parks is much more complicated, so most new residents are temporary workers hired for the ski season or over the summer. To the west of Banff, the lumber town of **Golden** is going through a billion-dollar makeover, and is becoming another important ski destination. Although located in the province of British Columbia, the main access point for that valley is Calgary and the area even operates on Alberta's mountain time zone.

Medicine Hat

Medicine Hat, in the province's southeast, is well known to some British because of a large military base nearby. Still part of Alberta's high desert, Medicine Hat enjoys the highest number of sunshine days in the country and the local economy is buoyed by thousands of British troops spending time off in pubs and restaurants trying to chat up the locals. A recent deal struck between Canada and Britain for the very controversial purchase of four submarines means training bases, such as the one in Alberta, will be used by British forces for some time to come. Rowdier elements in the forces have earned a negative reputation in the area.

Summary

As long as oil prices remain buoyant, Alberta should continue to boom, drawing business and expertise from around the world. House prices have risen sharply and the promise of well-paying jobs brings many Canadians from other regions. Unskilled workers do not always find it easy to adapt to Alberta. With rising costs and a professional, skilled environment, lower-income jobs are widely available but make 'getting by' difficult. Homeless shelters in Calgary and Edmonton are often full. Aid is available in the form of welfare, healthcare and food banks, but wandering wintry streets in the hope of finding work can be disheartening. Alberta has an established, open élite and a reasonably vibrant cultural environment, but the place also has a frontier feel to it. At weekends, cities like Edmonton and Red Deer come alive when visiting workers pour in from the ranches and oilfields. Many of these, mostly men, have plenty of cash and spend it on drinking and parties. Those who save their money a little more earnestly build impressive homes and enjoy the great outdoors by indulging in fishing, hunting, boating, golfing and travelling.

Saskatchewan and Manitoba

The two other prairie provinces to Alberta's east are vast and underpopulated, with fewer than two people to every square kilometre. Saskatchewan and Manitoba are so flat that it is said you can watch your dog run away for two days. The great plains and the Shield country to the north are famous for their enormous 360-degree skies with dancing clouds and northern lights. Despite having just over two million residents – slightly more than half in Manitoba –

Churchill's Bears

With a mere 800 permanent inhabitants, Churchill, Manitoba is an important port on Hudson Bay in the far north of the province. The town is only reached by aircraft, or on a marathon 37-hour train journey. In and of itself Churchill is an unremarkable northern town with a friendly population and harsh climate, noted for one of the largest and most accessible polar bear populations in the world. These magnificent creatures spend their summers inland, trying to stay cool and waiting for the bay to ice over so they can hunt their favourite food – ringed seals. Polar bears are not vegetarian and, unlike their grizzly and black cousins, these hunters of the north are not interested in berries or roots. They have an incredible sense of smell and can detect prey over 20 kilometres away. Not perfectly white, their special, hollow hair and black skin allows them to stay warm in the Arctic and they will cover large distances between and on ice floes.

With Churchill on their migration route, the bears are drawn by interesting smells and frequently wander into town. When this happens they are trucked off to 'jail' for 30 days without food or light. The first year the jail was attempted the bears were fed, but word got out and the number of offenders increased! Much of the thrill of living in the north is the outdoor lifestyle, but in Churchill activities such as skiing or dog-sledding mean travelling with a gun. No one, including the local Inuit population, wants to harm the bears and their numbers are closely studied, but the reality for all creatures – humans, foxes and seals – means taking as many precautions as possible when living with these mighty predators who will even eat their own kind.

Quick Facts: Saskatchewan and Manitoba

Population: Roughly 1 million in each province.

Largest cities: Winnipeg, Saskatoon, Regina.

Major ethnic groups: British/Western European, Ukrainian, German (Mennonite, Hutterite), Filipino, First Nations, Métis.

Physical highlights: Flat, farmland and rocky Shield country covered with lakes; floods are common in southern Manitoba; extremes of cold and heat.

Economic highlights: Farming, for better or for worse; oil; mining; tourism (lake-fishing, hunting, bear-watching).

Major events: Winnipeg hosted 1999 Pan-American Games; Saskatchewan is famous for rallying around its Canadian Football league team – the province's only professional sports team.

Issues in moving to Saskatchewan and Manitoba: Small economies, with Saskatchewan experiencing a recent boom; both provinces actively court new investment; housing remains affordable although rising rapidly; friendly.

---

the region has played an important role within Canada as a whole, leading political change and becoming home to many diverse ethnic groups.

Poetic images of wild skies framing stoic grain elevators only partially capture the beauty prairie people find in their land. As Canada's wheat belt, tiny communities still dot the landscape and harvest is the busiest time of the year. Despite challenges from Mother Nature and fickle markets, tonnes of wheat are exported annually and new, innovative crops keep farming alive.

Current economic realities have spurred significant growth in a region that has not traditionally enjoyed the sort of wealth and development seen in Alberta and BC. Oil in northern Saskatchewan and sharp increases in the price of wheat and other agricultural products are bringing life back to prairie communities. In 2007 **Saskatoon** and **Regina**, the two main cities of Saskatchewan, saw the largest increase in house prices in Canada and significant numbers of former residents are returnees, particularly from Alberta where the cost of living has shot up.

Swift Current, a small city in Saskatchewan, is named after the province. Saskatchewan means 'fast-moving river' in Cree, and three important rivers cross the province, including the North and South Saskatchewan rivers, which originate in the ice fields of the Alberta Rockies. The northern 40 per cent of the province is Canadian Shield and has literally thousands of lakes and a sparse population. The Shield constitutes an even higher percentage of Manitoba's territory and gives way to open tundra bordering the territory of Nunavut and Hudson Bay. The name Manitoba was first applied to Lake Manitoba and is of either Cree or Assiniboine origin – perhaps both.

Manitoba and Saskatchewan contain a peculiar mix of ethnicities, and although external immigration has been low during the last several decades, cultural identity and close families keep minority cultures alive. First Nations,

Métis and even a few Inuit populations are significant in Saskatchewan and Manitoba and as a result of natural increase their political and social relevance will only grow – Winnipeg has the largest urban aboriginal population in the country. French-speaking communities exist in the prairies and the community of St Boniface, located within Winnipeg's metropolitan area, has the largest Francophone population in the west. Ukrainians constitute over 10 per cent of the population in both provinces, as do people of German extraction. Winnipeg also has over 30,000 Filipinos, who remain the largest visible minority in the area. Economic opportunity draws new Canadians to larger centres, but strong social ties have kept Winnipeg growing through natural increase.

Saskatchewan's economy has recently turned an important corner. It is one of only two Canadian provinces to decrease in size over the last 10 years (Newfoundland has also suffered a net decrease), but people are now choosing to return home. As the country's largest grain producer, the difficult nature of that industry and the attraction of larger cities have driven people from the land. Others have stayed on the farms and even fared quite well, but small-town services have given way to those in larger centres. Saskatchewanians grow up with good levels of education and a rural work ethic and the many who leave the province often do well in their new homes – particularly in Alberta. As Alberta's oil boom is also being exploited inside Saskatchewan, the provincial government is beginning to address the infrastructure deficit and the province is actually debt-free. Politically, Saskatchewan (but not Manitoba) has made an important shift to the right, perhaps reflecting a stronger economic environment, influence from Alberta and a new approach to some deep social issues.

Winnipeg

The largest urban centre in either province is the city of Winnipeg, which in many ways *is* Manitoba. Over 600,000 people live in Winnipeg (or Winterpeg) and the city's metropolitan area houses the vast majority of the province's population. **Thompson**, the only sizeable Manitoban city outside the southern farming area, has a population of only 14,000, although it serves a region of around 40,000.

Winnipeg is an interesting and tough city and its residents are friendly and loyal. Bone-chilling cold settles into the city through the winter and scorching, humid, mosquito-plagued days are all too frequent over summer. In addition to these appealing qualities, Winnipeg is located in a flood plain, and since the first Red River settlement was established in the early 1800s the area has experienced numerous floods. After much of the city was submerged in the 1950 flood, plans for a floodway were put in motion and the ditch was completed in 1968. Now when the river breaks its banks it submerges the surrounding communities, but Winnipeg survives as an island. Flat and spread out, Winnipeg typifies the prairie city and, despite its natural challenges, has a great deal to offer.

Historically Winnipeg served as the gateway to the west and became a major hub after the completion of the railway in the 1880s right through to the First World War. Trains remain a dominant feature of the city and roughly divide the affluent south from the blue-collar north. Two of Canada's poorest electoral districts are located in north Winnipeg and the area remains staunchly working class, but it is not rough so much as simply not affluent. Housing remains extremely affordable in the city and throughout the prairies. Because of slower growth Winnipeg looks and feels like an older community, more so than Edmonton or particularly Calgary. The downtown has maintained a reasonable collection of impressive sandstone buildings that predate the glass towers of other cities.

Summary

While farming is the principal activity in the south of both provinces, northern Manitoba has a few major mines and Saskatchewan is enjoying an oil boom. Winnipeg and Regina (the Queen City) house the provincial governments and all three of the main cities (including Saskatoon) are important service centres. Winnipeg is only a little over a one-hour drive from Ontario and, as the northern communities of that province are more than a day's drive from Toronto and the population centres, Winnipeg is more relevant in their economic and social lives. Equally, North and South Dakota directly to the south are rural US states, and the weakness of the Canadian currency through the 1990s attracted many American shoppers – although the flow has now reversed.

Large lakes cover a significant portion of Manitoba's territory and many families own waterfront cottages. Northern Saskatchewan is also very popular for fishing and canoe enthusiasts and land remains affordable.

In either province you will be made to feel extremely welcome and can enjoy a high standard of living at a fraction of British costs. Farming is difficult but appears to have finally moved into a positive cycle. Both provinces actively court investment and are keen to attract new immigrants. Winters are harsh on the prairies, but curling and hockey are enjoyed throughout. The sense of community is strong and people continue to listen to Canadian Broadcasting Corporation (CBC) radio religiously, where the intricacies of making berry preserves may be discussed at length after the international news.

Ontario

With more than one out of every three Canadians living in Ontario, the province is Canada's economic and social heart, but not its soul. Ontario, like almost everything else Canadian, is vast, but the bulk of its population lives

> ## Quick Facts: Ontario
> **Population:** 12 million.
> **Largest cities:** Greater Toronto Area (GTA) 5 million plus; Ottawa (together with Hull, Quebec) around 1 million; London, Kitchener/Waterloo, Thunder Bay and Sudbury in the north.
> **Major ethnic groups:** Anglophone, Francophone (over 10 per cent); too many others to list; 2.7 million visible minorities.
> **Physical highlights:** Great Lakes; lush farmland in south; flat; thousands of lakes; Niagara Falls; summer smog around Toronto.
> **Economic highlights:** 'Golden Horseshoe' around Lake Ontario is the most industrialised area in Canada – verging on recession; Toronto Stock Exchange (TSX) – the country's most important exchange; banking; government in both Toronto and Ottawa; mining in north; services.
> **Major events:** Pope visited for World Youth Day; SARS; every major concert and theatre act visits Toronto.
> **Issues in moving to Ontario:** Traffic around populated centres can be as bad as in the UK; housing in Toronto is expensive, but affordable elsewhere; the Great Outdoors is further from population centres than in other provinces; transition from manufacturing to high-tech, banking economy.

around the so-called Golden Horseshoe along the eastern rim of Lake Ontario. The mega-city of Toronto is Canada's largest and North America's fifth largest urban conglomeration and sprawls out from the lake for what feels like an eternity. The national capital Ottawa hugs the eastern border with Quebec and spills over to Hull in La Belle Province. West and south of Toronto is an inland peninsula outlined by the Great Lakes and defined by excellent rolling farmland. Framed by water and the famous Niagara Falls, Ontario reaches further south than any other part of Canada. Across from tidy, safe Windsor is Detroit, USA, and an entirely different world. Northern Ontario goes on forever. Bordering James and Hudson Bays, it is a world of mining, lumber and aboriginal people. If you want to drive north from Toronto to see the west of Canada, find Yonge Street, drive north to Barrie and carry on northwest to the Manitoba border, 1,900km away.

Older than the western provinces, Ontario is still young in terms of European settlement, as it did not receive many settlers until the American Revolution. Loyalist Yankees moved north and those who relocated to the French province of British North America demanded their own laws and language. A staunchly British Upper Canada was born, later to become Ontario. The economy of the province expanded once the St Lawrence Seaway was constructed during the 19th century. Locks and a series of canals enabled large, ocean-going ships to travel up the mighty river and into the Great Lakes. Expansion of the system through the 1950s and 1960s increased the importance of the shipping route, not only for Ontario, but for major US centres like Chicago, located virtually in the centre of the continent. The Welland Ship Canal dates back to the 1820s and is an impressive route 44km route linking Lake Ontario to Lake Erie, thereby avoiding the Niagara River and its famous falls.

With the exception of farming settlements that were established in the fertile peninsula between the Great Lakes, the majority of Ontario's towns and cities lie dotted along the waterways and lakes. These towns and cities feel older than those in the west, and communities across the province have maintained the brick architecture familiar to people from the UK. Wealthier settlers constructed the extravagant loyalist (New England-style) houses that can be seen near Niagara (and in other eastern communities). Northern towns and cities remain resource-driven and do not maintain the same conservative outward appearance of those in the south.

Toronto

Toronto is a Canadian city, partly because it probably couldn't happen anywhere else. Internationally recognised for culture and business, it may not be London or New York, but it should be understood on that scale. Ontario's capital is huge and modern, yet interspersed with Georgian and Victorian houses. Not too long ago Toronto was as rigid as could be, with a strong Orange Order presence, restrictive drinking laws and a white population. Massive immigration after the Second World War and a general change in Canadian society have turned Toronto into a cultural mosaic, buoyed by a strong economy and a capital outflow from Quebec. Toronto is now the most ethnically diverse city on earth. Any one of a hundred languages can be heard on the streets and 44 per cent of Toronto's population were not born in Canada. What is perhaps even more amazing is that they all seem to get along fairly well and maintain the few quintessentially Canadian national traits such as politeness and

The Toronto Transit Commission

The Toronto Transit Commission is in charge of public transport throughout the Great Toronto Area and maintains a reasonably efficient system of buses, trams and a subway. The Toronto subway is clean and well run, although the lines are not terribly extensive and the tunnels quite small.

The transport highlight in Toronto is the street cars that rattle along tracks throughout the city. Distinctly red, the streetcars have right of way in most circumstances and cars stop to allow travellers to walk out to the middle of the road to get on to them. Subways, buses and trams are all linked and one ticket is accepted on all three modes of transport. Exact money is required.

Because streetcars run on tracks, newcomers to Toronto must learn to avoid slipping on the metal when crossing the street, and you may want to think twice about renting an apartment fronting onto a tramline, as the familiar clanking can rattle on late into the evening.

respect for authority. Regardless of ethnicity and country of origin, all Torontonians unite around the cause of the Maple Leafs – the city's hockey team. Win or lose (the latter more commonly), Torontonians are glued to their televisions during games and each year, when the Leafs are knocked out of the playoffs, the city mourns. Somehow by being a Leafs fan, one becomes a Torontonian.

The Greater Toronto Area (GTA) supports over 5 million people and continues to receive the largest number of new arrivals to Canada. This is in some ways surprising given the crowding, costs, terrible traffic and less-than-stellar climate. Fronting on to a large lake, Toronto is very humid and the humidity takes a toll. Summer temperatures have been known to soar above 40°C, with smog settling into the heavy air. Winter is cold, but fairly short in Canadian terms, with humid winds whistling between the tall buildings. Snowfalls are lower than in other eastern cities, but nevertheless clog routes, and freezing rain can make driving treacherous. Excluding the lakefront, geography has not limited Toronto's growth. A trip up the CN Tower on a clear day reveals flat expanses as far as the eye can see, and many of the homes are barely visible thanks to the greenery.

In addition to being Ontario's capital, Toronto is indisputably the business centre of the country, with dozens of glass towers standing as monuments to banking and commerce. The Toronto Stock Exchange (TSX) is important on a world scale and even the Bank of Montreal has its headquarters in downtown Toronto. Standing guard above the business centre is the CN Tower and beside it, the Skydome, now named the Rogers Centre – an impressive stadium with the world's largest retractable roof. This is typically Toronto – striving for bigger and better on a world scale – yet the community remains Canadian and surprisingly relaxed and friendly.

The least appealing aspects of living in Toronto are traffic and air quality. For a country with one of the lowest population densities in the world, the traffic around Toronto and Lake Ontario is horrific. Eight or even 10 lanes of freeway clogged with cars, each with but one occupant, are all too common, and rush hour carries on through most daylight hours. Add heavy snowfalls and expanses of suburban housing, and one can easily spend hours each day on the road. The 100km journey from Toronto to Niagara along the edge of the lake should take one hour, but can consume twice that amount of time. When passing though the industrial cities of Oakville and Hamilton, the views do not compensate for time wasted, although this changes once the orchards and vineyards closer to Niagara come into view.

The industrial cities on either side of Toronto are driven by the automobile industry and other heavy industries. A controversial Free Trade Agreement signed with the USA in 1994, followed by the North American Free Trade Agreement (NAFTA) which includes Mexico, has had mixed effects on the region. Many traditional blue-collar jobs have gone south, but new, high-tech industries have

The CN Tower

Toronto's most recognisable tower is 553 metres high, was once the world's largest free-standing structure, and dominates views of the city from almost all angles. When flying into Toronto the tower can be seen from a great distance, and when the weather is clear one can look across the lake to Niagara and even to New York State. The tower was built in 1976 in one continuous pour of cement and, although it has a genuine use as a radio tower, Canadian National was also boasting about size. With few physical limitations, communications were easy in Toronto until modern skyscrapers began to spring up in the 1960s and '70s. The tower was built to raise microwave receptors above the downtown, thereby freeing up the reception of communications. The receptors are now over 300 metres above the ground and the rest of the tower serves as an antenna.

The CN Tower is run as a crown corporation and is understandably one of Toronto's premier tourist attractions. The main observation deck is 340 metres high and the even higher Skypod 447 metres. Predictably, there is a revolving restaurant and plenty of views, but the prime attraction is to walk on the glass floor. Looking straight down from over 1,000 feet is quite a feeling and it is fun to watch adults peering from the edge of the floor as their children jump up and down – by not committing to walk on the glass completely, they presumably intend to jump back should one of the children break through.

put some shine back into the Golden Horseshoe, and the provincial government has grown dependent on cash-friendly casinos, offering deals to American visitors. The big three car-makers are still present and their Canadian workers earn good wages and form the backbone of the Canadian labour movement – the fate of these goliath manufacturers will directly impact the Ontario economy.

The car-making industry dates back to an earlier trade deal known as the Auto Pact, in which Canada and the USA streamlined automobile production between the two countries. In exchange for producing essentially the same vehicles, the Auto Pact guarantees that manufacturing for the Canadian market would take place in Canada. Since 1982 Canadian production has outstripped demand and many Canadian-produced vehicles are sold to the US market. Roughly 140,000 people are currently employed in automobile production in Canada, but the country produces no distinctly Canadian automobile, unless one counts the metric variation of imperially measured US brands. Buses and snowmobiles are designed and manufactured in Canada, but the country has no national car in the way that other countries claim cultural propriety of a product.

The sprawling communities and developments around Toronto reveal suburbia in all its glory – apartment living and a major waterfront redevelopment in the style of Vancouver's glass towers is under way in Toronto, but in general the Canadian ideal of a home, garage and patch of garden is desired. So-called 'soccer moms' (30–40-year-old, at-home mothers) constitute the backbone of Ontario's suburbia and represent an important political constituency. The suburban areas are reasonably affluent and tax cuts have helped. Toronto has many of the social problems associated with large cities, but the clean, prosperous suburbs are a long way from the inner city and crime rates remain low, particularly when compared with US cities. The GTA's remarkable ethnic diversity is not confined to the city centre and population growth contributes to new housing developments. Embracing a 'mosaic' rather than 'melting pot' model has encouraged the development of distinct communities, including several Chinatowns, Little Italy, Little Portugal, Little Greece, Little India, etc. Dining in and around Toronto is an adventure! Somewhat more negatively, crime rates and gang activities among some ethnic communities and areas are higher (a fact found elsewhere in Canada), but should not be exaggerated. Hints of radical Islam have also emerged, including a poorly designed bomb plot in 2006. As elsewhere, the extremist segment of the Muslim community is small, but the integration of the religiously observant into an increasingly secular (and egalitarian) society will raise challenges.

Outside Toronto

Niagara Falls is the closest and most popular day-trip from Toronto and may disappoint. The falls themselves are dramatic, but the old community is a gaudy tourist trap with wax museums and casinos. Its only saving grace is that across the river the American side is run-down and even less attractive. Hundreds of thousands of tourists flood over the border to 'see Canada' and accents on the street sound more New York than Ontario, but now, with a stronger dollar and restricted border, the important flow of American tourists will surely decrease. Watch that your mobile phone does not pick up the New York signal and incur roaming charges. Away from the glitz and noise, the Niagara Falls Parks Commission does an excellent job in maintaining parkland, and the clear, crisp days of autumn reveal the glorious colours associated with that season. Escape from the Falls area by travelling north along the Niagara Escarpment. Vineyards and impressive loyalist homes lead the way to Niagara-on-the-Lake, an attractive former capital and home to a George Bernard Shaw theatre festival. The entire area, first settled after the American Revolution, was extremely important in resisting American forces during the last major conflict, 1812–14.

Further inland, along highway 401 is a series of communities and smaller cities with good economies, great universities and a nice pace of life. **Kitchener/Waterloo**, **Guelph** and **London** may be dwarfed by Toronto, but would be considered large in other provinces. These cities are somewhat less diverse, but nevertheless reflect the Canadian mosaic and are an integral part of Canada's economic and cultural engine.

A beautiful, green world of trees, rivers and, above all, lakes lies north of the GTA. As an integral part of traditional central Canadian culture, thousands of small cottages perch along the lakes and it is here that many visitors will find the tranquil Canada of a different era. In 2005, **Barrie**, the largest city in 'cottage country', welcomed the world, as it was chosen over Toronto to host the Live 8 concert! Every summer weekend witnesses a mass exodus from the cities as factory workers and owners alike drive up to the wilds of Canada to fish, canoe, swim and relax. The agricultural land along the coast of Lake Ontario soon gives way to Canadian Shield, and small holiday areas continue to be scattered along the routes until finally distance from the population centres becomes a factor. Further north, the towns are distinctly resource-based, built around mining and hydroelectricity projects, and still further north communities become distinctly aboriginal.

The **Great Lakes** serve as Ontario's primary border with the United States. Ontario, Wisconsin and Minnesota share Lake Superior, the largest freshwater lake in the world. Only a few cities and towns dot its extensive coastline on either side of the frontier. The largest Ontario city along the lake is **Thunder Bay**; its location in the northwest of the province makes it an important service centre. Thunder Bay is a mining, steel and lumber city; steel-refining has historically been the major employer but weak prices through the 1990s led to serious downsizing. As is typical with resource cities like Thunder Bay, the municipal leaders have tried aggressively to attract other business and many communities are looking to the big city retirement population as a partial solution. Affordable housing and a spruced-up environment have attracted some internal migration drawn by the merit of the lifestyle. China's insatiable need for resources has also helped to breathe life back into resource economies. Generally larger regions with services, particularly fully equipped hospitals, survive, but when the major employers in smaller towns pull out, much of the local population gradually migrates away.

This trend to urbanisation is important in Canada, as elsewhere in the developed world, and is most obvious around the biggest population centres. Much is made of the fact that Canada is around 80 per cent urban, but by British standards this is a misleading statistic. Smaller municipalities in northern and central Ontario may qualify as urban but, in locations hours from more major centres, the cultural environment remains frontier in its feel. A 'village' in the UK may be five miles from a city of millions, whereas medium-sized cities even in well-populated Ontario can be a two-hour drive from the next hub.

Lake of the Woods district lies further west from Thunder Bay. The principal community is Kenora and the largest service centre is Winnipeg to the west. This dramatic, forested area is lumber country. The lakes are extensive and some residents will drive a boat, instead of a car, to the supermarket. The area has a large First Nations population and the region, while still Ontarian, is working class and not nearly as diverse as southern Ontario. Snowfalls are very heavy, and hunting is much more popular than theatre-going. There has been talk over the years of Ontario splitting, with the northwest joining Manitoba, as that urban and service area is more relevant to a region over 1,500km from Ontario's population centres.

Ottawa

Away from the Golden Horseshoe and the north, Ontario's other important population centre revolves around Ottawa, the national capital. Ottawa is a fine, attractive city with a low crime rate and a highly bilingual population. Many of Ontario's eastern communities are in fact French-speaking, and because the federal government functions (in theory) equally in both official languages, Ottawa does too. As would be expected, Ottawa is much more politicised than other municipalities and, with Montreal only two hours away, local activists draw on that population when they stage protests and demonstrations.

Ottawa sits along the Ottawa River and came to life in the 1820s during the construction of the Rideau Canal, which links the river to Lake Ontario. Originally named Bytown, Ottawa was chosen by Queen Victoria as the national capital because, at that time, it straddled the two Canadas. Spilling over into Hull, Quebec on the other side of the Ottawa River, the greater area is now home to around one million people. With average winter temperatures well below freezing, Ottawa may be the coldest capital city in the world. Warm summers always thaw the region. When the ice arrives, usually in December, the Rideau Canal becomes transformed into the world's largest skating rink and families and bureaucrats alike don their skates to enjoy extended lunch hours.

Beyond all the bureaucracy, Ottawa has a vibrant IT sector and good housing. An excellent educational environment has attracted many people to the region. Houses are more affordable on the Quebec side of the river, but taxes there are higher. As an almost predestined statement on governance, situated between the parliament buildings in Ottawa and civil service offices in Hull is a large toilet paper factory!

Summary

Ontario deserves significant attention when it comes to considering a place to settle. It is paramount economically in Canada, and socially much is driven from the province. Many families in western Canada trace their roots back to Ontario and the province is in many ways a microcosm of the nation. Progressively urban in some areas, rural and conservative in others and with undeniable weather extremes, Ontario has something for everyone – as noted on the vehicle licence plates, Ontario is 'Yours to Discover'.

Quebec

La belle province is the only French-majority jurisdiction in the country and, though it is not politically correct to say so, Quebec (Québec in French) is distinct within Canada. In some manifestations more truly *Canadien* than other parts of the country, Quebecers, regardless of politics, are without question Quebecers first and then, perhaps, Canadian. *Les Québécois* see themselves as a 'people' and speak in the collective 'we' much more than other Canadians do. The bulk of the province's population lives scattered along the shores of the St Lawrence River, as they have for nearly 400 years. About half the province's population lives on or around the island of Montreal (Montréal, in French), in the St Lawrence.

Quebec is a vibrant place: insular, yet worldly, all at the same time. As the oldest European-settled region of Canada, Quebec has a stronger sense of its own identity than points further west. Historically extremely conservative, modern Quebec society contains a peculiar mix of values. Intrinsic to the Québécois self-promoted history is the belief that French peasants fused with the Huron First Nation and emerged as a new cultural group. This certainly was the case with the Métis on the prairies, but a bit of a stretch in Quebec. Allegiances with the Huron were historically very important, but more recent provincial relations with aboriginal groups have been strained. Moreover, language laws centre on French and, while targeted at holding English at bay, they are by design not open to other cultures.

In addition to the classic Indian-peasant self-concept, Quebecers rally around the perception of speaking a Latin language and therefore believe themselves

---

Quick Facts: Quebec

Population: 7.5 million.

Largest cities: Montreal (second largest in Canada), Quebec City, Trois Rivières, Sherbrooke.

Major ethnic groups: French Canadian, British, Italian, Greek, Haitian, Jewish, others; First Nations and Inuit form a majority in the far north. Outside of the island of Montreal, communities are far less ethnically diverse than in Ontario and the west.

Physical highlights: St Lawrence River; Island of Montreal; Canadian Shield; autumn colours; rolling mountains.

Economic highlights: Hydroelectric production; manufacturing; resources; lots of government work; IT; tourism.

Major events: World Expo; Olympics (still paying off the debt); Quebec winter festival; festivals in Montreal including Just for Laughs.

Issues in moving to Quebec: Language – the province is officially unilingual (French); high taxes and dwindling Anglophone community; independent legal code and immigration rules; generally low cost of living.

to have those characteristics. Mixed with the bitter ideal of '*mon pays c'est l'hiver*' (my country is winter) is an outgoing, theatrical cultural environment. One example is the more frequent use of the familiar '*tu*' rather than the '*vous*' form, but this is really more Canadian than Mediterranean. Formality is not given a particularly high priority across a country that is noted in the English world for the common use of first names in business settings.

Quebec has a rich folk-music culture and a great theatre tradition known as 'improvisation'. In English this is better known as theatre sports, and leagues across Quebec and throughout French Canada take part. Montreal may be the only large city that will close main streets to traffic in order to host a festival. The Just for Laughs comedy festival, which has gained international notoriety, brings the city to life each summer, along with other, multilingual celebrations. Quebec City's winter carnival enlivens the coldest months and is a wonderful and genuine celebration of the harsh northern climate.

Montreal

If Toronto is Canada's heart, Montreal is certainly its spirit (its soul must always remain in the north). In understanding Montreal it is important to distinguish between the multicultural, multilingual island and the primarily francophone suburbs that surround the city's core. Often a little disappointing to British visitors at first sight, it must be said that Montrealers love their city. An eclectic mix of disparate cultures, drawn by trade and historical accident, the island is a fascinating place. Even its architecture exhibits the uneasy fusion of peoples, and an underground city spans out below buildings in deference to the harsh climate. Dominated by a mountain better described as a small hill, Montreal is a collection of several cities that were merged into one, and from which some have again separated. The rest of Canada may view politics as an irritation, but in Quebec it is a way of life. Montreal is a party city, with bars and restaurants open late into the evening, and young and old dress to impress. Smoking is still accepted, and driving styles resemble those of Italy more than Canada, perhaps because you need a PhD to figure out the parking regulations.

Montreal's largest ethnic group, the French Canadians, dominate the city's east side, but really live throughout. Because of its Francophone majority, Montreal is in fact the second largest French-speaking city in the world. Anglophones now constitute around 14 per cent of the city's population, but many more people come from bilingual or mixed families. Allophones are also an important group. Montreal's Italian community is ageing, but has maintained its language as well as speaking the other two. Greeks are also numerous, as is the Jewish community. Many Jews, not unexpectedly, come from the European Yiddish tradition, but historically there has also been a North African Sephardic population who migrated from former French colonies. Some of the Montreal–Jewish experience was well documented in the witty

The Murder of Women in Montreal

The worst crime against women in modern Canadian history occurred on 6 December 1989 in Montreal. Marc Lepine, who claimed to hate feminists, stormed into the University of Montreal's Ecole Polytechnique, separating the genders and slaughtering 14 young women. The brutal event has become a rallying point to raise awareness about violence against women. The fact that Lepine chose the engineering school has been the source of much discussion given the profession's strong male bias. Each year the tragedy is commemorated with marches, many by women only, to highlight issues of safety and independence for women.

Sadly a similar, though less targeted event again occurred at Montreal's Dawson College on 13 September, 2006, when an armed 20-year-old man went on a shooting spree, killing one woman and injuring another 19 people.

writings of local author Mordecai Richler. Richler lived for many years in London, but never lost his Montreal roots and on returning to Canada was swept up in controversy by exposing the province's historic Catholic anti-Semitism. A more recent ethnic group to arrive has come from Haiti – the oldest black republic in the world. Montreal's Haitian community numbers in the thousands and was drawn to the city by language, and it has given Canada its most recent governor general: Michaëlle Jean.

Many of Canada's élite families hail from Montreal, although an atypical class structure grew in the city. Each ethnic group had its own hierarchy and, while business was business, the different groups didn't really mix. The traditional Anglophone families, mostly of Scottish heritage, made their wealth in furs and liquor. Without question, prohibition south of the border benefited Canada economically. The French élite received their education in a handful of schools and their society maintained the French-colonial rigidity and religious hierarchy up to the late 1960s. Even today, the ethnic groups are somewhat divided, although Francophone supremacy is eroding diversity.

The early 1960s witnessed an emergence of French-Québécois society that will continue to be studied. Although the least educated, most religious and by some measures most backward society in North America, French Quebecers took the reins into their own hands and fired the traditional ruling party. In doing so, they dragged French Quebec into the 20th century. The Quiet Revolution, as it has been dubbed, was an almost totally non-violent rejection of the Church and the traditional power structure. In July 1967 President de Gaulle made no friends in the Canadian government when, during a visit to Montreal, he declared: '*Vive le Québec libre!*' Quebec's separatist party was still in its infancy at that time, but his declaration gave focus to the rising political movement and nine years later the Parti Québécois was elected. Differences between English and French Canada had long existed, particularly around the world wars, but the vacuum left by the collapse of the conservative Union Nationale party created space for a new articulation of French-Canadian identity.

The 1976 election of the Parti Québécois had a dramatic effect on the province. In addition to being openly separatist, the movement was also very left-wing, raising concern in the United States and triggering an outflow of capital. Montreal had long been Canada's largest city and prime financial centre, but money and much of the English community fled, primarily to Toronto. Montreal is only now recovering, or reinventing itself, and politically in Quebec the island has come a clear second to Quebec City in funding. Through the 1980s and 1990s Montreal continued to lose people, but the arts community grew and excellent universities and very cheap rents kept the student population loyal.

Montreal now ranks third, behind Calgary, as a business centre, but with 3.5 million people it remains important. The economy has begun to improve and people are returning. The island will never surpass Toronto in economic importance and the Montreal Stock Exchange recently merged with Toronto's, but it often surpasses its rival in terms of quality of life. The economy has now picked up and house prices are increasing rapidly to match those of the other regions. Montreal has well-maintained parks and easy access to the lakes, cottages and good skiing in the Laurentian Mountains to the north. Like Torontonians, many Montrealers own land north (or to the southeast) of the city and escape sweltering summer humidity to swim and relax in the country. When flying into Montreal, one can see what appears to be an infinite number of swimming pools attached to houses. Winter is as cold as summer is hot. In winter, the city receives large quantities of heavy, wet snow and the winds off the St Lawrence slam into the city and drop already-freezing temperatures into the bitterly cold category. Each season is distinct, and autumn colours are always worth looking forward to, even though they herald the coming of winter.

Quebec City

Three hours down the St Lawrence is the province's capital and one of Canada's jewels. Quebec City is North America's only walled city, and if you can get past the almost sterile feel of every protected brick, it is indeed a wonderful place, full of life, restaurants and an active local culture. Quebec City perches on a point at the narrowing of the mighty river. Not very large as a city, the greater capital region has nearly 700,000 people. The area is not particularly wealthy, but the overall standard of living is high. Tourism is very important to Quebec City's economy and the magnificent Château Frontenac hotel dominates the skyline from all angles. In all tourist areas service is available in English, though greater Quebec City is over 98 per cent French-speaking. Government is a major employer, as is the port, plus farming and lumber in the surrounding areas.

The river is a dominant feature at all times of the year and the mountains close to the north offer great hiking and surprisingly good skiing within easy

Quebec Independence

The move to create an independent nation in Quebec has always been a complicated one. Two referendums have been held on the subject in 1980 and again in 1995, with neither passing, albeit by the slimmest of margins the second time. Although independence is talked about in the media, Quebecers have never been asked if they really want to become a separate country; rather the term 'sovereignty' is used. The so-called Sovereignty Association proposed by the 'sovereigntist' movement would allow Quebecers to maintain the Canadian currency, Canadian passport and most other trappings of the larger country. The idea floated is to make Quebec an equal partner, instead of one of ten provinces, or three of nine Supreme Court judges. Without question about one-third of Quebecers support outright independence, but that figure, while important, has never managed to climb much higher. Those in favour of a new partnership, on the other hand, often represent a small majority.

Although the separatist movement is serious, it has taken on few of the trappings of other such movements around the world. The one period of violence occurred in 1970 when an extreme group called the Front de Libération du Québec (FLQ) kidnapped and killed the British trade commissioner James Cross and a Quebec minister, Pierre Laporte. The federal government's response was swift, imposing the War Measures Act (the only time in Canadian history) and detaining hundreds of people. With the murders support for the FLQ dissipated and there has not been violence since.

The question of national unity will always hang over Canada, and not only in Quebec. The nature of such a large, diverse nation will always foster regionalism, and with legitimate political movements in Quebec so frequently raising the matter, it logically enters the political mainstream. Recent political shifts in the province have relegated the separatists to third place in a minority government and seen the rise of an alternate and more socially (and econo-mically) conservative political voice, the 'Democratic Action Party' (ADQ – Action Démocratique du Québec). Neither separatist nor fully federalist, the ADQ has served to fill a political void for disenfranchised francophone voters who do not feel represented by a traditional two-party dialectic in Quebec.

access. Housing has traditionally been extremely affordable in the region, even around the old, walled town, but Quebec is in the process of being discovered and prices are rising quickly. Systemic unemployment is reasonably high and finding good employment as a new immigrant could be quite difficult: the cultural environment is not racist, but is somewhat closed; visitors are very welcome, but a clear 'us and them' outlook exists.

An even more culturally insulated region known as the **Saguenay Lac St-Jean** lies north of Quebec City. With its largest city, Chicoutimi, at the centre of the region, this is the heart of independent Quebec. Some romantics want the

---

Quebec's Birthday

2008 is a year of great celebration in Quebec City as Quebec's capital celebrates its 400-year anniversary. Already a major tourist destination, Quebec has spent several years preparing for this anniversary. While the Old City of Quebec has been lovingly (and perhaps excessively) restored, life in modern Quebec must be so much more pleasant than in its early days as a distant outpost of the French crown. Sadly, a 19th-century armoury and one of the city's beautiful buildings was lost to fire in 2008, but will surely be restored.

---

region to separate from Quebec. The Saguenay is an attractive place with a limited number of surnames. Further east, the St Lawrence broadens out, opening to the Gulf of St Lawrence and the eastern maritime provinces. The north coast is sparsely populated with small fishing communities while beluga whales frequent the estuary at certain times of the year. The south coast, called the **Gaspé**, is slightly more populated and has gained renown for its spectacular fall colours. The Gaspé region, with a different accent from other parts of the province, resembles the maritime culture of Acadia to the east and south.

Southwest of Quebec City is a more open region centred on **Sherbrooke**. The Eastern Townships, or **Cantons de l'Est** as they have come to be known, were settled by loyalists, but slowly converted to French. The small communities spread along the many lakes near the Vermont border have fused British–New England and French-Canadian culture. Montrealers have cottages throughout the area, but enough permanent residents keep the region vibrant year-round.

Summary

Northern Quebec comprises roughly three-quarters of the province and is larger than many other provinces. Bordered by Ontario, James and Hudson Bays to the east and Labrador to the west, the north has provided huge wealth to the province in the form of hydroelectricity. Quebec is a net exporter of hydro and nationalists take great pride in the government corporation's success. Damming rivers and exploiting hydro potential involves negotiations with Quebec's First Nations and has given aboriginal people an important say in the province's development. When a majority of French Quebecers voted to secede, over 90 per cent of aboriginal people did not support the cause. Quebec's north remains a vast and wild place, home to the Cree and Inuit.

For British migrants, Quebec is a world apart. Linguistically different, the province nevertheless carries as much of a British tradition as a French one. The big city, Montreal, is cosmopolitan and fun while the rest of the province combines charm and style as it embraces its northern environment. Quebecers come from hardy settlers with a long memory, as demonstrated by the words on every licence plate: *'Je me souviens'* (I remember).

Atlantic Canada

Canada's east is divided into four provinces, three of which – Nova Scotia, New Brunswick and Prince Edward Island (PEI) – are collectively known as the Maritimes. The fourth province is 'the Rock' – Newfoundland – and its partner territory, Labrador. Atlantic Canada is a beautiful region, with deeper roots than other parts of English Canada and a very relaxed, friendly population. Weighed down by weak economies, highlighted by the collapse of the cod fishery around Newfoundland, the region is beginning to re-emerge, with new businesses, offshore oil, tourism and remittance money from western Canada. Traditionally, many people from these four provinces have moved to central and western Canada for work, thus the region has not developed the sort of immigrant-based ethnic diversity that is seen in other parts of the country. Fort McMurray, the booming community at the heart of Alberta's oil industry, has many Newfoundlanders whose lilting accents can be heard over the nasal western voice. A popular 'Newfie' band, the Irish Descendants, has a song about the reality of Newfoundland life called 'The Rock and a Hard Place'; the 'Rock' refers to Newfoundland and the 'hard place' to where there is work, namely Alberta.

Life has certainly been difficult on **Cape Breton Island**, the northern third of Nova Scotia. Islanders are a culture apart and speak both accented English and a complex Acadian-French dialect. An additional 500 Cape Bretoners continue to use Scottish Gaelic, which is even taught in some local schools. Once a major coal-mining region, the industry has all but shut down and the island has levels of unemployment that rank among Canada's highest. These difficulties are offset somewhat by a rich folk and cultural tradition and great tourism potential. The 'Cabot Trail' drive along the north coast is one of the most

Quick Facts: Atlantic Canada
Population: Nova Scotia, 900,000; New Brunswick, 725,000; Newfoundland, 500,000; Prince Edward Island, 135,000.
Largest cities: Halifax (NS), Saint John (NB), St John's (NFLD), Charlottetown (PEI).
Major ethnic groups: British, French (Acadian), First Nations, Inuit (in Labrador), Afro-Canadian group in Halifax, developed from escaped slaves.
Physical highlights: Dramatic coastlines, rocky and forested in areas; much of Newfoundland is barren; very heavy snowfalls; ocean ice.
Economic highlights: Fishing industry in decline (wiped out in areas); important offshore oil drilling; tourism; call centres; seasonal work; manufacturing.
Major events: Collapse of the cod fishery; 500-year anniversary of Cabot's voyage; received thousands of stranded travellers during 9/11.
Issues in moving to Atlantic Canada: High unemployment in areas; French is spoken widely in New Brunswick; economy is beginning to pick up; housing is affordable in most areas.

beautiful anywhere on the continent and historic sites like the former French Fort Louisburg capture history and create jobs.

Having survived economic upheavals, the Atlantic economies are improving. Offshore oil drilling has brought great promise to Newfoundland and also looks positive for Nova Scotia. With effective marketing, New Brunswick has attracted international call centres and the Confederation Bridge now links PEI to the mainland, resulting in increased tourism; *Anne of Green Gables* is now just a short drive away.

Nova Scotia

Halifax

Atlantic Canada's largest and most cosmopolitan city is Halifax. Fused with Dartmouth across the harbour, the greater area has over 350,000 inhabitants and is an animated yet relaxed place. Perhaps because of successes in Montreal, Halifax hosts a comedy festival that is growing in stature. Maritimers are reputed to have a great sense of humour and some of the festival receives airtime on national television. The city's most enduring image is of the *Bluenose* schooner. The majestic tall ship that currently embellishes Halifax Harbour is *Bluenose II* – a replica of the original racing ship. The ship's image is shared nationally on most Canadian dimes (the ten-cent piece) and on automobile licence plates in the province.

Halifax's port is vital to eastern Canada and to Canada's limited Atlantic naval fleet. As a country with a long tradition of peacekeeping, Canada's ill-equipped troops, festooned with United Nations' blue berets, often wave farewell from Halifax – more recently Canadian troops have left for the controversial NATO mission in Afghanistan. Within Halifax, Nova Scotia's provincial government is the largest single employer, although manufacturing is the largest contributor to the local economy. The province's largest service centre, Halifax caters to both Nova Scotians and the tourists who crowd the city's attractive harbour front. With an important student population, Halifax maintains a party atmosphere and, while the city is yet to have its own professional sports team, university-level sports, including Canadian football and of course hockey, enjoy enthusiastic support.

One of Halifax's most interesting communities has American slave origins. Despite a short period of slavery in parts of Canada, British North America developed as a logical destination for the Underground Railway's escaped slaves. African-Americans who moved to Nova Scotia during the US War of Independence and the War of 1812 were promised much, but received little. Loyalists even travelled north with their slaves and indentured servants, but found the land to be unsuitable for slave-driven agriculture. Some black Nova Scotians eventually went to West Africa, but those who stayed made a home in

Case Study: Jeanette Sproson

Jeanette and her husband Carl emigrated to Canada in 2000 and decided to settle in Halifax, Nova Scotia. Now with a home and five-year-old Canadian-born daughter, Jeanette is feeling ever more Canadian, without losing her Birmingham roots.

Why did you choose Nova Scotia as your new home?

My first exposure to Canada was in 1995 when we visited Cape Breton Island, which constitutes the northern part of Nova Scotia. We went for one week to visit some distant cousins on my husband's side and we instantly fell in love with the place. We returned to Canada the following year and visited Toronto, but found the city's size and pace to be not much different from Birmingham. In 1998 we returned to Nova Scotia to research Halifax, which we decided would be the place for us to settle.

How has the process of settling into Halifax been?

Setting in was quite easy and we found a nice home, but two weeks after landing a job Carl was laid off. Before coming we were unaware that seasonal lay-offs were so common in the Maritimes. Carl had been working steadily since leaving school at 16 in Britain, so the shock of various temporary jobs was difficult. For me it has been up and down. [For a time] I was a legal cashier working for a lawyer doing his accounts in the UK; this changed dramatically for me, as I now have had to revert back to reception and administration work that I did when I first left school, so I'm still trying to find that permanent position.

Despite work challenges do you enjoy living in Nova Scotia?

Absolutely; it's great that there are beaches only a short drive away in the summertime and it's wonderful to see the tourists flock here – the place is buzzing. The winters are probably the hardest aspect to overcome; it has taken us eight years to become accustomed to it, but we know that the snow is now our way of life. Coming from a multicultural society to Nova Scotia there were and are differences and this is now being put forward, with the government letting Nova Scotians know that this province is in need of significantly more immigrants in order to maintain a steady economy. Gradually Nova Scotians are starting to warm up to this idea, but it is a slow process.

As an additional comment, I am not sure if Canadians realise how friendly and polite their country is. Even for myself I forget this fact until I return from a trip to Britain or elsewhere. People on the street, in shops and grocery stores all take the time to ask how you are and to be helpful.

Would you recommend others to move to Nova Scotia?

Overall, yes. The cost of living is lower than in the UK, although house prices are rising here, too. Halifax has a nice mix between small town familiarity and city sophistication. There are many festivals and people become very involved in the community. It's a great place to live and the economy is improving.

Oak Island – Nova Scotia's True Money Pit

Covered in oak trees more common in southern climates, this small island in Mahone Bay continues to be the site of one of the world's most import treasure hunts. Since 1795 people have been looking for buried treasure that seems ingeniously well protected by a series of booby traps and tides.

The search for treasure has now cost many lives and millions of dollars, yet, despite the lack of any real success, people continue to sink money and holes into the island and are encouraged by legend, hope and a series of peculiar clues. There are many theories as to where the treasure may have come from. In the 1600s pirates regularly frequented Nova Scotia's waters, with William Kidd being the most famous. When he was hanged in London, much of his buried treasure was lost – and some of it may still lay beneath Oak Island. Or indeed the treasure may even predate Kidd, dating back to the Spanish or even the Knights Templars! Who knows?

'Africville', just outside Halifax. Sadly and inexcusably, Africville was levelled in the 1970s.

Rural Nova Scotia and the Coast

Except for Halifax, Nova Scotia is mostly rural, and defined by a long, indented coastline and central valley. Much of the province has trees and, despite being almost totally surrounded by water, the climate is defined as continental as most weather develops from the west. When storms form to the east, somewhat diminished hurricanes can hit the province. Forestry, fishing and mining are all notable elements of Nova Scotia's economy, whereas farming remains minor. Small-scale agriculture has persisted and even a few vineyards are bearing fruit, but the general climate has not aided farms. Manufacturing is the largest contributor to the provincial economy, and services employ the largest percentage of the workforce.

Nova Scotia's dramatic coastline is ideal for small fishing ports and villages and was important for booze-running during prohibition and even piracy in earlier days. In a landscape similar to that of western Britain and Ireland, some of Canada's most photographed and painted towns perch along Nova Scotia's shore. For visitors, these communities elicit romantic visions of wild seas and painted houses, stilted on bare rocks. Sadly, attention was drawn to the coast near Halifax when Swissair Flight 111 crashed into stormy seas.

Some newcomers have successfully established bed-and-breakfasts or small hotels catering to the artists and tourists who are drawn to the coastal towns. Lobster is a mainstay of the local and tourism diet and in fact Nova Scotia and Atlantic Canada is quickly becoming a culinary destination. Indeed, if you are considering relocating to anywhere in Atlantic Canada, affordable and beautiful housing can make up for fewer employment options, provided you have, at the very least, financial resources and creativity.

New Brunswick

New Brunswick is located to the west of Nova Scotia and was once part of its territory. Founded by loyalist settlers, New Brunswick is, remarkably, the only fully bilingual province in Canada. Roughly one-third of the province is French-speaking. Be careful, though, the Atlantic Francophone community is not Québécois but Acadian. Centred on **Moncton** and spreading across much of the north of the province to Edmonston, the Acadians are an echo of a larger population that predates British settlement. In the mid-1700s the British expelled most of the Acadians in the belief that they would side with the French in the battle for Canada. Many ended up in Louisiana, where Acadian became Cajun. Those who either managed to stay or returned to their traditional fishing life along Canada's east coast have maintained the language and their enticing folkloric traditions and music. Now loved by the federal government, the Acadians are a Francophone population that is distinctly pro-Canada. To that end, despite constituting a population of only around 350,000, they receive considerable attention during national celebrations like Canada Day on 1 July.

Moncton is a busy, functioning bilingual city, which has hosted the Francophone Games (similar to the Commonwealth Games). The city is also referred to as the 'hub' of the Maritimes, as all trains and a lot of shipping pass through the city or enter its port. Consequently, Moncton has hosted several important concerts, including the Rolling Stones in 2005, and would be a logical choice for a professional sports team. Moreover, Moncton was declared Canada's friendliest city.

Around 50 per cent of New Brunswick's population lives in urban areas, which is far below the national urban average of over 80 per cent. The provincial capital, **Fredericton**, is a quiet, conservative place that has some of the best loyalist architecture anywhere in the country. The largest municipality is **Saint John**, located on the southern coast of the province. Home to 125,000 people, the port is the main employer. The surrounding area is New Brunswick's primary agricultural region. Potatoes are grown extensively, and one well-known inter-national company that grew from New Brunswick, McCain, has become famous for its chips and other frozen products. With 83 per cent of its territory forested, lumberjacks really exist, in spite of a weak paper market and difficult relations

Magnetic Hill

Moncton, New Brunswick is home to one of Canada's most visited natural wonders – or optical illusions: Magnetic Hill. Not totally unique, but certainly well promoted for over 60 years, it is a place where people leave their cars in neutral just to watch them roll uphill! It is otherwise known as a gravity hill, and water also gives the impression of flowing uphill. This spectacle has attracted enough tourists over the year to spawn the development of a tourist park, and it remains one of New Brunswick's most visited sites.

Case Study: James Hoyland, Academic

James was born in Lancashire and brought up in Darlington, County Durham. James is in his 30s and has experienced life in both eastern and western Canada; he currently lives with his Canadian wife in smalltown New Brunswick, after moving from Vancouver. James studied applied physics to PhD level at the University of Hull. As a physicist he has specialised in the area of laser applications in the semiconductor industry and materials science and more recently in microbiology.

James' wife Judith is a doctor of social anthropology whom he met while studying in England. Together they lived for three years in Guildford, before moving to Canada. Initially James came to Canada on a work visa for the British Columbia Cancer Agency and subsequently applied for permanent resident status through the spousal programme.

What attracted you to Canada?

I have been interested in Canada since I was a child. When I was about 14 I had a big map of Canada on my bedroom wall. I always got the impression of a relaxed, socially progressive country. I was also fascinated by the images of the landscape in *National Geographic* magazines. It just seemed like a good place to live.

How have you found living in both the far west and east of the country?

British Columbia really was the Canada I had imagined – mountains, forests, cosmopolitan city life. Living in Vancouver just off Cambie Street was wonderful; we had Thai, Japanese and half a dozen other restaurants just round the corner – including a crêperie, which was open until midnight. The 10-minute walk to work with the mountains towering over the city skyline ahead of me was beautiful. We met some really nice people and made some good

with the US industry. Almost the entire coastline is dedicated to fishing, and the lobster season anywhere in the Maritimes is an event. Both Saint John and Moncton are located off the **Bay of Fundy** (Moncton via the Petitcodiac River), which holds claim to the world's largest tides.

New Brunswick has been aggressive in developing new industry and has succeeded in attracting call centres. A bilingual population and a gentle, enjoyable accent, combined with positive incentives, have drawn business to the province. World markets being what they are, serious competition is coming from call centres in India and the Philippines, where workers are called on to answer any number of queries regarding high-tech products.

Prince Edward Island

To the north and east of New Brunswick in the Gulf of St Lawrence lies Prince Edward Island, now joined to the mainland by the 13km Confederation Bridge. In 1997, to great fanfare, this 13km connection between mainland Canada and friendships. Unfortunately, my job didn't really turn out to be what I thought it was going to be, and so when Judith was offered an assistant professorship at Mount Allison University in New Brunswick we decided it was the smart choice and went for it.

New Brunswick is certainly very different from British Columbia. A lot colder for a start. The first January we were here, we had to dig ourselves out of a two-metre drift of snow just to get out of our house. For a couple of weeks that February the temperature dropped to minus 26°C. But I enjoyed all that for being so different from the UK. The lifestyle here is slower but we've found the people very friendly and have made lots of friends. Also we can afford to own a house here, something we could never have managed on one salary in Vancouver. Generally most things are cheaper in the Atlantic provinces, but it's harder to find unusual items.

What are some of your impressions of the academic environment?

In Canadian universities there is much more of an emphasis on teaching than in the UK where research is king. There is also much more of an 'audit culture' in the UK, with professors continually have to take part in endless research assessment exercises and teaching-quality reviews. In Canada it may be a bit too far the other way, with little apparent accountability. Finally if you're applying for a job in a Canadian academic institution, don't hold your breath for news of your application or indeed acknowledgement that they've received it. The hiring process can take up to a year from the application deadline to the start date. Even the interviews can take months to line up. Also, they rarely if ever contact anyone but those called for interview – something I've found very irritating.

Prince Edward Island was completed. Spanning the Northumberland Strait, the bridge was a significant undertaking, having to withstand harsh winter conditions and ice floes. As one would expect, there was some opposition to the link for cultural and employment reasons. Although construction created many jobs, these would no longer exist once the bridge was completed and ferry routes terminated. Culturally some islanders attached a great sense of identity to their perceived isolation and therefore opposed construction on emotional grounds. The other major concern was environmental: people worried that such an intrusion on lobster habitat could be very damaging. The jury remains out on the lobster, as so many pressures have negatively affected the Atlantic fisheries, but there have been quantifiable economic gains, particularly in tourism and real estate. The bridge's construction, however, has swollen the number of visitors to the island to over one million annually and has boosted tourism to the land celebrated by Lucy Maud Montgomery's *Anne of Green Gables* books.

Canada's smallest province, both in population and size, is historically important as the site of Confederation, but the economic relevance of the

Case Study: Judy and Trevor Pye, Innkeepers

Judy and Trevor are in their 40s, from Reading, UK. They moved lock, stock and barrel to Prince Edward Island, Canada's smallest province, in July 2003, where they now run the successful and attractive Shipwright Inn in Olde Charlottetown. The Pyes' move involved giving up their good jobs and life in the UK and was motivated by a trip to PEI and their daughter's choice to study at the provincial university.

How much of a risk did you take in coming here?

We really did 'burn all our bridges' and took a huge risk in buying property here in Canada, selling up everything in Great Britain and coming here only on a year's work permit. The promise of provincial nomination made it easier to swallow but until we got our landed immigration status in June 2004 we really didn't feel too safe... We also brought my mother with us (86 years old) whom we are now sponsoring to become a Canadian resident.

How easy was the process?

Surprisingly quite simple, although the provincial nomination streamlined the process drastically. Not being able to speak with a person at the Canadian High Commission is difficult and dealing with automated voices annoying, but it all worked out fine. Good tip – get your fingerprints and police clearance done before leaving Great Britain – it took Ottawa six months to process mine,

island has diminished in relation to other regions. Fishing and lobster-trapping are important industries and Prince Edward Island is well known for its excellent potatoes grown in the distinctive red soil.

Beyond the obvious resource and tourism industries, government is an extremely important employer. Little Prince Edward Island, with fewer than 140,000 people, must have one of the highest ratios of representation in the world. The Provincial Assembly has 32 elected members and the island has four federal members of parliament, as well as four appointed senators. To round out the administration, communities all have mayors and councils, albeit functioning mostly on a part-time basis. Some other individual federal constituencies or 'ridings' in Canada contain as many people as all of Prince Edward Island, so Islanders certainly have a voice.

Because of its size and economy, the Island has a long tradition of emigration. Economic growth has not kept up with high birth rates so young people move to other parts of the country. Conversely, some mainlanders and immigrants choose Prince Edward Island precisely for its tranquillity and unhurried pace.

Newfoundland and Labrador

Really two distinct entities, Newfoundland is a rocky island, whereas Labrador is a sparsely populated territory of mainland Canadian Shield north and east of as I left Britain and then spent more than six months in Canada and therefore had to get both English and Canadian clearance.

What have been some of the highlights of your move?

There have been numerous highlights: the success of our business – better than we could have ever dreamed given that neither of us has ever done anything like this before. The way the Maritimers have gone out of their way to help us – they are an amazing group of people. Having our own house built out on the waterfront – something we could never have done (or afforded) in Great Britain. Our first hurricane – Juan, September 2003, and then White Juan in February 2004 – 40 centimetres of snow overnight.

What have been some challenges?

Our credit rating in Canada was the equivalent of a 15-year-old's. You cannot give references as you haven't had dealings with anyone and without references they won't give you credit – a vicious circle. In the end we deliberately took out a hire purchase for a car and built up our credit that way.

The other difficulty we encountered is probably pertinent to the Island and not all of Canada. We had to wait about nine months before we were allocated a family doctor (the delay was caused by the shortage of doctors in the Maritimes). In defence, the Island has a very good series of walk-in clinics, which means that you can get always access to a doctor if needed.

Quebec's own sparsely populated Shield region. The entire province has slightly over half a million people, almost all of whom live on the 'Rock'. Its population ravaged by the two world wars, Newfoundland completed Canada by joining the Confederation in 1949. Newfoundlanders represent a mix of peoples from Britain and Ireland whose establishment on the island occurred separately from loyalist settlements elsewhere in Canada. As a result of isolation and distinct immigration patterns, Newfoundlanders (and Cape Bretoners) retain a noticeable accent. The culture is more Celtic than American and holds on to a rich musical tradition.

St John's

The bulk of Newfoundland's population is located around St John's on the Avalon Peninsula. This charming capital has the dubious distinction of being North America's foggiest and wettest city and, with fewer sunny days than any other provincial or territorial capital, the risk of melanoma is much reduced. Sitting south of 48 degrees north, St John's latitude is below that of Southampton, but the strong continental effect and northern currents result in an unmistakably harsher environment. Icebergs descend into Newfoundland's harbours, and barren rock and tundra make up a large portion of the island's interior. So much snow will fall in St John's that it must be dumped in the ocean, as there simply is not enough space along the narrow, hilly streets to merely

St Pierre and Miquelon

Located off the southern coast of Newfoundland, the tiny archipelago of St Pierre and Miquelon is France's last remaining outpost in North America. Traded back and forth between Britain and France, the islands were secured as French first at the treaty of Paris in 1763 and again in 1814. Today the islands are home to nearly 7,000 French citizens who use the euro, fish and sell discounted liquor and cigarettes to Canada.

For obvious strategic reasons the islands have an important fishing industry whose boundaries have caused numerous conflicts between Canada and France. The collapse of cod stocks and an international moratorium on fishing have rendered the debates all but academic.

plough. Given these physical limitations, Newfoundland's economy and culture is conspicuously maritime in appearance and style. For much of its history, rural Newfoundlanders lived in tiny 'outport' villages scattered along the indented coast. Since joining Canada many outports have closed and some houses were literally floated to larger centres. Saint John's is commonly referred to as 'Town', as its greater area has 40 per cent of the province's inhabitants.

The Rest of the Island

Newfoundland appeals in the way that Ireland's west does. It is culturally warm and has a strong, independent identity. The collapse of the cod fishery – once the world's greatest reserves – has devastated an already marginal region. Early explorers talk of so many fish that it hampered their ships' movements, yet today, owing to gross international over-fishing, the waters are all but bare. Slowly the economy of the Rock is improving, with the promise of offshore oil reserves. Many jobs will have to be created in order to bring the Newfies back from other parts of Canada and the world and before the area will attract economic immigrants. Nevertheless, tourism does offer some opportunities and the idea of spending several months on Newfoundland's coast, or perhaps studying at the university, may draw some to this interesting and unique region. To ensure many return visits, some British have chosen to invest in holiday homes at Marble Mountain ski resort near Corner Brook, in western Newfoundland.

Labrador

Labrador has a population of only 30,000. Excluding those living in mining communities, the majority of the population are Cree or Inuit. Some of the coastal Inuit communities attracted international attention for having the highest suicide rates on earth. Substance abuse and the loss of cultural identity after government-forced relocations plague many of these communities. With very few roads, air and sea provide the main forms of access. At some point a bridge may link Newfoundland to the mainland, with an ultimate goal of extending a route south through Quebec.

Summary

Atlantic Canada has a great deal to offer and should see relatively stable growth during the next decades. Close to major population centres in the United States and a mere hop over the Atlantic from the UK, Canada's far east may again emerge as an important trade centre as it did during the colonial period. More importantly, however, the cultural integrity of the region remains strong and the wild, battered coast is a constant reminder of North America's grandeur. Fish stocks will never recover, but alternative activities are filling the economic gap and a hardy population should enjoy the fruits of good government and a unique home in the world.

The North: Yukon, Northwest Territory and Nunavut

As embodied in the national anthem, Canada *is* the 'True North Strong and Free' and, while the majority of Canadians may never see their true north, Canada's soul lurks in the wintry polar lands. For, in the words of the bard of the Yukon, Robert Service: 'there are strange things done in the midnight sun...' The north is magic and unique and should be approached with reverence, but never with fragility. Life is hard in the north – almost everything is extreme, with long dark winters giving way to the endless sun of summer. July heat can be barely tolerable and walking in the woods requires either an iron skin, or long clothes and mesh to fend off the swarms of mosquitoes and blackflies.

The people of the north are special – Inuit hunters with eternal faces speak perhaps the world's most complex language. The Athapaskan nations along the Yukon River will catch and dry thousands of salmon during their long run from the Bering Sea, and hardy prospectors wander into Dawson City to pay for their beer in actual gold nuggets. Elsewhere, workers earn excellent money working in major mines and driving heavy equipment on the ice highway – for much of the year no roads exist in the north until the great freeze, when ice becomes more stable than muskeg and tundra.

Few paved highways are found north of the 60th parallel. The **Alaska Highway** starts in northern British Columbia and then passes by Whitehorse on its way to the 49th state. Heading north from Whitehorse, the **Klondike Highway** leads to Dawson City and its historic goldfields. Just south of Dawson the Dempster veers off, and a mostly unpaved route goes several hundred more kilometres above the Arctic Circle to Inuvik in the Northwest Territories. The trip to Inuvik

> *Quick Facts: The North*
> **Population:** 101,000 spread over 3.5m sq km.
> **Largest cities:** Whitehorse (YT), Yellowknife (NWT), Iqaluit (NU).
> **Major ethnic groups:** European, First Nations, Inuit.
> **Physical highlights:** Cold; mountains in Yukon and parts of Nunavut; tundra; Shield; ice; huge coastline; extremes – dark winters, bright summers; dry; trillions of mosquitoes.
> **Economic highlights:** Some communities still pursue a traditional lifestyle; mining, famous for the Klondike goldfields, diamond mining; oil exploration; government; tourism.
> **Major events:** Yukon Quest dog sled race; creation of Nunavut as a new territory in 1999; global warming.
> **Issues in moving to the north:** Brrrr; isolation; seasonal depression (SAD); very expensive; incredible sense of community; important resource-driven opportunities.

requires two ferry crossings and when ice is forming or thawing the rivers become impassable.

The **Dempster Highway** is the only permanent road in Canada to cross the Arctic Circle. A few roads lead to the Yukon and Northwest Territories, whereas Nunavut, the new territory of the eastern Arctic and Canada's largest political jurisdiction, does not yet have road access for its 30,000 people.

The north has seen more changes in the last 10 years than perhaps anywhere else in the modern world. Once totally isolated, northern communities now have television and the Internet. Modern governments function in numerous languages and Canada's Arctic has become the third largest diamond-producing region on earth – although Nunavut's only mine has recently suspended operations. Large families contribute to population growth, as do resource trends and increased metal values are bringing people back into Yukon and the Territories. The north has Canada's youngest median population, as ageing joints suffer from the cold.

The Yukon River

The Yukon River starts in the beautiful lakes in the southern part of the territory and continues for 2,500km to the Bering Sea. It is central to the most likely route of migration from Asia, and people have been living in the region for thousands of years. The Yukon, as understood in the western concept, came alive with the discovery of gold in 1896, which brought more 'stampeders' into the territory in two years than live there today. These hardy dreamers mostly boarded ships to Skagway, Alaska, hiked the Chilkoot Trail, then rafted or mushed several hundred more kilometres to Dawson City and the hope of wealth. Few became rich, but the Yukon was discovered as a land of extremes and a land of magic. **Dawson City** is the most authentic frontier town anywhere in North America, supporting over 2,000 residents, 400 of whom continue to mine. **Whitehorse** is younger and named for the river rapids that resembled the mane of a white horse. It really gained life during the construction of the Alaska Highway. Until construction of the Klondike Highway in the 1970s, the only way to reach Dawson City was by paddle-wheeler or dogsled, so the capital was moved to Whitehorse, which remains the largest city in the north.

Whitehorse and Other Towns

As a rather new, government-driven centre, Whitehorse has a lot of functional rather than beautiful buildings, but the central core has maintained some frontier architecture and the spirit of the city cannot be denied. Home to 25,000 of Yukon's 30,000 people, it is undoubtedly the centre of life for the territory and even Wal-Mart (Asda) has pushed into the local economy. But people do not really move north for the urban experience. They accept it as a necessity, but never love it.

Most other non-aboriginal northern communities are a microcosm of Whitehorse, with spiritless buildings and a general store that carries many

Hunting Seals

Many images are promoted in the UK and around the world scolding Canada for the continued hunting of seals. Greenpeace's famous photo of a beautiful white baby seal aroused emotion in all circles and celebrities such as Brigitte Bardot and Heather Mills have grandstanded about saving seals, but the issue is much more complicated than it is often presented. There is almost universal agreement that seals and particularly baby seals are extremely cute, but they are a sustainable resource for humans and polar bears alike. In the north of Canada – Greenland, Alaska and Siberia – the Inuit have been hunting seals for thousands of years, so much so that humans are part of that eco-system. As with the pelts of other animals, European demand fostered a market for seal skin and numbers have been affected by over-hunting.

Over-hunting last century threatened seals in much the same way that whales were also endangered, but current seal populations are healthy and may require a cull. Surprising to many Europeans, the killing of white-coated baby seals has actually been illegal since 1987 – the use of stock footage of adorable baby seals being clubbed has proven to be an effective fundraiser for some organisations. While images of the hunt are difficult to defend, prime minister Stephen Harper did a good job by clarifying that the hunt is simply another form of animal husbandry as practised the world over.

Rising fuel costs and a decrease in pelt values may yet end the debate prematurely, wiping out some northern communities, and relieving Canada of some negative publicity.

different provisions. Because of the permafrost few streets are paved, and people live in scattered settlements with little in the way of urban planning.

Yellowknife, the second-largest centre, has around 15,000 people. Located roughly due north of Edmonton, Yellowknife sits on the north coast of Great Slave Lake and is the capital of the ever-diminishing Northwest Territories, having recently given up the entire eastern Arctic. Once, all western and northern Canada, apart from lower British Columbia, was called the Northwest Territories, thus the birth of Nunavut continues the same process that led to Manitoba, Yukon, Alberta, Saskatchewan and numerous other border readjustments. Yellowknife owes its existence to a major goldmine, services and government. In the 1990s a sometimes violent strike tore the community apart, and only new industry and time will heal some of the social wounds. This conflict was exceptional in the north – a region where people are scarce, conflict is avoided and peculiarities are perhaps a little more accepted. A few adventurous souls really do disappear in northern Canada, but many more find a closer community than anything they knew in the south.

Summary

Living and working in Arctic Canada could well be the subject of a study unto itself, as the majesty and isolation of the land is encountered in only a few other places on earth. Northerners know what is going on in the world, but they don't have to care. In European communities fitting in is easy, as everyone is welcome, but the ancient indigenous cultures are complicated and, although they have mastered the north, merging that lifestyle with the modern world is not easy. Some find religion, others drink, yet more seek spirituality in the eternal light and the aurora.

Iqaluit, the capital of Nunavut, is developing into a modern, isolated city governing a region primarily in the Inuktitut language, as well as English and French. Treeless, snowy and cold, it faces many social challenges, but is destined to be an important centre for Arctic peoples and hopefully a model of Canada's indigenous heritage. Opportunities abound throughout the north, but one must leave behind prejudgments and have the ability to adapt to an extreme world. Boredom and loneliness plague many settlers and those in search of ice and snow can find it much more easily elsewhere in Canada, but in the north you become part of something and very much leave something else behind.

Canada Today

03

Modern Canada is a first-world nation, often ranked in the top five for quality of life. On several occasions Vancouver has been rated as the world's best city in which to live, and Toronto, Ottawa, Calgary and Montreal are usually placed in the top 25. As an economic power Canada sits firmly within the G8. The strong position against inflation pursued by the Central Bank and (belated) fiscal restraint at all levels of government has resulted in Canada's being the only G8 economy to maintain budget surpluses, albeit at the cost of higher systemic unemployment and reduced services.

Having shed, for the most part, its colonial roots, the modern country is regionally a multicultural entity caught up in a quest for its own identity and a debate over unity. The Queen is portrayed on the currency and is represented by a governor general, but many Canadians pay little attention to that arrangement. The periodic threat of Quebec's secession and regional discontent in other regions results in much navel-gazing and flag-waving.

'Sleeping next to an elephant' (in the words of Pierre Trudeau) has benefited Canada. The United States is the country's largest trading partner, receiving over 80 per cent of its exports. Canada has become rich as a result of this market. Many Canadians are vocally anti-American or, more specifically, anti-US government, and the country has foreign policy distinct from its neighbour. Canada did not support the war in Vietnam, nor did it take part in the most recent incursion into Iraq and, although it is increasingly less merited, Canadians proudly hold onto their broad peace-keeping tradition.

Major Political Parties and Themes

The three levels of government – federal, provincial and municipal – share an uneasy distribution of power. The Canadian system is based almost entirely on the British parliamentary system, with a prime minister and terms of up to five years. Provincial governments operate in the same manner, but moves are afoot to reform the system. Ontario, for example, has adopted fixed election dates, and British Columbia may experiment with some form of proportional representation, instead of the current 'first past the post' system. The federal Conservative government has also recently introduced four-year terms with fixed election dates, although its minority status almost guarantees an election before 19 October 2009.

The most arcane element of the political system is an appointed senate, designed around the British House of Lords; Canadian senators are not elected, but chosen by the prime minister. Therefore, Liberal governments result in Liberal senators. Originally appointed for life, senators must now step aside at the age of 75. Distribution of senate seats favours the older provinces and, as a result, western Canada, particularly Alberta, has vocally advocated a 'triple E' senate – effective, equal and elected – a system based more on the American model. Others simply want to abolish the upper house, arguing that elected provincial assemblies counteract the federal parliament's power. Changing the structure of the senate means revisiting the constitution, a painful and tedious affair involving all the provinces, egos and separatists. As prime minister Stephen Harper pointed out on a visit to Australia's parliament, 'the mandate to govern, when it is given to you directly by the people, is a great honour and a great responsibility. It's the very essence of responsible government, and it is the minimum condition of 21st-century democracy.' As senate reform is fundamental to the Conservative platform, changes such as term limits and perhaps provincially administered elections should be implemented, while avoiding complicated constitutional amendments.

Flamboyant former prime minister Pierre Trudeau left his most significant legacy in 1982 when he patriated the constitution from Britain. With it came his image of Canada as a Just Society, which included a charter of rights and freedoms that ostensibly protects the rights of all individuals. Also enshrined in the document were multiculturalism, bilingualism and a complicated formula that requires the agreement of at least seven provinces and 50 per cent of the population in order to modify any part of the charter. Although patriation represented an important progression in the country's history, Quebec did not sign the constitution, and thus left open the question of national unity.

Political Parties

Liberal Party

Pierre Trudeau was a member of the Liberal Party, which has ruled nationally for over 70 per cent of Canada's history and is sometimes called 'Canada's natural governing party'. An amorphous lot, driven more by governance than ideology, the Liberals sway to both the left and right according to current issues and political pressures. Ideologues are often offended by the party's malleability, but generally the party will receive 35 to 45 per cent of the national vote as it slides between polarities in the political spectrum.

Defining the Liberal Party in Canada is not easy. One politician described them as campaigning like socialists while governing like Tories. The party can generally be seen as centrist, or centre left, but much like the Labour Party in Britain it often sits slightly to the right in actual administration. (Unlike Labour in Britain, an entirely different party, the New Democrats, carries the banner of the trade unions.) This centrist governance typifies Canada – fiscally responsible while maintaining social programmes. The term 'liberal' is understood differently in Canada from in the United States, as even the Democrats south of the border would sit to the right of the Canadian political spectrum.

Currently the Liberals sit in opposition – a position they have not been in since the early 1990s. The party's leader, Stéphane Dion, again comes from Quebec and is far more articulate in French than in English. An ardent federalist and ostensibly an active environmentalist, his appeal in Quebec and across Canada has remained limited.

Conservative Party

Currently in government, the Conservative Party is the only other political party to rule at the federal level. The Tories have existed under a variety of names since Sir John A. Macdonald led them to the first national government in 1867. Following the Conservative reign from 1984 to 1993 under Brian Mulroney and then the brief tenure of Canada's first female prime minister, Kim Campbell, the party has undergone a rebirth after a fractious division.

Elements of the reincarnated Conservative Party have returned to a long-abandoned socially conservative stance, which limits electoral appeal. The few voices that favour such issues as the death penalty and restricting abortion had little say in previous Conservative (PC) governments, but were able to acquire representation under the banner of the Reform Party, which grew from a western protest base. Trapped regionally, the Reform Party morphed into the Canadian Alliance in an attempt to attract Progressive Conservative voters in the east, but failed to do so in any definite way. By 2002 it had become abundantly clear to conservatives of all shades that a split vote would result in eternal Liberal governments, and therefore the two groups attended marriage counselling and came together under the conservative banner. With previous mergers in its history, it is interesting to note that the new name, Conservative Party, was the official name of the party at Confederation.

The new party essentially abandoned many of its populist policies and was elected on simple ideas of good governance, fiscal management and a general appetite for change. The small religious vein of the party that opposed gay marriage and even bilingualism has gradually been silenced or drowned out in deference to the national electorate.

New Democratic Party, Bloc Québécois and Green Party

Nationally two other political parties have members sitting in parliament. The leftist **New Democratic Party (NDP)**, which has never held power, has nevertheless been very influential on social issues and during minority governments. Often referred to as 'Canada's social conscience' the NDP continues to raise important and controversial issues, such as opposing Canada's role in Afghanistan, abolishing the senate and addressing the increasingly potent issue of homelessness. The other significant federal party is the sovereignist (separatist) **Bloc Québécois (BQ)**, which runs candidates only in Quebec but still managed to form the official opposition from 1993 to 1997. The BQ is currently polling poorly, but some members should manage to hang on until the next big issue involving Quebec emerges – whatever that may be. Some political observers anticipate a **Green Party** breakthrough, particularly in

British Columbia, and it is conceivable that the Greens may yet achieve an elected voice. The Party's leader, Elizabeth May, has chosen to run in Nova Scotia against prominent Tory Peter MacKay, a potential future prime minister, thereby virtually guaranteeing she will not win.

Other Trends

Right-wing populism is a by-product of western Canadian culture. With less loyalty to tradition, westerners have introduced most new political movements in Canada and have been the first to turn their backs on ruling parties. In the early part of the 20th century a 'United Farmers' movement rose to provincial power in all three prairie provinces. Federally, the **Progressive Party** won support in the west and eventually merged with the Tories to form the **Progressive Conservatives** back in the 1920s. **Social Credit**, a bizarre political ideology invented by Scot C. H. Douglas, promised hope during the Depression and rose to power in Alberta in 1935. The Social Credit (Socred) idea of dodgy banking didn't last long, although the movement became the firmest expression of true conservatism in English Canada. It achieved power in Alberta and British Columbia and developed a reasonable presence in Quebec. Social Credit and Quebec's **Union Nationale** had the most overt religious tones of any political ideology in the country's history. The Union Nationale in Quebec, which died with the Quiet Revolution of the 1960s, gave way to a secular liberal government. The Socreds hung on in name in British Columbia, but really as the non-socialist option, rather than an ideology.

On the left, Canadian socialism also developed in the west, growing from discontent during the Great Depression. While Social Credit gained ground in rural Alberta, the **Cooperative Commonwealth Federation** was making political

Danny Williams

Newfoundland's famously aggressive premier has virtually gone to war with the last two Canadian prime ministers, while remaining loved in his own province and generally respected across Canada. The premier first gained notoriety in 2004 when he removed all the Canadian flags from provincial buildings over a dispute with then minority prime minister Paul Martin over offshore oil revenues. Moving next onto the world scene, Williams appeared on *Larry King Live* and debated the seal hunt with Paul McCartney and Heather Mills. During the discussion he exposed inconsistencies in their arguments and defended the historic industry. Although a Conservative, Williams will actively campaign against the federal Tories in the next election. He has openly accused current prime minister Stephen Harper of lying, once again with regard to oil revenues and transfer payments.

A successful businessman and Rhodes scholar, Williams is one of Canada's most colourful politicians and a great booster of Newfoundland and Labrador.

inroads in Saskatchewan and Manitoba. Forming the provincial government in Saskatchewan in 1944, the CCF had nationalised healthcare by the 1960s. Provincially and federally, the CCF became the New Democratic Party (NDP) in 1971 and, although the NDP have never won a national election, most Canadians feel positive about their presence in parliament. Traditional support for the NDP comes from parts of the prairies and the unionised areas of Ontario and British Columbia, although it is shifting to parts of Atlantic Canada and urban centres. Some support for the Greens comes from NDP and Conservative voters as well as traditional non-voters.

Healthcare and Quebec Separation

Healthcare remains an extremely relevant theme in Canadian politics, with no party openly discussing privatisation of the system. Canadians see access to healthcare as part of their national identity and, while problems exist in the system, neither provincial nor federal governments question the universality of basic services. The system is provincially administered and is in crisis in some areas due to understaffing and an infrastructure deficit; Edmonton alone has recently recruited 500 British nurses.

Another constant theme or irritation on the national political scene concerns the perpetual time bomb of Quebec separation. Since the formation of the Bloc Québécois (BQ), Quebecers have been offered a nationalist option on the federal scene. Recent Tory successes in Quebec have dulled the debate somewhat. Provincially the issue has been similar, with a provincial Liberal Party (currently in power) and the separatist Parti Québécois (PQ). A third party, the Action Démocratique du Québec (ADQ), with its strong focus on balanced budgets and tax reform, is gaining in popularity, and has altered the balance by placing second in the last provincial election.

The rest of Canada, often referred to as ROC, has tired of the unity debate in Quebec. Francophone Quebecers tend to view Canada as a duality of English and French, but the reality is far more regionalised. Most Canadians do not want to see Quebec leave, but are weary of the debate and the strain the uncertainty places on the economy. The fact that separatism remains an option within the Canadian political landscape means other regions banter it around from time to time. Up to a quarter of Albertans state they do not feel a significant allegiance to Canada, and ideas about a new nation are sometimes raised academically in British Columbia. Newfoundlanders have always been Newfies first, and Maritimers have a deep sense of regional identity.

Politics Since 1993

The 1993 national election wiped out the Tories and reduced the party to two seats. With the Conservative vote split, Jean Chrétien's Liberals swept Ontario, which has nearly a third of the seats in parliament. Chrétien remained in power for 10 years and oversaw a balancing of the budget, a second referendum in Quebec and strained relations with the USA over certain trade disputes and the war in Iraq. With his distinctive accent and folksy style, Chrétien had always been on the left of his party, promising great reforms to the electoral system and the elimination of poverty. None of this happened during his tenure and, under the guidance of his finance minister Paul Martin, the party and government took a step to the right. With Chrétien finally out of the scene, Paul Martin took over the reins of the Liberal Party, and the government, in 2003.

The 2004 election was to be Martin's coronation, but, swept up in scandals over misused funds, his party could only manage a minority government. Less than two years later the government fell, and on 23 January 2006, sick of Liberal governance, Canadians gave the new Conservative Party a chance at minority government. Amid concerns about hidden social and corporate agendas, support for Stephen Harper's Tories was tepid. For their part the Conservatives ran on an simple five-point anti-corruption platform and have managed to maintain a reasonable level of support and approval so far.

Current Themes

Having balanced the budget, controlled inflation and settled the Quebec question for at least a few years, the government is turning its attention to governance itself, tax reduction and, grudgingly, the environment. A severe economic downturn in the United States will be bound to affect Canada – primarily in the manufacturing centres of central Canada. A stronger dollar certainly feels good, but hurts exports and encourages cross-border shopping. Melting ice in the north is opening shipping routes that will raise sovereignty issues. Demand for Canadian resources from Asia will offset decreased demand from the USA, continuing the significant economic growth in regions such as Alberta and Saskatchewan. The border remains a challenge to trade as citizens of Canada and the USA will soon require a passport (instead of just a driver's licence) to cross between countries. General relations with the USA have already improved, and the post-Bush era should help. Some Democrats want to reopen aspects of the North American Free Trade Agreement, but it will be surprising if that really happens. Canada intends to withdraw its troops from Afghanistan by 2011.

Socially, Canada remains quite progressive. Gay marriage is now legal in all jurisdictions and the Tories consider the issue closed. Homelessness is on the increase and the number of children living in poverty continues to rise, despite low unemployment and budget surpluses. While wages have increased, house prices have virtually doubled in some areas. The three western provinces have seen spectacular housing booms and vacancy is at an all-time low in a few cities. Childcare remains expensive and spaces are limited in many areas.

Funding for healthcare will always elicit debate, particularly about federal government transfer payments. The federal government in Canada, via taxes, takes money from richer (have) provinces and subsidises poorer (have-not) provinces. The largest per capita donor is oil-rich Alberta and the largest per capita recipient is Newfoundland although, in terms of actual amounts, Quebec receives the most money. In balancing the national budget, the federal government transferred many of its costs to the provinces, which in turn passed costs on to municipalities and individuals. The ongoing fight between juris-dictional powers and programme funding is often lost on 'normal' Canadians, who care more about the quality of services than they do about the division of power.

Politics in Canada may appear mundane at first sight, but the intricacies of a federal system are complicated and such a vast territory is difficult to unite. Voter turnout during elections is average on a world scale and regional biases run deep. It can be assumed that Canada will likely remain a mostly intact nation in the 21st century. It is not a corrupt nation, but, with one party so often in power, misuse of resources occurs. Canadians tend to vote regionally, leaving to the federal government the role of speaking for the entire country, difficult as that task may be. *See* also 'Internal Issues', pp.96–100.

Economic Background

Once a land of furs, fish and forests, modern Canada is a prosperous G8 nation whose services and manufacturing industries dwarf traditional resources. Inextricably linked to its rich southern neighbour, the Canadian economy sends over 80 per cent of its exports south and also receives 60 per cent of its imports from Uncle Sam. This close relationship, or dependence as some might say, is not without its problems, but is important enough to the United States that both countries make the flow of trade operate as smoothly as possible. Britain and France, the historic parents, are relatively minor players in the Canadian economic picture, but Mexico and Asia are grabbing much more attention.

Canada is inherently rich, with a relatively small population and many resources. Atlantic fish stocks brought the first non-native migrants. Lumber and furs drove the push inland, and good soil in Ontario and the vast plains in the west attracted farmers. The British Columbia and Klondike gold rushes encouraged a mining tradition, which continues in much of the country. But, as in the Klondike, the money was made by 'mining the miners'. And, as in all developed economies, services in Canada employ the most people – over 70 per cent of the labour force. Resources will always be important to the country's economic health and the fresh-water story is yet to be fully explored: possessing by far the world's largest reserves of salt-free water, Canada controls an essential supply of a resource that in bottled form already retails at a higher price per litre than oil.

In terms of oil, the western province of Alberta (and to a lesser extent Saskatchewan) contains one of the largest oil reserves on earth, and the north is a source of all manner of resources. Abundance defines most natural resources, save for Atlantic fish stocks that have all but disappeared as a result of poor management and over-harvesting.

Beyond romantic images of noble ranchers or sculpted lumberjacks, most Canadians veer towards brains rather than brawn. Good education characterises the modern Canadian workforce and Canada claims to have one of the highest levels of tertiary education in the world. Although Canadians have manual-labour occupations and many earn their living in the great outdoors, overall the nature of the economy requires specialisation.

The New Economy

Canadians fully embraced the so-called New Economy of the 1990s. Recent slowdowns will undoubtedly affect growth in the high-tech industry, but predictions suggest that by 2010 information technology will match resources in percentage of the gross domestic product. Once an IT goliath, Nortel Networks has gone through some punishing fluctuations and Enronesque accounting concerns. Shares that traded at well over C$120 per unit around the turn of the millennium sell for less than C$10 in 2005. Research In Motion, owner of the addictive BlackBerry, is probably Canada's best known IT company at the moment.

Without doubt, the tech bubble has burst, but the computer age is well integrated into Canadian life. The industry employs many people in graphic design, software development and IT servicing. All large companies have IT departments, and lone contractors manage to survive after making small fortunes during the run-up to 2000.

At a more tangible level, goods production represents about 30 per cent of gross domestic product. All the traditional Canadian resources, such as wheat, lumber, oil and minerals, make up a significant part of that percentage, but are by no means the country's sole products. The county's vastness means that big industry is generally not that obvious. The industrial corridor around Lake Ontario, however, is dense with factories, clogged with vehicles and sometimes choking on smog. Areas on the island of Montreal and around steel, mining and lumber towns certainly look industrial, but urban areas are not nearly as closely linked to factories as in parts of the UK. Apart from in heavily populated areas smokestacks are refreshingly rarely visible, and cities are marked by endless suburban developments and shopping centres.

Services in Canada include a mixed bag that ranges from supermarkets to government. Healthcare stands out as a major government-run service, as does the mostly public education system. Government in its many manifestations is a chief employer and, despite cutbacks during the 1990s, many professionals still move to the public sector. Healthcare funding is hotly debated and the majority of costs fall to the provincial governments although the system is subject to the requirements of the federal Canada Health Act. Despite embracing a market-style economy, Canadians love socialised healthcare, and poll after poll indicates their reluctance to accept the privatisation of services.

Regionally, government can also be one of the largest employers. Obviously around Ottawa the federal government, operating in English and French, is fundamental to the local economy. In smaller jurisdictions (the North and Prince Edward Island) government in its many manifestations is the largest employer. Yukon, for example, has about 30,000 inhabitants who are administered by the federal government, a territorial government, city government (in Whitehorse) and a series of First Nations governments. Given the extent of public services such as healthcare, education, policing and so on, it would almost seem surprising to find someone who isn't a government employee.

The Canadian Economy since 1939

During its history the Canadian economy has gone through several major shifts. The Second World War precipitated the move from agrarian to industrial, as significant military production moved over from Britain. In 1939 and 1940, when the USA was still a spectator and the UK facing such serious threats, Canada, under the direct management of C. D. Howe, a minister in William Lyon Mackenzie King's government, did what the Soviets never really managed to do: he successfully developed and managed industry from a central government perch. By the end of the war Canada had one of the largest economies on earth, and through the 1950s and 1960s Canadians gained considerable wealth. Much of this now-decaying industry was developed around Lake Ontario for access to shipping and steel. Oil was extracted in Alberta, lumber in British Columbia and the east, and fish stocks were abundant.

Socialism's ascent to power in Saskatchewan by the end of the war led to the nationalisation of healthcare, the development of crown corporations, pensions and other trappings of socialist democracy. The 1970s were generous times. Pierre Trudeau's Liberals spent and spent and, as in the rest of the developed world, high oil prices and government deficits triggered soaring inflation and consequent interest rate hikes. From the late 1960s through to the middle of the 1980s two economic ideologies became firmly rooted in the Canadian psyche. Quickly Canadians became attached to public healthcare and other generous government programmes, yet from the western-based Reform Party came a greater abhorrence for debt than in any other Western country.

By the mid-1980s Canada's debt ratio was terrible – similar to that in Ethiopia – and Canadians were losing their homes because of interest rates in the high teens. This also happened elsewhere, but in Canada the independent Central Bank sets targets on inflation that it has now maintained for over 15 years. Brian

Mulroney's Conservative government was elected in 1984 to balance the federal budget, but the books did not make it back to the black until the mid-1990s, when Jean Chrétien's Liberals adopted a clearly Tory façade and cut spending in earnest. To offset much of the cost of balancing the federal books, the government decreased transfer payments to the provinces, which in turn cut government services and offloaded costs to the cities.

The Economy in the 1990s and early 2000s

Through the 1990s and early 2000s Canada was the only G8 country to run government surpluses and to keep inflation, for the most part, under 2 per cent. This has not been achieved without cost. Unemployment has dropped below 7 per cent, but sat firmly above 9 per cent for many years. Homelessness, previously rare, has become a serious problem in major centres; a temperature of minus 30°C does not afford the luxury of sleeping under the stars. There has been minimal investment in government infrastructure and the state of the environment in some areas is atrocious.

Each province has fared differently. Ontario, the economic centre of the country, went from distinctly left-wing governance to the firm right and massive cutbacks. The Ontario economy grew, but at major social cost. Quebec witnessed little growth through the same period, caught up in its own quagmire of politics and extremely high taxes. British Columbia went through a peculiar housing boom, which was driven more by Hong Kong investment than by government policy, and Alberta flourished, with oil production generating the largest internal migration in the country. The Atlantic provinces struggled through to the end of the century, with negative growth in Newfoundland. Stable government and innovation helped elsewhere, and Nova Scotia has begun to emerge as a 'have' province (meaning it will soon contribute more financially to Canada than it takes out).

Two free trade deals were signed in recent years. First, the Free Trade Agreement increased cross-border traffic with the USA, and it was followed by the North American Free Trade Agreement, which includes Mexico and, to some extent, Chile by association. After its protectionist, mixed-economy era of the

A Mad Cow in Canada

In 2003 one case of BSE was discovered on an Albertan ranch, devastating Canada's important cattle industry. On the animal's discovery, despite its having been successfully screened from the food chain, import bans were immediately raised around the world. The US blockade was by far the most damaging as the two industries are so intertwined and the political process of removing the ban has been long and costly – the Canadian cattle industry has lost somewhere around 5 billion dollars. A case of BSE was also discovered in the United States, but tracked back to an Albertan ranch.

1970s, Canada has become a free trader, for better or for worse. As a percentage of its economy, Canada is the largest trading nation of the G8. An extremely weak Canadian dollar in terms of the US dollar boosted exports during the early years of the new millennium, but by 2007 it had reached parity with and even briefly surpassed the US dollar.

The largest trade union is the Canadian Union of Public Employees (CUPE). Other organised labour groups tend to operate provincially. British Columbia, with its large resource and port sectors, is the most unionised province in the country, followed by Quebec. Ontario's automobile sector is also highly unionised and strikes do occur, but labour strife seems to create frequent news headlines only in Quebec and British Columbia.

With government now worrying more about the bottom line than its role in people's lives, the modern Canadian economy has become more liberal than in the past. Large casinos exist in some provinces, and contribute significantly to government finances in Ontario and Quebec. Alberta and, to some extent, British Columbia have privatised liquor sales, which previously acted as a source of government income. With taxes paid both federally and provincially and professional bodies governed at a provincial level, Canada sometimes resembles a union of independent countries rather than a single nation. The economies of the various regions vary greatly and as much trade travels from north to south over the US border as flows from east to west across the provinces.

The Economy Today

The Canadian economy of today is performing very differently from the way it did in the past. Perhaps because of strong Scottish roots or memories of previous depressions, Canadians traditionally emphasised personal savings and fiscal restraint, while the government did the spending. In an almost concomitant manner, government has pulled back and Canadians have taken on extremely high levels of personal debt. A slow economy during the early 1990s and relatively high interest rates capped inflation but created higher rates of systemic unemployment. Subsequent interest rate reductions led to an increase in house sales and new house starts. Furthermore, benign neglect by the Central Bank permitted the dollar to fall in value against the American greenback and resulted in less capital flowing south and a large increase in the opposite direction.

Just as interest rates began to creep up in a healthy, steady manner, the twin towers in New York were attacked and came crashing down and, along with them, interest rates. Thus, in the hope of preventing a major recession and in response to the bursting of the technology bubble, money poured back into housing, and personal debt soared. Canadians now have lower personal savings than at any time since the Great Depression. The housing market is cooling and Canada cannot be immune from global trends, but as a result of conservative

September 11, 2001

One of those rare events where almost everyone knows exactly where they were, the terrorist attack in New York had a profound effect on Canada and its relations with the United States. When the US government closed the skies the planes had to land somewhere. Some landed in Mexico, but the majority were grounded in Canada. All Canadian airports received jets, and the airport that took most in was Gander, Newfoundland. Historically important as a refuelling stop for transatlantic flights, the Gander area with around 10,000 inhabitants became home to thousands of stranded travellers.

The closing of the land border followed by severely restricted movements had a major effect on the economy. Lower interest rates by the US Federal Reserve, followed by the Bank of Canada, encouraged an already vibrant housing market, and military actions abroad opened a rift between the two countries. When George W. Bush gave his famous post 9/11 speech naming Britain and other important allies he didn't even mention Canada, although Canadian forces participated in the actions in Afghanistan, with troops being killed by bombs and friendly fire from a US aircraft.

Retreating to its traditional peace-keeping stance, Canada did not participate in the action in Iraq and some polls suggest that, among Canadians who have an opinion, nearly 90 per cent prefer the Democrats in the USA. Traditionally Canada is the first international destination for a US president after an election, but it wasn't until Bush's second victory that he made an official visit to Canada.

Economic and geographic realities dictate that there is a close relationship between Canada and the USA – with over US$400 billion spent in trade with Canada, the two countries need each other. Relations will always be smoothed over, but differing world views have become clear in the post 9/11 world, and passports are now required for travel between Canada and the USA.

banking traditions at least few Canadians are exposed to so-called sub-prime mortgages.

The strong dollar is affecting Canada's export-driven economy. Exchange rates with most other major currencies have remained relatively steady, but the Canadian dollar's substantial increase in value against the US currency has had a direct negative effect on export profits. Nevertheless, Canada maintains a reasonable trade surplus, but the boom of the early 2000s has passed.

Canada's economic future will remain regional. Unless oil prices should miraculously plummet, Alberta will continue to lead growth and investment in the country. Internal migrants will continue to flock west to jobs where BC, Alberta and Saskatchewan are short of skilled trades. With the improved economic environment on the east coast, some Newfoundlanders and Nova Scotians are returning home. As recession settles in the United States it appears central Canada will fare least well.

The Tar Sands

Focused around the community of Fort McMurray in northern Alberta and spilling over slightly into Saskatchewan, the oil reserves tied up in the Tar Sands could account for as much as one-third of world reserves. It is expensive to strip-mine, and separate from the bitumen, but high oil prices have led to significant capital investment into the region. As conventional sources of oil are depleted, more energy is focused on the Tar Sands in Alberta. All the reserves are not as yet proven and technological advancements will be needed to access the majority of the predicted 1.6 trillion barrels of oil mixed in the ground. Current production yields around 120,000 barrels per day and this should more than double by 2010. Production from the Tar Sands accounts for slightly over half of the province's extraction and has caused an economic boom in a not particularly hospitable area.

The community of Fort McMurray is a mecca for workers from eastern Canada, and house prices are higher than in Edmonton. Oil royalties have balanced the provincial budget and paid off all outstanding debts. Now the debate is what to do with the money pouring in. Environmentally the strip-mining of the Tar Sands is extremely damaging, and work is contingent on cold weather for freezing the ground and moving large machinery across tundra and muskeg.

Internal Issues

Canadian society is relatively stable and major issues are few and far between. After the constant constitutional debates of the last 30 years, Canadians are taking a breather and focusing more on making a living and dealing with issues as they arise. The climate is predictably unpredictable, and every year some dramatic weather-related events seem to occur. In 2004 a hailstorm lashed Edmonton and in just 1½ hours managed to inflict damage to the tune of C$160 million. Later that same year a hurricane somehow slipped past the USA and slammed into Nova Scotia. More recently Vancouver's Stanley Park lost over 100 trees to wind storms (*see* p.37).

Regionalism

On the world scene Canada is a stable, even boring country, which likes to lend a hand and promote trade. Internally, on the other hand, it can be a seething political swamp, with regions pitted against the federal government and even against each other. The constant threat of Quebec's secession weighs on Canada politically, and provincial governments are often elected on anti-Ottawa platforms. In the Canadian parliament the largest block of seats from Quebec is separatist and, although many represent protest votes, their presence constitutes a destabilising force. In fact the same regionalism that defines provincial–federal relations is repeated in the national parliament. Apart from Alberta and Saskatchewan, the governing Conservatives did not win seats in any of the large urban areas. It appears as though federally Canada may be entering a prolonged period of minority governments, with support for the various parties remaining fairly consistent.

Discontent in western Canada has eased somewhat now that the Conservatives are in power. Ontario's Liberal government has had some open disagreements with Ottawa and anger in eastern Canada is only beginning to take political form, with palpable feelings of resentment in Newfoundland and to a lesser extent Nova Scotia.

The most interesting element about all of the regional debates is that a clear majority of Canadians see themselves as just that – Canadian. The jurisdictional debates that make the news tend to be lost on most regular citizens, who rarely stop to consider which division of government manages which services. Recent political trends suggest the majority of Canadians are moving away from a regional perspective, as is the country's economy.

See also 'Major Political Parties and Themes', pp.84–90.

Defence

Outside Canada many people may be vaguely aware of Canada's tradition of peace-keeping, but it may come as a surprise to discover how important the theme is internally. Even though the Canadian military has been severely reduced in recent decades, Canadians repeat the mantra that they are a peace-keeping nation. Certainly Canada introduced the Blue Beret peace-keepers to the UN and has served in numerous conflicts around the world, but the current state of the military severely weakens the armed forces' ability to respond to the various crises. The purchase of faulty submarines from Britain and a fatiguing 15-year debate about the purchase of new helicopters has done little to renew faith in Canada's role on the world stage.

A greater source of pride focuses on Canada's opposition to war. Canada did not take part in the Vietnam conflict, but did receive thousands of Vietnamese refugees who are now well integrated into modern Canadian society. Recently, relations with the United States became strained when Canada refused to go along with the invasion of Iraq. Relations with the USA will thaw, and Canadians take pride in their government's fortitude in this one instance.

During a 2004 visit to Canada, US president Bush raised the issue of missile defence. Supporters of the scheme want Canada and its thousands of kilometres of Arctic territory to join in, but the majority of Canadians oppose participation. Additionally, aspects of Arctic sovereignty have been challenged by the USA and even Denmark (Greenland). Part of the Tory agenda is to increase Canada's military presence in the north – as clarified by prime minister Harper: 'use it or lose it'.

The Environment

To receive the attention it deserves, the environment promises to force itself, one way or another, on to the national scene in coming years. Certainly the Green Party is receiving more votes and may even win a few seats, but the effects of global warming are already apparent in Canada, with the north melting and pollution increasing. Canada supported the Kyoto Accord, but has not achieved its targets.

It is quite possible that the mighty glaciers (pronounced 'glayshers') in the Rockies could be gone by the end of the century and extreme weather phenomena, such as droughts and *El Niño*, will increase in frequency and severity. Even closer to daily life, smog is a reality in major centres. In Toronto, air quality can be poor enough to cause respiratory problems. Montreal can be almost as bad, and other urban centres like Calgary, Edmonton and Vancouver are developing a notable layer of haze on certain days. Governments in Canada have not acted quickly or effectively on environmental issues and it will be interesting to see how Canadians respond. A national poll recently declared the country's most famous environmentalist, Dr David Suzuki, to be the fifth greatest Canadian, as much for political reasons as in honour of him individually. Suzuki tends to be somewhat extreme in his analysis and predictions, but makes a solid argument for resource management when he uses the depleted Atlantic cod fisheries as an example. In British Columbia, hotly debated issues include fish farms and offshore drilling, while a pine beetle devastating the forests is only part of the environmental discussion. In 2008 the Liberal (although right-wing) government in BC took an important environ-mental step with a first 'green' budget that gradually introduces carbon taxes. The Conservatives are not an environmentalist party and have their core

Global Warming

Notwithstanding the assertions of certain governments and industries, the earth's mean temperature is undoubtedly rising and the effect on Canada and its icepack is significant. Whether entirely caused by natural cycles, or purely by pollutants, the scientific evidence is clear that there are human-caused contaminants throughout the Arctic and still waters across Canada. Rivers freeze more slowly and thaw faster than in the past, and some predictions suggest there will be no non-polar glacial ice within 50 years. In the south, smog is increasing and droughts and excess rainfall are common. For the Inuit people of the north, global warming could result in the destruction of their entire culture. Polar bear and seal populations may be wiped out and coastlines will recede as more water is exposed. What this will all mean for the world in general is open to debate, but, as Canada has the largest volumes of fresh water on earth, the contamination and melting of these reserves will have serious environmental consequences.

support in Alberta – where the oil industry is Canada's largest emitter of greenhouse gases. The Tories have however introduced a clean air act, which may be seen as a positive step.

Social Issues

Socially Canada is changing. The idea of two solitudes – English and French – as the basis of the country has given way to diversity and regionalism. Gender issues have begun to fade as women enjoy greater equality and pay equity. Issues surrounding First Nations society will persist but some progress has been made. Perhaps the more important fact is that First Nations governments are, in some instances, on the offensive, asserting their rights through education and the legal system.

Two of the prominent social issues under discussion in recent years were gay marriage and the decriminalisation of marijuana. **Gay marriage** is now an institution, but pot is a little more complicated. Canada has legalised **marijuana** for medical purposes and generally will not arrest people for possession of 'small amounts' of cannabis, but is a long way from introducing joint-vending machines. Much of the impetus for decriminalising marijuana comes from British Columbia, where dope is a multi-million-dollar industry. Cannabis is consumed openly in a few establishments, which the police raid from time to time. 'British Columbia bud', as it has come to be known, is very strong and equally popular south of the border, where a much less tolerant attitude towards drugs continues to hold sway. Debate on the issues has calmed, but public opinion tends to view it as inappropriate, expensive and unhelpful to burden with a criminal record someone who chooses to smoke a little weed. Conversely, police are aggressively pursuing and destroying the marijuana grow-operations (ops) found in basements across the country.

Demographically, the growth of the Canadian population relies heavily on **immigration**, and that growth is concentrated in a few large urban areas. The ageing of the population has not reached the crisis point it has in Italy, but some good accounting and planning is required. Because seniors continue to be consumers, an ageing population is not necessarily more expensive. Seniors tend to 'give back' a great deal in volunteer work, but they draw from the Canada Pension Plan (or Quebec Pension Plan in that province). A few years ago, fears that the pension plan was going broke generated much hype, but good investment returns, as well as lower unemployment, have resulted in the programme being secure for some years to come.

Sadly, **homelessness** remains a growing issue despite government promises to eliminate poverty. Deep cutbacks in Ontario's government programmes during the 1990s and the sale of subsidised housing boosted the economy but left many falling between the cracks. Homelessness has increased steadily in booming Alberta where people move to find work, but cannot pay market price for rent. The Lower Mainland of British Columbia and Victoria has attracted vagrants because the warmer climate allows them to sleep outside, but government cuts to welfare have left many turning to food banks and shelters. Canadians are proud of their social programmes but these have failed to take into account the state of the poorest in society. Frequent political talk about housing projects remains talk, and volunteer organisations have been left to do much of the work of caring for the needy and disenfranchised.

Crime

Because crime rates are relatively low, crime does not receive the level of attention that it does in either Britain or the USA. Murders do occur, of course, and gang activities are on the rise, but overall (despite sensational media reports) Canadians generally feel quite safe. More homes are locked than in the past and alarm systems have become more common, but there is no national fear of evildoers freely roaming the streets. Women should be careful, but it is doubtful that the need for such caution is any greater than in the past.

The so-called roughest area of Canada is in Vancouver's downtown eastside, which has all the trappings of a port city. Prostitution (of all ages) and hard drugs abound and the condition of its residents is depressing, but one can still walk through the area in relative safety. Most cities will have their 'rough' districts but, for the most part, none deserves a 'no-go' label.

See also **Living in Canada**, 'Crime and the Police', pp.194–7.

Religion

According to recent polls, it would appear the largest-growing faith in Canada is Jedi, going from a presumed zero followers to over 20,000. While it is not clear what this new force in Canadian faith might bring, it does belie the fact that Canada is not, by world standards, a very religious country. Over 16 per cent of Canadians purport to have no religion and the majority of those are young. British Columbians are the least religious, with 40 per cent claiming no faith at all. The most religious place in the country is Prince Edward Island, where slightly over half (53 per cent) of the population attends church at least once a month.

The apparent secularisation of Canadian society represents an important trend. Moderate Protestantism has seen the most significant decline in church attendance, although some statistics have noted a slight increase in religious observance in recent years. Overall, however, it is clear that fewer Canadians than ever before feel compelled either to attend church or declare a religion. Among new immigrants, about one-fifth claim to have no religion and an ever-greater percentage of those who do observe a faith are not from the Christian tradition. Another interesting trend is the number of Canadians who claim to be Christian, without identifying a particular denomination.

Catholicism

Catholicism continues to have the most adherents, with over 40 per cent of the country's population, although regular church attendance figures are certainly lower. French Canada was strictly Roman Catholic for much of its history, but since the 1960s church attendance has fallen off dramatically. Where once 88 per cent of Quebecers attended Mass weekly, less than 20 per cent now do so. The statistics are not much different in other parts of the country where 32 per cent attend once a week.

The Church's most important role in daily life remains at an educational level. Many provinces have a separate Catholic school system and taxpayers may redirect their payments to those schools. Catholic schools must fulfil the education requirements outlined by the government, so the religiosity of the system is limited and non-Catholics and believers alike attend the schools. As in other parts of the world, the Church has been caught up in shocking abuse scandals resulting in major lawsuits.

Protestantism

Protestantism is not faring much better. Although 35 per cent of the population claims to be Protestant, church attendance has been declining for decades. The largest Protestant flock belongs to the moderate United Church, which was born of a fusion between Presbyterians and Methodists. The second largest Protestant church is the Anglican **Church of Canada**, with 7 per cent of Canadians as members. **Evangelism** has a foothold in Canada, with many denominations represented. The largest crowd ever to gather in Toronto's Skydome stadium went to see American preacher Billy Graham. Stockwell Day, who for a short period in the 1990s was leader of the federal opposition, is a fundamentalist and former preacher, but his opposition to evolution, abortion and other such attitudes were generally scorned nationally. The rise of Day within the Reform-Alliance party was the first time since the decline of Social Credit that Canada's religious right had a political voice. The unceremonious dumping of him as leader confirmed that, unlike south of the border, Canadians simply do not equate government and religion.

Statistically less relevant, but nonetheless interesting, is the mosaic of minority Protestant faiths. In 1887 polygamist **Mormons** fled Utah and one group, led by Charles Ora Card, settled in southern Alberta. The Canadian government quickly responded by banning bigamy, but the community remained, building the first temple outside the United States in Cardston. Another more extreme group of breakaway Mormon polygamists has survived in Bountiful, British Columbia. The group, living in an isolated southern valley, regularly excommunicates its young men, which results in a surplus of potential wives for the older community leaders. Because they are not legally married, the community's many 'unwed' mothers receive significant financial aid from the government.

Other Religions

Persecution in Europe resulted in large numbers of agrarian **Anabaptist** groups coming to Canada in the late 1800s and early 1900s. The largest group are the German-speaking **Mennonites** who are dotted throughout central and western Canada. **Hutterites** continue to live collectively and speak an old German. These communities lead an almost self-sufficient existence devoted to farming and educating their young. Women and men have very defined roles, and, though community members do learn to speak English, it is heavily accented. A limited gene pool has resulted in a disproportionate occurrence of certain ailments such as cystic fibrosis.

Also living in the west, the **Doukhobors** gained renown for protesting by marching without clothing. As avid pacifists the Doukhobors came to Canada from Russia after refusing to convert to Orthodoxy. Instead of taking up arms to defend their cause, they simply burnt all weapons.

Canada's non-Christian community is growing both in actual numbers and as a percentage. The only non-Christian faith to make it into the top 10 is **Islam**, with around 600,000 worshippers. This number represents a large increase, as the Muslim population has more than doubled in the past 10 years. Currently Muslims represent around 2 per cent of the national population.

The next-largest non-Christian faith in Canada is **Judaism**. Just over one per cent of Canadians are Jewish, the majority of whom live in Ontario. As elsewhere in the Christian world, Canada has a dishonourable history of anti-Semitism, although it has been far less apparent since the Second World War.

Buddhists, **Hindus** and **Sikhs** each represent slightly less than 1 per cent of the national population, although it is important to understand their distribution. Almost half of Canada's Sikh population live in the city of Surrey, in British Columbia's Lower Mainland, and constitute the largest ethnic group in that expanding city. Therefore, despite being a relatively minor voice nationally, Sikhs have become a voting block in British Columbia. Buddhists and Hindus also concentrate in areas such as Greater Vancouver and Greater Toronto.

Summary

Canada's religious make-up will continue to change as the number of non-Christian immigrants into the country increases. The secularisation of society seems inevitable, based on percentages among youth, and suggests that

Canada may have a majority non-religious society within this century. The elderly maintain the highest levels of religious observance. In their many manifestations, Christians have declined from 80 per cent to 72 per cent of the population, giving up most ground to non-believers. In a multicultural, immigrant society, faith will be respected but will not find much earnest political support.

The Family and the Role of Women

Over the last several decades Canadian families have been going through the same sort of transformation found in western European nations. The traditional model of a man working outside the home while the wife brings up the children has given way to fewer children and double incomes. Canada liberalised its divorce laws in 1968 and, since a peak in 1987, roughly one in three marriages will end in divorce. The percentage is lower than in the United States or Britain, but this isolated statistic does not reveal the deep changes in Canadian society.

More and more Canadians are simply choosing not to marry, but rather to live in common-law relationships. This reality is particularly true in Quebec and the Territories, where a majority of people will never marry. As common-law relationships become more widespread there may be a statistical, yet irrelevant, decline in legal divorces. Non-married couples are far more likely to terminate their relationships and a lack of legal restrictions expedites the process. Common-law relationships are nevertheless legally recognised in Canada, even for immigration purposes.

The Canadian family is not large and, as with other developed societies, natural population increase is negligible. Historically, families in French Canada did their Catholic duty by procreating exponentially, but they turned their backs on tradition during the 1960s and now Quebec has one of the lowest birth rates in the world. The highest birth rate in Canada is in Nunavut, but even that is only 2.3 children per family. With a national average of 1.7 children per family, Canada's population would decline without immigration.

The Family

Urban Canadian families are nuclear and small. Extended family traditions remain stronger in rural areas, but with family members spread across large distances, and often in other countries, modern Canadians define family as a mother, a father, children and perhaps grandparents. Women (and men) are choosing to have children later in life and more and more are not reproducing at all. The number of single-parent families is increasing and recent homosexual marriage laws are again redefining 'family'; 74 per cent of Canadian households fall into the traditional category, but increasing numbers of households are single-parent, common-law or 'blended', a term defined as including children from previous relationships.

As women live significantly longer than men, there are more widows than widowers. While some senior parents will live with their adult children, the majority of seniors stay on their own or in some form of assisted living. Only in conservative communities and among some immigrant groups do multiple generations of one family commonly live together. Families do not abandon the elderly, but it is assumed that seniors, with family and state help, will provide for themselves as they grow older. While some nursing homes can be depressing affairs, many retirement and senior communities provide a good quality of life.

Gender Equality

Reforms in women's rights have resulted in important advances towards gender equality. The introduction of the birth control pill, the legalising of abortion and pay-equity legislation are among the more recent advances. In 1900 Canadian women had very few rights. Although prairie women were absolutely fundamental to the homesteading experience, they were sometimes left destitute because the man was the sole proprietor of the land and he could dispose of land and assets without any obligations towards his wife. Early last century Nellie McClung advocated for women's equality and by 1916 female suffrage had been attained in Manitoba and Alberta. In 1917 Louise McKinney was sworn into the Alberta Legislature and became the first woman elected anywhere in the British Empire. Nationally, women gained the vote in 1918, but not provincially in Quebec until 1944. In 1993 Canada, for a brief time, had a female prime minister, Kim Campbell.

On a world scale Canada has achieved a high level of gender equality, but there is still a long way to go. Levels of education are in some cases higher among women, but violence persists both inside and outside the family. Only Quebec has a provincial childcare programme and, although maternity benefits across the country will last up to one year, women can fall behind professionally when they leave the workforce for even that short period. An ever-increasing number of single-parent families live in poverty, with the majority of these headed by the mother. A female lone parent heads 15 per cent of Canadian families, but only 2 per cent have a sole male as head.

Professionally the proverbial 'glass ceiling' endures, although it should decline in significance as women rise to higher positions of power. Division of labour remains unequal and, although their incomes are extremely important to family finances, women continue to carry a disproportionate load of household responsibilities. The balance of duties is changing, albeit slowly.

Major Media

Geography and language make the media situation in general reasonably complicated. It is difficult for the 'national media' to speak for, or to, all Canadians, or to discuss relevant country-wide issues. The two official languages result in obvious duplication, or translation. There are 5½ time zones in Canada (the half being Newfoundland), which greatly affects the scheduling of programming and publishing times. When families sit down to watch the news in Montreal, people are still at work in Victoria. Live programming for events such as sports becomes particularly difficult, as easterners have to stay up late just to watch their hockey team play out west.

Weather varies throughout the country and national reports are usually rather general. Canadians watching the weather reports in the UK are amused to see the little country divided into so many different weather patterns. In Canada, an entire province could well be granted one sun or cloud.

Canada's proximity to the United States also has an impact on the media. The country does have the Canadian Broadcasting Corporation (CBC), plus several private servers, but the viewer can access dozens of channels based in the United States, as well as those from other countries. In addition to television, Canadians continue to listen to radio, read a limited selection of newspapers and magazines, and spend hours surfing on the Internet.

Television

TV has come a long way since its inception and the days have long since passed when everyone discussed the previous night's programme – because that was the only viewing choice. Homes regularly receive more than 50 channels, and only during the hockey play-offs can you assume many people are tuning into the same channel. Satellite dishes and digital services are popular and provide viewers with literally hundreds of choices. The bulk of programming comes from the United States, but most homes will also have British, French and even Spanish options. Canada has a reasonably well-developed system of national programming administered by the CBC (Radio-Canada in French). In addition to regional and national news programmes, the CBC develops and airs shows with Canadian content. No channel is commercial-free. Some private channels broadcast nationally and, although much of their programming is purchased from abroad, they must include a certain amount of Canadian content.

Broadcasting is governed by the Canadian Radio-Television and Tele-communications Commission (CRTC), and through a complicated equation guarantees a Canadian presence on television and radio. Generally Canadian networks are required to fulfil a 50–60 per cent Canadian-content quota. Bonuses are given for Canadian dramas aired during primetime. A programme

The Greatest Canadian

In 2004 the Canadian Broadcasting Corporation (CBC) held a long-drawn-out competition to name the greatest Canadian. The process wasn't really 'one person, one vote' and communities rallied around their native sons, but in the end the list was reduced to a top ten and the final winner was found to be palatable to most in the country: Tommy Douglas, former premier of Saskatchewan and first socialist premier in the country, received the most votes. Born in Scotland and raised on the prairies, Douglas was moved by the plight of returning soldiers from the First World War and then the hardships brought on during the Great Depression. As leader of the socialist Cooperative Commonwealth Federation in Saskatchewan (later the New Democratic Party), the small, boxing Baptist preacher did much for equality in Canada, but beyond a lifetime of achievements he won votes because he nationalised healthcare, seeing medicine as a right not a privilege.

There were no women in the top ten, but other finalists were Terry Fox (a victim of cancer who set out to run across Canada and raise money for cancer research; he died en route), Pierre Trudeau (charismatic and controversial former prime minister), Frederick Banting (discoverer of insulin), David Suzuki (renowned environmentalist, author and presenter), Lester B. Person (former prime minister and Nobel Peace Prize laureate), Don Cherry (loud, nationalist hockey coach and commentator), Sir John A. Macdonald (first prime minister and father of confederation), Alexander Graham Bell (inventor of the telephone) and Wayne Gretzky (the all-time-greatest hockey player and coach of Canada's gold-medal-winning teams; see p.117).

is considered 'Canadian' if it was created by Canadians and 75 per cent of costs were paid to Canadians.

There are no **TV licences** in Canada and every house should be able to receive CBC. Access to other channels and networks is offered by private cable providers. Generally in the English market, most homes will receive Canadian 24-hour news programmes such as *Newsworld* (CBC). The well-known American networks such as CNN and its affiliates are available, as are the BBC and France's TV5. In addition to national and international broadcasting, CBC and other private networks air regional news programmes and shows. Perhaps the most unique programming comes from the north, where Inuit and First Nations language television may be subtitled in Cree, English or French.

Funding cutbacks have affected public television in Canada and the CBC struggles to remain relevant. It still leads the way in news programming and from time to time creates a popular drama. All the Canadian networks provide regional programming. The larger cities have local news hours during prime time, or this service may be province-wide.

All the US situation comedies have a following in Canada, as do the much-touted reality shows. Canadian versions of some programmes such as *Canadian*

Idol have been well received. Comedy, on the other hand, differs markedly between the two countries. The Canadian sense of humour, much more irreverent than in the USA, tends to be closer to that in Britain. The *Comedy Network*, featuring Canadian and US comedians, has appealed successfully to a TV audience.

Canadians watch a lot of television but actual hours are declining slightly, possibly because of increased Internet use. French Canadians spend more hours in front of the TV than their English-speaking counterparts and watch more Canadian programming. As might be suspected, viewers watch significantly more TV during the winter months. Francophone Canadians have fewer programme choices, but will find at least one French-language channel in every part of the country. As is often the case with smaller markets, French Canadian television concentrates on local dramas and talk shows. Newer programming can be obviously Franco-centric, or Quebec-centric.

As in the UK, DVDs have replaced video cassettes and movie rental or purchase is popular. Films and pay-per-view programming are available directly from digital servers, cutting deeply into video rental businesses, and DVDs can be purchased easily and affordably. British PAL videos do not work on Canadian machines and not all DVDs are playable on Canadian machines (*see* p.175).

Radio

During the Second World War almost every household in Canada listened to CBC radio religiously, and although some people continue to function at home with CBC in the background, they have become a minority. As elsewhere in the world, television, and now the Internet, have displaced radio as a medium, but not entirely. In a country as large as Canada, people can drive for hours at a time and therefore many will listen to the radio then. CBC broadcasts throughout the entire country, but on different frequencies. Signs indicating available radio frequencies are posted along highways.

News and talk radio are available, as are all the various music styles. Radio also serves as a tool for keeping multicultural Canadian communities informed, as programming is more affordable than on TV. CBC is often the only French radio available in those parts of the country where English-speakers form the majority. The quality of discourse on CBC is excellent, however quirky. From science to gardening, CBC radio has time to dedicate to discussions and is perhaps the one national institution that brings together voices from across the country in real time. Obviously language-biased, it addresses subjects separately in the two markets, but the general content is Canadian and no subject is too obscure for coverage.

In conjunction with national broadcasts, the CBC maintains regional networks, which remain involved in the local culture. Major cities have a local CBC station that competes well for listeners – often private-vehicle commuters.

Canadian content regulations also govern radio, but fortunately, as a result of a strong musical tradition, music-based radio is not much restricted.

Print Media

The newspaper market in Canada is not particularly diverse and the country does not have the great broadsheet tradition found in the UK. A few companies own the majority of Canadian papers in both the English and French markets. Almost all dailies are distributed in the morning and home delivery is common. General readership is declining and in this age of 24-hour news, papers are going online.

Within the English market only two papers can claim to be national – the *Globe and Mail* and the *National Post*. Both are produced in Toronto and have been accused of being Toronto-centric, but they make a genuine effort to present articles from across the country. The *Globe* is the oldest national paper and is fairly centrist in its views. The *National Post* was started by Lord Conrad Black, who is now finding jail a 'bore' in the United States after being convicted of misuse of investor funds as the head of Hollinger International. Black, along with his flamboyant wife Barbara Amiel, is well known in the UK as the (former) owner of the *Telegraph* and *Spectator*. Through the 1990s Black's Hollinger group was the third-largest newspaper publishing group in the world. In his quest for supremacy, Black was offered a title by the British government. Prime minister Jean Chrétien blocked this move, citing the 1919 Nickle Resolution, which prevents foreign governments from granting titles to Canadians. As a result Black renounced his Canadian citizenship to become Lord Black of Crossharbour. As part of the divestiture of his many Canadian holdings, Black sold the *National Post* to CanWest and the newspaper retains its right-of-centre perspective. Had Lord Black not surrendered his Canadian citizenship, he might have enjoyed a much shorter prison term. His friends in the British Conservative Party and the House of Lords were very quick to dissociate themselves from the scandal.

CanWest Global Communications is a large and controversial corporation that has acquired an impressive percentage of the Canadian print and television market. Started by the late Winnipeg booster Izzy Asper, CanWest owns many of the major papers in Canada, including the two largest dailies in Vancouver and Quebec's last important English daily.

The situation for the French media is not very different, and Quebec has only a few major publications. Most are owned by Power Corporation of Canada, with only *Le Devoir* remaining independent. *Le Devoir* is well respected for taking a balanced approach to the separation question, but has been seriously criticised for historic anti-Semitism in its editorials.

Most cities in Canada have two daily papers, with one usually less sensational than the other. The Canadian market does not produce much in the way of tabloids such as the *News of the World*, so Canadians must look either south of the border or to Britain to find out if aliens have arrived, or who is marrying whom. Nudity cannot be shown in newspapers, but the less serious papers carry photos of attractive people in various poses. The sensationalist papers cover the usual crime and tragedy stories and provide limited analysis of issues, but fortunately such papers are not the only source of news.

Canada's one national news magazine, *Maclean's*, has a reasonably broad readership. Not particularly academic, *Maclean's* does nevertheless provide an arena for Canadian writers and issues. The magazine attempts to present different viewpoints and has been in existence for over 100 years. The *Globe and Mail* and *National Post* produce magazines for distribution with their papers, and many special-interest publications exist.

The Internet

Canada is very much online, and has one of the highest personal computer ownership rates in the world. High-speed connections are common and most Canadians, particularly those younger than retirement age, are computer-savvy. Canadian web pages end in '.ca', but others have managed to claim '.com' or even '.org' status. Anything to do with the government will end in '.gc.ca' or '.gov.ca' ('.gouv.ca' in French-speaking territories). Provincial governments will tack the provincial abbreviation before the Canadian one.

As the general population becomes more acquainted with and dependent on the Internet, print media and television will continue to lose customers. To cope with this, media companies are attempting to achieve greater degrees of integration and to develop new revenue streams.

All the well-known Americans sites such as MSN, Yahoo and Google have .ca addresses servicing the Canadian market, but Canadian-made sites are also ubiquitous. CBC has a reasonably good site with an excellent archive. All the major newspapers have websites, and subscriber information services that provide full website access at a cost. Some newspapers are also tied to larger media sites such as Canada.com, which is part of CanWest Global Communications Corporation.

Those Canadians who so choose have the option of being extremely well informed. Whatever is lacking in the print media is readily available on television, radio or the Internet. Canada's role as a middle power is reflected in the media, and international issues receive almost as much attention as internal ones. Certainly, not all people are well informed and, without question, geographic isolation permits personal indifference. From time to time some accuse the CBC of left-wing coverage, but, with the American media so readily accessible, a counterweight exists. Access to the European media is also readily available, and Canada's ethnic make-up directs attention to countries such as Ukraine and Haiti, which might otherwise receive less coverage.

Culture and Art

Canada's culture remains one of those hotly debated subjects for which there is no definitive answer. A vast young country made up of numerous ethnicities and wedged between the world's last superpower and a melting Arctic is not easy to define, but nor is it impossible. Canadians are proud to be Canadian and often speak for the country as a whole, without really knowing it. Language obviously defines part of one's identity, and unilingual Canadians, whether English, French or allophone, miss much of what goes on within their own nation. When asked what it is to be Canadian, people often enter into a tirade about what makes them different from Americans. When the CBC tackles the question, it either drones on about Canadians being polite peace-keepers, or defers to a personal account of growing up in small-town Canada.

Pierre Trudeau had a clear vision for the country's future as a Just Society, respecting the individual as well as collective groups. This idea probably developed from the less-than-cohesive Montreal of his youth, where different ethnic groups retained their identities and languages while participating in the greater whole. Unfortunately Trudeau's Quebec-based image included some dubious economics and only partly accepted that other parts of the country interpreted their home in a separate, though similar way.

The American influence on Canadian culture is obvious, but so is that of Britain and France. Unlike other countries where these powers have imposed their will, Canada has had the luxury of being able to evaluate the actions of the USA and Europe and, by being on the periphery, choose the beneficial aspects of those societies while turning away from those seen as negatives. The Canadian accent is sort-of American, but not fully. The government is British in construct, but not really in action, and unfortunately the food is really not French at all.

A few facts unite Canadians in spirit and action, but in an unintentional way. Snow falls everywhere. The cold north means most Canadians live with snow and sub-zero temperatures for at least some of the year, and the extremes of the climate have kept the population relatively small, while encouraging a sound infrastructure. A northern work ethic prevails and visitors often notice a gentle courtesy. A sense of all being 'in it together' exists, whatever 'it' is. People take pride in their homes and themselves, but generally shy away from flashy demonstrations of wealth. This may come from stern Protestant or farming roots, or perhaps is driven by the fact that, regardless of how much your haircut cost, you still need a toque (warm hat) in the winter.

Canadians love hockey, television, music and eating out. Very high levels of education affect public discourse positively and, while pretension is frequently cast aside, many Canadians are very well-informed. Some are not, though, and opt for the shopping mall and fast food over ballet and caribou in red wine sauce. There is no doubt that the consumer society has reached the Great White

North, and the larger cities are home to distinct cultural groups who feel quite Canadian but know little about the rest of the country.

If one is attracted by the arts, Canada has a lot on offer. Alternatively, umpteen American TV channels and all the North American sports provide a different sort of entertainment. In discussing the arts in Canada it must, as always, be noted that Quebec and other Francophone regions have a separate cultural expression from that of English Canada. Some forms of First Nations art have entered the mainstream and Nunavut is, by its very existence, supporting Inuit and Arctic culture.

Literature

Canada produces a respectable number of writers who have earned national and international acclaim. Both federal and provincial governments support writers through grants and prizes and several large publishing houses exist. In developing their trade, Canadian writers face a number of choices including whether to use Canadian, American or even British spelling, where to publish and how country-specific their subjects should be. The large US market just to the south appeals to artists, as well as all other professionals, and while some Americans are happy to read Canadian themes, it is fair to say they do not dominate American discourse.

As in Britain, the publishing industry has its problems, authors find it difficult to get published and royalties remain modest. A recent trend towards enormous bookshop chains has concentrated much of the control of distribution into a few hands. For writers and publishers, making money depends significantly on selling through these stores. The English-language market is around 22 or 23 million and potential French readership is much smaller, at perhaps nine million. Bestsellers in Canada do not bring great wealth, but some fiction writers and journalists have managed to build good careers. A few writers have become national personalities; **Farley Mowet**'s name is prominent on an anti-sealing ship, busy disrupting hunters.

Better known to the British market is the recently deceased Montreal writer, **Mordecai Richler**. With an impressive command of language, Richler captured his Jewish-Anglophone-Montreal upbringing and wove it into numerous books and stories such as *Joshua Then and Now*, *The Apprenticeship of Duddy Kravitz*, *Barney's Version* and the popular children's story *Jacob Two-Two and the Hooded Fang*. In Richler's most controversial work, *Oh Canada, Oh Quebec*, he lambasted the nationalist movement in his home province and exposed deep, historic anti-Semitism in Quebec's media.

Fortunately not all great Canadian writers are either dead or male. Ottawa-born **Margaret Atwood** has written many novels, short stories and poems during her distinguished career and has won many awards for her fine work.

Lucy Maud Montgomery's stories about *Anne of Green Gables* live on, drawing thousand of visitors to Prince Edward Island. On the west coast, author and visual artist **Douglas Coupland** coined the much-abused phrase *Generation X* and declared Vancouver to be the *City of Glass*. **Michael Ondaatje** was born in Sri Lanka and now lives in Toronto. Best-known for his work *The English Patient*, Ondaatje manages to capture much of the multicultural experience of his life and his home. A few other well-known Canadian writers include: **Farley Mowat**, **W. O. Mitchell**, **Alice Monroe**, **Jack London** (an American who wrote about the Yukon), **Margaret Laurence**, **Leonard Cohen** (whose music crossed over into poetry), **Robertson Davies**, and the late, American-born **Carol Shields**. Far from being exhaustive, this list just highlights some of the better-known writers; many more contemporary authors work in both official languages writing novels, prose and short stories.

Books about Canada or based on Canada can usually be found in the 'Canadiana' section of bookstores and the variety is impressive. Every province and territory has produced writers, and all have their own biases and experiences. From small-town Newfoundland to the Klondike gold rush, long cold winters have fuelled literary expression. It is worth visiting local bookshops when travelling, as regions will stock works relevant to the local area.

Numerous special-interest magazines are published in Canada, and some of them offer a forum to new writers. The CBC also hosts a broad-based literary competition each year and the Governor-General offers writing awards.

Art

By its very nature, Canada is a land of art. Far from other centres, Canadians look inward to their own ethnicities and environment for artistic expression. Robert Service, the 'Bard of the Yukon', suggested that God may have been tired when he made that northern land, but the enormity of Canada's wilderness is an artist's dream. As is perhaps true of all colonial environments, it took some time for Canadians to look around and start capturing the fabulous beauty of their world. Founded in the 1920s, the Group of Seven branded themselves as a truly Canadian school of painting with their interpretations of the environment. Members of the Group of Seven were not the first to paint Canada, but their emphasis on landscapes, and the positive reception given to their work, drew attention to Canadian art as an independent discipline. In British Columbia the paintings of **Emily Carr** (1871–1945) fused her European studies with the indigenous world she experienced along the coast. The Emily Carr Institute of Art and Design in Vancouver is a degree-granting institution, which embraces Carr's non-conformist artistic outlook while supporting a British Columbian art tradition. Painter and naturalist **Robert Bateman** still receives frequent acclaim and he has many permanent exhibits throughout Canada. The more affordable prints of his work adorn the walls in many homes.

Fine art in Canada often reflects the region in which it is produced, with more avant-garde works shown in Toronto, Montreal and Vancouver. Picturesque fishing villages along the Atlantic coast have been painted and photographed thousands of times, as have the cobbled streets of Quebec City. The east also enjoys an artistic migration each autumn as the forests explode into colours. Art on the prairies focuses on the open land, the huge overarching skies and white winter images. A sculpting tradition has also developed nationally, with stone and metal images of buffalo and First Nations peoples common subjects.

Native Art

Native art is enjoying a renaissance throughout Canada and becoming so incorporated into the mainstream in parts of the country that lines between native and non-native art are no longer clear. British Columbian artwork most clearly demonstrates this trend, and the University of British Columbia's Museum of Anthropology celebrates and encourages totem-carving. Inuit art has migrated south with the popularity of Inuksuk statues (a statue of a stylised person, constructed with stones). To some extent the Inuksuk is replacing the maple leaf and will serve as the symbol for the Vancouver 2010 Olympics.

Galleries and Museums

All major cities have art galleries and, though they do not compete with ice hockey rinks for attendance, they survive. The National Art Gallery of Canada is in Ottawa and exhibits Canadian works, as well as those from abroad. Unfortunately, given the country's size, it is not easy for most Canadians simply to nip over to the capital to peruse the collections. From time to time the National Gallery will spend what seems like a fortune on a contemporary piece, much to the chagrin of less cultured Canadians.

Museums abound and are sometimes quite eclectic. Some universities have themed museums attached to them, and visitors and locals will find city, provincial and federal museums to visit. Subject matter varies but the Canadian Museum of Civilisation (located across the Ottawa River from Parliament) tries quite successfully to tackle the collective whole. Some of the most enjoyable museums are in small towns. Not great cultural affairs, these museums tell the stories of local settlement. The first European immigrants to Canada were a hardy lot, and in these days of high-speed communication it is worth discovering their stories of exploration and, often, misery.

Film and Television

There have been films about Canada, made in Canada, by Canadians, but the story centres on the large American productions. Vancouver, Toronto and Montreal all vie for the title of 'Hollywood North' and great sums of money have been made producing American cinema. The film infrastructure that has developed in Canada is used for everything from big productions to automobile advertisements. Film schools have also sprung up, creating a greater focus on the genre, and although the industry is slowing, a production culture, with all its affectations, has emerged.

On a more cultural note, the National Film Board of Canada has existed for over 50 years and currently operates with a budget of nearly C$70 million. The Film Board promotes and helps to fund movies, documentaries and other programmes about Canada. The Canadian Broadcasting Corporation, another Crown corporation, and private broadcasters are also producing some good Canadian programming and cinema. Some urban artists in Canada complain about an overemphasis on rural stories and childlike nature documentaries, along the lines of 'The beaver builds a lodge for his family...' Another frequent and somewhat merited grumble draws attention to the inequity of funding, which favours French-speaking Canada. Nevertheless, you should watch *Jesus of Montreal*, one of the best films ever to come from Canada. *See* also **References**, pp.256–7.

It is difficult to confine one's viewing just to Canadian programming, but not impossible. A few films are released each year and made-for-television documentaries and series do quite well. One of the heavier examples, *The Boys of Saint Vincent*, was aired in the UK and won awards for its excellent depiction of a true story of abuse. At the lighter end, *Anne of Green Gables* was also well received and left most viewers smiling and happy.

Toronto's annual film festival ranks among the biggest and draws many international stars. High in the Rockies, the Banff Mountain Film Festival brings together works dealing with mountains and other outdoor-orientated themes at the Banff Centre. Located just above the town, the centre describes itself as an incubator of creativity that is designed to promote artistic expression and mountain culture. In addition to film, it hosts a literary festival and supports composers. Vancouver's festival is growing and has acquired a reputation for showing more innovative films, while other cities hold smaller festivals, which are really just an excuse to go to the movies.

Canadian actors are numerous and include such personalities as Michael J. Fox, Jim Carrey, Kim Cattrall, Donald and Kiefer Sutherland and America's silent movie sweetheart, Mary Pickford. It is also worth noting that California beach bombshell Pamela Anderson grew up on Vancouver Island and, at whatever cup size, is a strong animal rights supporter. Canadians turn up all over US television as actors and news presenters. Some of their silver-screen success can be attributed to the flat Canadian accent and also to their ability to adapt to different roles. A few are discovered at home, but many go south before their careers really take off.

Performing Arts

Theatre is well attended across the country. Many small and creative companies exist in larger cities, with Montreal leading the way. Quebec and French Canada have a wonderful tradition of improvisation (improv, or theatre sports), which is enjoyed across the province and throughout Canada. Improv is a participatory activity in which teams must act out subjects according to various rules (non-verbal, singing, dancing and so on) and the audience votes for the winner. Improv, at first glance, can appear very rudimentary, but the art is developed and enjoys a keen following.

All cities have performing arts centres of varying quality where a predictable selection of acts from *The Sound of Music* to *The Nutcracker* will pass through. Toronto's version of *The Phantom of the Opera* was widely considered to be the best, even by non-Torontonians. From time to time more risqué productions will visit less cosmopolitan centres to mixed receptions. The Ontario town of Stratford (not surprisingly) holds a Shakespeare Festival each year, which draws over 600,000 people to the municipality. Niagara-on-the-Lake celebrates George Bernard Shaw with a festival, and small towns on the prairies will put on their own interesting, if not celebrated, productions.

The Royal Winnipeg Ballet ranks among the best in the world and receives considerable support. Symphony, on the other hand, struggles. The Roy Thomson Hall in Toronto provides an excellent venue for classical concerts, but support for classical music is weak. Canada has produced some good composers and musicians, but they struggle to make an adequate living. Many orchestras survive on philanthropy, rather than ticket sales.

One of the most active emerging genres is old-fashioned comedy. Fortunately Canadians don't seem to take themselves too seriously, and Montreal's comedy festival is achieving world fame. Halifax residents now enjoy their own festival, and comedy clubs thrive throughout the country. Canadian comedy pushes more boundaries than in the USA and it is one of the rare times that Canadians will come together to really laugh at themselves. In a country where the goings-on in the rest of the world often top news headlines, it is enjoyable to sit back and find humour at home.

Stratford Shakespearean Festival

The aptly named southwestern Ontario community of Stratford has gained international acclaim for its summer-long classical theatre festival. Dating back to the 1950s, the festival now stands as one of Canada's most important cultural events, luring world-class actors and between 600,000 and 700,000 visitors annually. While the festival is clearly based around the works of Shakespeare, many other classical and contemporary works are exhibited. The economic significance of the festival is enormous and has transformed this farming community of 30,000 into an important cultural and service centre.

Popular Music

It may come as a surprise to discover that Canada is one of the largest music-exporting nations on earth. Many performers who are taken for 'Americans' are Canadian. There are many sociological reasons why Canada is such a good breeding ground for popular artists, but without question most have to go south, or perhaps to Europe, to 'be discovered'. Many of Canada's great performers hail from smaller communities – growing up connected to the outside world, but with the stability to develop their craft. Few move back to their home towns, but fortunately they don't forget their roots.

It is generally well known that Céline Dion and Anne Murray are Canadian, but there are many more. The following list is far from comprehensive, but indicates the depth and popularity of Canadian artists: Brian Adams, the Guess Who, kd lang, Avril Lavigne, Alanis Morissette, Neil Young, Gordon Lightfoot, Shania Twain, Leonard Cohen, Joni Mitchell, Kim Mitchell, Diana Krall, Tom Cochrane, Bruce Cockburn, Paul Anka, the late Jeff Healy, Tragically Hip, the Barenaked Ladies, Crash Test Dummies, Triumph, K-os, Feist and many, many more...

Sports

Ice Hockey

Any discussion of Canada's sporting life must be divided between ice hockey and everything else. The 'ice' in the title is virtually redundant, as field or grass hockey has few followers in Canada, whereas 'real' hockey dominates the sports media and unites the country during the Olympics. As sad as it may sound, many Canadians would trade all other Olympic medals for gold in hockey; after success in Salt Lake City, Turin was a dismal failure for the men's team. There are thousands of hockey teams across the country, beginning with children learning to skate all the way up to senior citizens. British spectators who are unfamiliar with the game will be excused if they think they have gone to see a fight, but the game requires a great deal of skill and teamwork. Hockey is a tough sport, played by tough people, who for the most part are good law-abiding citizens in their private lives. Born from long winter months and frozen ponds, hockey is quintessentially Canadian.

The foremost professional league is the National Hockey League (NHL) and its teams vie each year for Lord Stanley's Cup (unless there is a strike). The quest for that particular cup attracts more attention than the battle for the World Cup of Hockey and eclipses all other sporting events in the country. On the rare occasion when a Canadian team reaches the final, the country stops, watches and cheers. In reality, the National Hockey league is made up of teams from both Canada and the United States, with only six of 30 teams located in

The Great One – Number 99

Canada is a country where hockey players can command more media than politicians, but without the tabloid sensationalism surrounding footballers in the UK. A name that every new Canadian must learn is Wayne Gretzky – the undisputed greatest hockey player of all time. Gretzky was not the strongest skater, or toughest player, but he had an uncanny ability to evaluate and make plays. During his heyday with the Edmonton Oilers, the National Hockey League changed rules to try and even the score.

Gretzky endeared himself to Canadians with his relaxed, folksy style and for bringing together the 2002 Olympic gold medal team, but disappointed after the performance in Italy. Not discussed quite so often is that he lives in the USA, is married to an American and is part-owner of a US hockey team. Residence aside, Gretzky is a common feature on Canadian television and is supportive of hockey development and charities in his home country. When he retired from playing hockey, the mourning and tributes carried on for days; it was as if a saint was moving on to other things. His face is plastered on numerous product endorsements, but even with his millions he remains a nice guy from small-town Ontario – and the greatest player the game has ever seen. His jersey number, '99', has been retired, not to be worn by any other player.

Canadian cities. This reality has more to do with money and market size than with hockey culture. Over 60 per cent of players in the league are Canadian, with the remainder coming from the rest of the hockey-playing world – Scandinavia, Eastern Europe and the USA.

It is possible to meet Canadians who quietly admit to not loving hockey, but most people have at least some sense of what is going on in the NHL. A high percentage of Canadians know how to skate, and outdoor ice rinks dot the landscape. One of the few pleasures of the long, cold winters is the ability to skate outside. Ottawa's Rideau Canal freezes (almost) every winter and becomes the largest skating rink on earth. The Montréal Canadiens is probably the most famous hockey team, or at least is the team with the most Stanley Cup wins. Some of the most dedicated followers cheer on the Toronto Maple Leafs, but their patience for a cup has been tested since the last victory in 1967. The other Canadian teams are located in Vancouver, Calgary, Ottawa and Edmonton. This last city has the smallest market and an amazing 1980s legacy for being the best team in history.

American Football

American football, Canadian style, is played throughout the country at an amateur level and by nine teams in a professional league. The Canadian version of the game, slightly different from the US brand, uses a longer field and has three, not four, downs (attempts to carry the ball 10 yards). The quality of play in Canada is average and the game's most fanatical fans are in Saskatchewan, where the Roughriders are the province's only professional sports team. The glory of the game occurs late in the season when large numbers of American players and Canadian fans face bitter temperatures in outdoor stadiums. For British spectators who have trouble following the game, or who are annoyed by the many pauses in play, it is helpful to view a team as a whole, rather than a group of individual players. Football is a game of tactics, much like chess, where two coaches try and out-strategise each other.

Lacrosse

A truly Canadian game that rivals hockey and hurling for sheer toughness is lacrosse. Traditionally known as Canada's national sport, lacrosse developed from the First Nations' game of Baggataway, which has origins dating back hundreds of years. Played on foot, with the ball passed between netted sticks, lacrosse was the most popular game in the 1800s, but gradually lost this place to hockey. Fortunately for lacrosse fans, whose numbers are swelling, the sport is making a comeback and a national league is expanding. The game has updated its rules and for the most part is played in a turf-covered hockey rink, and parallels with ice hockey are obvious.

Speed Skating and Figure Skating

Back on the ice, Canadians love all things that involve skates. Speed skating brings many international championships to the country and a surprising array of fans watch and enjoy figure skating. Kurt Browning and Elvis Stojko, both popular world ice-skating champions, continue to draw large crowds to their professional shows. Jamie Sale and David Pelletier attracted the attention of the world media during the controversy that surrounded their Olympic pairs-skating gold medal during the Salt Lake games.

The Canadian figure-skating system is excellent and competitive. Hockey players will often study figures to improve their own skating techniques and those with obvious ability will be drawn into the system. As a sport, figure skating demands an astounding commitment, as well as the uncanny ability to continuously bounce back after falling on ice. Some have called for figure skating to be pulled from Olympic competition until a better system of judging can be developed, but fortunately improvements are on the way.

Curling

Make sure not to laugh at the men with brooms, as curling is remarkably difficult and is taken very seriously. This chess on ice is now an Olympic sport and has a huge national following. Similar to golf as a lifestyle sport, curling can be played well into one's senior years and is a mainstay of small-town culture. Curling rinks and clubs are as common as hockey areas. The heavy rocks are made of granite and the sweeping affects trajectory and distance. Every second world cup is hosted in Canada, and a curling competition is called a *bonspiel*.

Skiing

Snow blankets Canada for several months each year and people enjoy it on skis, toboggans and snowshoes, as well as dog-sleds and powerful snow-mobiles. Cross-country skiing is arguably the best cardiovascular work-out that exists, and is a wonderful way to enjoy winter. Downhill skiing is extremely popular, particularly in the western mountains, although all ten provinces have some facilities. It is a less pretentious sport than in Europe; some people in Alberta and central British Columbia will ski in jeans.

Skiing in Canada can be cold, but the snow conditions are usually excellent. There are several developed resorts including Whistler (BC), Mont Tremblant (Quebec), Blue Mountain (Ontario) and a few ski towns, of which Banff is the most famous, but many other ski areas have limited serious development, few crowds and real snow. Skiing is expensive and the sport's future is challenged by climate change, yet maintains a national and international appeal. Those serious skiers not restricted by limited resources can take advantage of helicopter skiing in British Columbia and access some of the best conditions anywhere on the planet.

Ski Resort Development

The mountains of western Canada offer some of the best skiing in the world and may eventually, if global warming continues, offer the only skiing on Earth. Even mighty Whistler, often the world's top-rated resort, frequently sees rain, rather than snow, at lower elevations.

With such climatic trends in mind, resorts further inland have seen significant expansion, and the associated communities continue to grow with more and more people choosing small town resort living. Kicking Horse resort in Golden, BC is much closer to Calgary than Vancouver, and with improved roads through the Rockies its famous powder and more affordable housing will surely encourage growth.

On an even larger scale, the attractive and historically isolated town of Revelstoke, on the Columbia River, has seen its community ski area transform into a remarkable new resort that now boasts the highest vertical in North America and virtually guaranteed metres of snow. The development is quite a gamble, but the developers believe the European market will look west as snow becomes increasingly rare in the Alps.

Other Sports

Beyond hockey (if one can find that place) many other sports are enjoyed both in winter and summer. Canadians, although generally quite active, are not as sports mad as their Australian cousins. Toronto has the one professional **basketball** team in the country (despite the fact that the game was a Canadian invention), as well as a professional **baseball** team. Both teams play in US leagues. The American owner of Montreal's professional baseball team recently moved the team south. English **football** is played and semi-professional teams do exist, but coverage is minimal, despite Canada's hosting of the 2007 FIFA Under-20. Canadian children grow up playing soccer but the game holds little of the stature that it does in the UK. **Cricket** is hardly known, but is played at a few outdoor ovals and within immigrant communities. **Rugby** does have a following and forms part of the sports curriculum in some schools, but generally plays second fiddle to American football. **Tennis** is not pursued as keenly as in the UK. The climate requires covered courts for some of the year, so the game attracts fewer players than in other countries. **Golf**, conversely, is extremely popular, reasonably affordable and easy to access, despite short seasons.

It is possible to go on and on about the myriad sporting opportunities in Canada, and anyone considering living in Canada should factor sporting or outdoor activities into their plans. Cities have **cycle** paths, and **walking** and **hiking** opportunities abound. Recreational facilities with **gyms**, **racquet courts** and **swimming pools** are available at most universities and through municipal organisations. **Sailing** and **kayaking** are enjoyed not just on both coasts, but also on lakes where cottages dot the shorelines. In Vancouver it is possible to ski and sail in the same day, or simply jog along the seawall – which perhaps explains why it is the healthiest place in the country.

Holidays

In many ways, Canada's vacation culture is quite different from that of Britain and Europe. Working professionals often begin their careers with only 10 days' vacation and may wait years before earning the equivalent of four weeks off. When choosing where to travel Canadians are faced with huge distances (at home and abroad) and often an unfavourable exchange rate. Travelling across Canada is much more feasible by air than by land and working families frequently don't travel far from home (in Canadian terms).

As an outdoor-orientated culture, Canadians enjoy their lakes and rivers, building cottages within easy access of the cities. Canadian families will happily drive three or more hours to reach their family cottage, yet only stay for the weekend. People will even regularly drive two hours each way for a day of skiing. Larger vacation expenditures are often reserved for escaping the Canadian winter by travelling to Mexico, the Caribbean or even the USA, where Canadian colonies exist in warmer states such as Florida and Arizona.

As Canada is so large, each region is a trip unto itself and, while brave families and individuals may set out to cross the continent, the Trans-Canada Highway is far from a universal Canadian experience. A sizeable percentage of Canadians have never been outside their own province or region and, as a consequence, have a limited understanding of the true nature of their country. People on the east coast can fly to Heathrow faster than to Vancouver and many westerners head south or across the Pacific for their holidays, rather than east in their own country. The population centres of southern Ontario benefit from comparatively easier access to all parts of the country.

Much of Canada is accessible by road, although alternative modes of transport also exist, including boat, bicycle and even dogsled. During the winter months, many Canadians chase the sun, yet Canada naturally provides a plethora of winter-specific destinations – none perhaps as evident as the Ice Hotel outside Quebec City, which is given back to the land each spring. The mountains of Alberta and British Columbia attract the most skiers, although there are ski runs in every province. Some of the resorts in Quebec are world class, and even in the flat prairies what is lost in elevation is made up for in enthusiasm.

As seen on Canadian tourism posters, there are several 'must-see' places that are as exciting to Canadians as they are to foreigners. The Chateau Frontenac Hotel perched above the St Lawrence River in Quebec's old city may be the most photographed building in the country, and Lake Louise in the Alberta Rockies may be the second most frequently captured natural image – after Niagara's famous falls. Driving or even cycling the rugged Cabot Trail on Cape Breton Island is a delight and can be incorporated into a broader trip through the Maritime Provinces, or north to Newfoundland.

The Canadian Rockies are not the biggest mountains in the world, but they are the most recognisable and are beautiful and diverse enough to be visited again and again. In one form or another, anyone living in Canada should explore as much of British Columbia as possible, in conjunction with or in addition to the Alberta Rockies.

Canadians living on flatter lands have long enjoyed the country's hundreds of thousands of lakes. Families in every part of the country flock to the water – both fresh and salt – every summer to fish, swim and barbecue as well as fight mosquitoes. Cottages, particularly within easy reach of Toronto, have increased significantly in cost, but remain the focus of summertime activities in Canada's most populated province.

Beyond the better known tourist spots such as Quebec City, Halifax, Banff and Vancouver Island, there are many other regions worth travelling to at any time of year. The Yukon is simply magical – long summer days and long winter nights frame the vast northern land first exposed to the world through the Klondike

The Greatest Outdoor Show on Earth

Dating back to 1912, the Calgary Exhibition and Stampede is Alberta's biggest annual event and draws upwards of a million visitors. Essentially the Stampede is the world's largest rodeo, including cattle shows and midway with shows, rides and as much greasy food as one could ever desire. Replete with gambling, a strong First Nations presence and a city-wide western conspiracy, the Stampede is a big event. Each July the oil tycoons of modern Calgary, of whatever ethnicity, celebrate their city's heritage by donning cowboy hats, boots and blue jeans. Free breakfasts are offered all over the city and bars stay open extra late. Only a fraction of the celebrants watch the rodeo itself, but cowboys from around the world come to break bones and chase after the impressive prize money.

The event kicks off on the first Friday of July with a large parade led by First Nations leaders, and roars along for ten days. Urban cowboys emerge from all corners of the city and locals show off their two-stepping and line-dancing skills. Although modern Calgary is a diverse, international city, ranching and farming communities are nearby, so, while there is undoubtedly a promoted quality to the entire event, the Stampede does link rural and urban Alberta. The boom feel to the Stampede would be heartening to the city's early visionaries, who imagined just such an event.

gold rush. Dawson City is frozen in time, and with miners still working claims it remains a special and 'real' place. Vast and isolated, Canada's newest territory, Nunavut, is only just developing tourist infrastructure, and the lack of any road access results in high costs, but fascinating rewards.

Further south, Canada's road network is very good, despite constant post-winter reconstruction, and each region offers natural tourist circuits, albeit some requiring a little backtracking. Little Prince Edward Island owes much of its economic life to tourism and therefore is an easy and enjoyable place to visit.

While much of Canada's attractions and tourist activities revolve around the great outdoors, most Canadian cities come alive with festivals over the summer and various celebrations throughout the year. Montreal may be one of the greatest party cities on earth and during the hot summer months the island always seems to have some event going on. Out west, Edmonton is working to develop a festival culture including an excellent folk festival and many sporting events, but topping the prairie calendar is the lively Calgary Stampede.

With the world's longest coastline, both the Atlantic and Pacific coasts offer attractive villages as well as true wilderness. Surprisingly the water is not always too cold for swimming, and the lobster on the east coast should be enjoyed as often as possible.

See **References**, pp.245–6, for a list of national and provincial holidays.

First Steps

04

The decision to move to another country requires emotional fortitude, as well as good planning. This chapter will attempt to address some of the positive reasons for making a move to Canada – either permanently, or for a predetermined period of time. It is not easy to leave one's home and culture and, regardless of how attractive the eventual destination may be, frustrations will arise, especially when things are done differently from the way you are used to.

When asking yourself if you will like the people in your new home, it is worth examining whether you liked them in the last place you lived. For British travellers and migrants, Canada represents a reasonably easy option – a shared language and heritage, good services and a population that enjoys and welcomes British newcomers. The strength of sterling can make the settling-in process somewhat smoother, and modern telecommunications help maintain links to home. Needless to say, winter can come as a shock, but more affordable air travel brings the sunny climes of Mexico ever closer.

Getting to Canada is very easy these days. The flight from London to St John's is shorter than that from St John's to Vancouver. The story is not the crossing of the ocean, but rather where to arrive in Canada. Staying for the long term is somewhat more complicated, and subsequent chapters will address this issue.

Why Live and Work in Canada?

Canada's size is daunting. To say you are moving to Canada is a bit like just stating that you are moving to 'Europe' in terms of distance – whether that be Finland or Spain. It takes several days to drive from the big eastern Canadian cities to the Rocky Mountains, so if you are looking for the great outdoors, consider wisely. A central location like Winnipeg may seem logical until you discover that Toronto is a two-day drive in one direction and Calgary a day and a half in the other. This vastness and diversity allows newcomers to visit and experience a world that is completely different from home, but getting there takes time. Life in small-town Canada can be rewarding despite the isolation – should you choose Churchill, Manitoba, for example, you will find no road access, but hundreds of polar bears.

For most, economic prospects are the principal factor when choosing where to locate in Canada. Obviously, the more diverse larger centres contain all the first-world business models. Ski resorts can be popular spots for a year or two, but opportunities for advancement are few and it is difficult to settle permanently in mountain resorts. Provincial regulations govern many aspects of professional life, so internal moves can take longer than expected. Choosing Canada involves selecting a region and a lifestyle.

Canada is bureaucratic, and adapting economically to the country can take time. You make a personal decision when you choose to leave your home, but what draws you to Canada may be based on an intangible concept, rather than the cold reality. The big cities are big, and the towns are isolated, but, precisely because of that, residents make do and contribute to their own physical and cultural environment.

Without a doubt, the sheer grandeur of Canada explains, in part, why the Great White North has long been a destination of choice for British migrants. Sure, winters are colder than in the UK, but many parts of the country enjoy long stretches of blue skies and the Canadian infrastructure is distinctly more winterised. In fact, prairie cities that can seem a little plain and empty in the summer are, in some ways, designed around winter living. It would be wrong to suggest that those who made the historic trek to the New World came to behold meadows of glistening snow – it was opportunity that brought Brits and other Europeans. During the colonial period the United States was understandably more attractive both climatically and economically, except perhaps to those with interests in fishing or furs. But for different periods over the last 200 years Canada has received waves of Europeans. The early settlers deserve a degree of reverence – when they left Liverpool or Glasgow it really was goodbye, and the new land daunting and unknown.

Living Standards

In modern times economic migrants have come from poorer or less stable regions of the world, whereas Britons come to Canada for lifestyle choices as much as business ones. Sometimes they come to rejoin family, and occasionally they come for love.

Unemployment in the UK is lower than in Canada, but the general costs of living in the UK are higher. By most measures, Canada has a higher standard of living than Britain, in terms of basic services and living conditions. In no way does this denigrate personal history, family or a simple enjoyment of one's present place of residence, but the basic elements of a modern economy tend to be either more affordable or more accessible in Canada. Cities have been planned and developed with residents' needs in mind. In booming Calgary all new housing divisions contain designated parkland, schools and professional services. Less romantic than the Mediterranean, Canada demonstrates a mix between American exuberance and Nordic planning.

Of course if international living standards were the only reason for moving, we would all end up crowded into Vancouver, Geneva, Melbourne and a few other cities. But there is more to daily life than just statistics. Among wealthier nations, differences between purchasing price parity and other measures become less significant and home is defined as much by friendships and belonging as by economic indicators. Canada, therefore, offers all the basic standards of the first world, in addition to its particular way of life.

Ethnic Diversity in Canada

The British fit well into Canada and, for the most part, find Canadians receptive and polite. The lack of an obvious class structure and the (fading) prestige that a British or Irish accent carries make for an easy transition. Canadians tend not to be terribly outgoing, but they are warm and helpful. The culture offers a nice halfway point between the more reclusive elements of British society and the sometimes overzealous US world. Parts of Canada retain a frontier feel, but not in a gun-slinging way. Resource workers live in harsh conditions and can blow off steam during time off, but generally Canada is not rough and rules are obeyed. Large numbers of British-born people live in almost all areas of Canada and they have forged good lives socially and economically.

Canada's ethnic diversity is not the contentious issue that it is in Britain. Except for the First Nations, everyone is an immigrant, and, while some of the older guard undoubtedly cling to a feeling of propriety, most people get along quite well. Stop anyone in Toronto (black, white or green) and ask for directions and you may end up in a friendly chat about where you are from and how you are enjoying Canada. Even the big cities haven't completely lost their small-town beginnings.

Living in Canada is Pleasant

It would not be fair to say that Canada has a *joie de vivre* that matches the Mediterranean or Caribbean use of the term (not even in Quebec), but Canadians are happy and friendly. Away from busy city streets you can expect a 'hello' from passers-by, or perhaps a slight wave if jogging. European and even American standoffishness when it comes to talking to strangers surprises Canadians. This doesn't mean divulging one's personal history, just a friendly nod or hello. Even more surprising to visitors is the Canadian attitude towards pedestrians. Unless otherwise signed (with lights for example), a pedestrian standing at a street corner always has right of way. You may not want to test this in Quebec, but elsewhere it is fantastic. Three lanes of traffic will screech to a halt in Edmonton, just so you can cross the road.

Of course crime exists, but the same philosophy that respects pedestrians and resists the use of slang in the language underpins a broad trust. Slowly but surely, steps to upgrade levels of security are increasing, but one can still shake hands with a bank teller. Banks do not use protective screens to separate the customers and staff and any guard who might be on duty will usually smile and nod in a friendly manner. This trustful society is pervasive. People are inclined to lend a hand and small-town volunteerism remains strong.

It is easy to find exceptions to all examples, but visitors frequently comment on the overall pleasantness of Canada. To gain a better understanding of the various parts of the country, refer to Chapter 02, **Profiles of the Regions**, which provides a regional breakdown. Overall, as in Britain, life speeds up in the larger centres, and ranges from a veritable crawl in parts of the Atlantic provinces to the sometimes frenetic pace of greater Toronto. Although western Canadians thought that Vancouver epitomised the big-city lifestyle, the business people who began to move in from Hong Kong had a very different opinion. Accustomed to the 24/7 world of Hong Kong, they found it took some effort to slow down to British Columbia's pace. It is interesting to note that families will keep their traditions, but within one generation will also adopt the much more relaxed Canadian lifestyle.

Bilingualism

To the British migrant, Canada's bilingualism becomes a factor only in Quebec, parts of New Brunswick and for employment with the federal government. Some knowledge of French is required in Montreal and is absolutely imperative in the rest of the province. Unilingual people (English or French) do live around the Ottawa region but probably do not have government jobs.

Familiarity with the peculiarities of Canadian French opens the way to enjoying a bonus culture. The basic lifestyle in Quebec does not differ much from the rest of the country, with ice hockey commanding more headlines than politics. The linguistic/cultural environment is rich and quite different from that in France. The folk songs which most Quebecers still know have a sort of old-world charm.

The Seasons

In Canada one is acutely aware of time. Seasons are distinct and turn over at a surprising speed. Most Canadians live at latitudes similar to southern England and therefore sunlight hours are virtually the same; however, winter and summer temperatures are more extreme. Autumn in the east is dramatic. Frigid conditions mean that outside construction is often postponed to the warmer months and long, bright summer evenings draw Canadians out of doors to barbecue and imbibe. Seasons lend themselves well to festivals and annual scheduled events so more does go on during the warmer months. And although many take southern vacations during winter, the Canadians who are left behind do not hibernate.

One of the most enjoyable times is the Christmas and New Year period. Needless to say, consumerism abounds, and Father Christmas miraculously visits all shopping centres to hear what the children expect to receive. But this is also a time of beauty. Lights adorn houses and, when snow falls, a rainbow of colours illuminates the shortest days of the year. For some, Christmas remains a religious event; for others it is a time to visit family and celebrate winter. Schools close down for around two weeks and, after the frenetic pre-Christmas shopping, the day itself is quiet, only to be broken by even madder Boxing Day sales the next day.

Value For Money

As long as sterling stays strong against the dollar, Canada offers good value. Not everything is cheaper, but people coming from Britain do feel they are getting better value for money. Meal servings are larger, menus offer greater choice and petrol (gas) is less than half the UK cost (but distances are more than twice as far). Choice can in fact be a little overwhelming and take some getting used to.

Immigrant societies, which are less coded than older cultures, take for granted that there will be differences in personal taste. Breakfast provides a great example. Good, affordable breakfast restaurants are all over the country, but you must know how you want your eggs cooked – simply fried does not do it in Canada. No, you must decide whether your eggs should be over-easy, over-hard, poached, basted, scrambled or even boiled. Service is friendly and for the most part genuine – and not just for the tip.

Activity

Moving to Canada alone or as a family involves a very different set of decisions. For the footloose and fancy-free, towns like Whistler or Banff, which are located in beautiful mountain settings, offer a party culture and plenty of outdoor activities. Skiing is the principal draw, but biking and climbing are also popular. Single people may also be interested in a stint in the north, where smaller populations engender closer communities. Far more men than women live in the north, so single women need to be aware that the odds are good, but the goods are odd.

Nightlife

For the most part, the clubbing scene bears no resemblance to that in Britain, but all the bigger cities have plenty of bars and dance clubs. Dress codes in showy Montreal can be quite strict, but generally entrance fees are low, booze is expensive and how you look is your business. This freedom of style occurs throughout the country. Utilitarian dress outdoes flash and, consequently, fashion has adapted to comfort and the climate. All the upper-end products are on offer, but the general population just doesn't care all that much.

A pub culture exists, but not to the same extent as in Britain. British and the ever-popular Irish-style pubs are easy to find and, as the country has gone non-smoking, the air can be quite clean. Coffee houses have become an institution and many Canadians wander the streets with an insulated cup in hand. *See* also **Living in Canada**, 'Life in Cafés, Bars and Restaurants', pp.185–8.

Schooling

A family move obviously creates more complications, especially when the family includes school-age children. Individual provinces administer the school systems, which are generally very good. Private schools exist, but they are not very numerous and are less exclusive than the British equivalent. In Toronto your children may sit in a classroom where a dozen languages are spoken, and in less diverse settings their accent will attract interest and even a little popularity. Children do not wear uniforms and the educational philosophy is quite broad. This seems to be paying off as education levels in Canada rank among the world's highest. *See* **Living in Canada**, 'Education', pp.207–15.

Summary

While Canada is very distant from the many conflicts around the world, its location, perched above the mighty United States, can be both aggravating and reassuring. Spacious, friendly, clean and modern, Canada combines functional sophistication and nature. Its size works against the concentration of cultural activities in just a few cities and each community generates its own fun. It requires some effort to take advantage of all that the country has to offer. People move to the big cities for work and often spend little time in the wilderness. To some extent this is understandable.

All Canadian cities have large park areas that include walking trails and the facilities for numerous activities. You do not need to go to nature because it comes to you, in the form of snow, wind and heat. A drive to the smaller towns or to the many parks is rewarding. Depending on where you live, acquiring a cottage or vacation property, or at least going off on a camping trip, reveals a whole new world.

Unfortunately vacations are depressingly short and bank holidays (statutory holidays) are somewhat infrequent. Long-distance internal travel can be expensive, while trips to exotic destinations cost more than they would in the UK. These are the trade-offs you make for good economic opportunities and reasonably priced living costs. Average working people in Canada can save some money and do not have to do without much.

Getting to Canada

Travelling to Canada is quite easy and relatively affordable. Reaching your final destination, however, can be somewhat more complicated and involve several connections. By air, Toronto is the country's principal hub but, depending on the final destination, internal flights can be routed through any one of several different cities. Market size has restricted significant airline competition and the development of mass land transportation to the more remote areas is simply too costly.

By Air

Except for the very adventurous or extremely creative, the only realistic way to get to Canada from Britain, Ireland or mainland Europe is by air. Aside from the neighbouring United States, the only other countries that are geographically close to Canada are France (via the tiny St Pierre and Miquelon Islands) and Danish-protected Greenland – not known as a major hub. Someone particularly pedantic could point out polar proximities, but almost all of Canada's main points of entry and population live within 200km of the US border. Only Edmonton stands out as a large city located far from the border, although it must be pointed out that all three prairie provinces sit atop some of the least-populated areas of the United States and therefore remain quite distant.

Toronto's Pearson airport is Canada's largest and most important gateway. Other eastern Canadian airports with direct flights to the UK include Ottawa, Montreal (Trudeau airport in the west part of the island), Halifax and St John's, Newfoundland. In western Canada Calgary, Vancouver and Edmonton all have daily non-stop air services to Britain.

If you are flying to any other cities, connections must be made through one of these airports – and that is where the challenge begins. While several major airlines (Air Canada, British Airways and other European carriers) and some charter outfits fly to at least one of the major cities, only Air Canada maintains a full network of internal connections. Smaller national airlines do service a reasonable number of cities, but are not partnered with international carriers.

Flying through the United States offers a further option for reaching points in Canada, but all the new security and visa requirements can make this a time-consuming and not very enjoyable alternative. To fly via Houston or Chicago in order to save £50 may not be worth the effort and, frankly, you will be likely to spend the savings on food and drink while filling in time in airports.

Flights to Canada leave from London Heathrow and London Gatwick, and from Manchester, Glasgow, Edinburgh, Belfast, Dublin and Shannon (frequency varies depending on the time of the year). In terms of predictable frequency, Heathrow has by far the most flights, and it is often worth flying through

London rather than messing around with long and complicated connections in Canada.

Air Canada

The decision about which airline to use is easy because of the limited choices available. The main airline, somewhat unsurprisingly, is Air Canada (AC). The national flag carrier has been through multiple reincarnations, bailouts and bankruptcy protection. Up to the end of the 1990s, Air Canada's main domestic competition came from Calgary-based Canadian Airlines, which was partnered with British Airways. Either as a result of management issues or market realities (probably both), Canada could not sustain two national carriers. Though the story at the time was more complicated, the final result saw Air Canada absorb Canadian Airlines. This merger, people believed, would make Air Canada fabulously wealthy and cause ticket prices to soar. In the end, consumers did not do too badly as internal competition kept prices down. Instead of seeing huge profits, Air Canada found itself burdened with Canadian Airlines' debt. Then the September 11, 2001 events in New York City knocked the wind out of the airline and the industry in general. Air Canada slid into bankruptcy protection and its main competitor at the time, Canada 3000, went bust. The currently reincarnated Air Canada operates as a fully private company and seems to be making some money, so buying a ticket represents no great risk.

Air Canada belongs to the Star Alliance network of airlines, which is part of the reason why British Airways' service to Canada is limited. As a member of Star Alliance, Air Canada is partnered with British Midland in the UK and United Airlines in the United States as well as numerous other carriers.

Internally, Air Canada has an extensive network of subsidiaries and partner airlines, although very few of them show up on Air Canada's website. If you are flying to a more remote destination it may take a bit of hunting to discover which airline flies which route. Many smaller places do not appear on regular online databases.

Purchasing tickets with Air Canada is easy and can be done safely through the Internet. For the most part the airline's website (**www.aircanada.com**) is user-friendly (unless you use a Mac) and quotes prices quickly; note that a price is not a price until all the extra taxes and fees are added. Although the site is Canadian, prices for flights originating in the UK will be quoted in sterling. Quotes may also be obtained from **British Midland** (**www.bmi.co.uk**) or on many travel websites.

British Airways and American Airlines

Once upon a time, **British Airways** had a reasonable presence in Canada, but having lost its partner, Canadian Airlines, it now flies only to Toronto, Montreal, Calgary and Vancouver. With a bit of creativity it is possible to link flights with

American Airlines through the USA, or by using one of Canada's regional discount carriers. British Airways' website can be accessed easily through **www. ba.com**, but the only options offered are for cities to which it has direct flights.

American Airlines' somewhat less clear website (**www.aa.com**) offers a little more creative routing.

Charter and Discount Airlines

Companies offering charter flights to Canada come and go, and prices vary. Unless purchased as part of a package, charter deals rarely cost less than a regularly scheduled service. One advantage is that charter flights will sometimes fly in and out of smaller airports, which in Europe can be a nuisance but which could represent a huge saving in cost and time when flying to Canada. Most charter companies schedule their flights around seasons or activities. The newest player on the discount market is **Zoom** (**www.flyzoom. com**) with flights between the UK, France and North America. Montreal-based **Air Transat** (**www.airtransat.com**) runs a moderate fleet that flies Canadians south to the sun during winter months and over to Europe from May through the summer. Its flights leave from a variety of UK and Irish airports and usually go to Toronto. Air Transat even has a more affordable, scaled-down version of business class. **Canadian Affair**, which is part of the Transat group (**www. canadianaffair.com**), offers a similar service.

Skyservice (**www.skyservice.com**) gears its service towards package operators and flies mostly to sunny climes, but has flights to Europe. Also in the charter business is Halifax-based **Canjet** (**www.canjet.com**), which sells through package holiday companies.

Internal Airlines

The number two Canadian carrier at the moment is western-based **WestJet** (**www.westjet.com**), which boasts live television on its flights. Most of its flights are to destinations within North America, and the airline's friendly service has engendered a loyal following. As yet, this low-frills company has not expanded to Europe, but is flying to the USA and Mexico. For short-haul trips within Canada, WestJet provides a very competitive service and some Canadians use the airline specifically in order not to fly Air Canada.

Halifax-based **CanJet** (**www.canjet.com**) flies discount routes in eastern Canada and to a few US cities.

Dozens of other small and tiny airlines fly throughout Canada. Some stick to corporate routes (such as Calgary to central Edmonton), while others serve distant northern communities. Furthermore, many of the regional airlines that Air Canada or Canadian Airlines established as subsidiaries now operate as semi-distinct entities. The following list is far from an exhaustive, but includes some of the larger regional carriers:

- **Air Canada Jazz:** really just Air Canada.
- **Air North (www.flyairnorth.com):** Yukon-based.
- **Bearskin Airlines (www.bearskinairlines.com):** Northern Ontario.
- **Calm Air (www.calmair.com):** Winnipeg-based; services central north.
- **Canadian North (www.canadiannorth.com):** flies north from Alberta and Ottawa; some routes are expensive and cater to business travellers in the mining and oil sectors.
- **Central Mountain Air (www.centralmountainair.com):** British Columbia and Alberta.
- **Provincial Airlines (www.provincialairlines.com):** Atlantic Canada.

US Airlines

All the major US carriers fly between the United States and Canada, but none is permitted to offer routes entirely within Canada. **United Airlines** is Air Canada's major partner in North America and therefore the two airlines share some check-in facilities and run co-shared routes. **American** flies to more destinations than British Airways and is also affiliated with **Alaska Airlines**, which has several access points in western Canada.

The Cost of Flying

After you factor in inflation, the cost of flying internationally has either decreased or stayed the same in the last few years. All airlines sell seats based on a variety of fares that range from the lowest-cost, no-frills ticket to executive class. Full-fare tickets can usually be changed or refunded without cost, but the actual ticket price is often prohibitively expensive. Charter flights have a more straightforward pricing system, but are typically less flexible. Discount airlines

Flying in Winter

Flights from or within Canada during the winter can often be delayed because of inclement weather. Large storms bringing high volumes of snow usually hit southern Ontario a couple of times a year, disrupting traffic from Toronto's airport. Even larger accumulations occur in the Atlantic provinces, which have to be cleared before flights can take off. De-icing (spraying anti-freeze over the wings) takes place everywhere with freezing temperatures, but no one seems to mind the slight inconvenience.

If delays or flight cancellations occur as a result of the weather, you will be rebooked, but not compensated. Frustrating as the process is, the industry simply cannot afford to pay for the hotels and meals passengers need as a result of bad weather. Air Canada is in the process of developing an inclement weather insurance scheme, offered for yet another additional cost.

have reduced ticket prices even further and, while they may not offer refunds, unused trips can be banked or changed for a fixed fee, plus the difference in ticket price. On busy routes, such as London–Toronto or London–Vancouver, low-season flights can be obtained for around £300 (plus a fuel surcharge). The busy summer months are more expensive, although competition increases as the charter companies redirect flights from the tropics to Europe. Flying to Canada's largest cities should not break the budget, but the £1 deals found in Europe are simply not available. Flights to smaller cities can prove costly, particularly when not booked as part of a larger itinerary.

Buying tickets to Canada in advance still results in some savings, despite the plethora of last-minute deals advertised in the UK. Bargains can be found, but they involve a lot of hunting and numerous phone calls. Because so few airlines fly to Canada, choice is very limited, whatever travel agents and online marketers tell you about their ability to search hundreds of airlines.

Internal flights to remote areas can cost as much as international flights, which explains why flying to cities that require a connection can be so expensive. Getting to the Canadian north is extremely expensive and, once there, everything remains expensive. The airline industry is based on volume. Small operators will run a few aircraft for a few people, but still must maintain international safety standards.

Although the following examples provide a very general idea of costs, it is worth keeping an eye out for special offers and phoning different travel agents. The return flights shown in sterling are typical advance-purchase fares for flights on major airlines in May 2008 – considered the shoulder season.

London (any airport) to:

- **Calgary (direct or indirect): £500+ (all airlines).**
- **Halifax (via Canada or USA): £650– despite a shorter distance.**
- **Toronto (direct): £400+ with lots of competition.**
- **Vancouver (direct): £450–650.**

Baggage

Most major airlines have strict regulations about the size and weight of the cabin baggage that is permitted on aircraft, but are more generous about checked luggage. Air Canada and British Airways allow passengers to check two pieces of luggage not weighing more than 23 kilos (50 pounds) each, per person. Overweight charges range from £25 to £40.

The Views

Clearly, western Canada is much further from the UK than eastern Canada, but flight lengths are shorter than a Mercator projection map suggests. While flights to Alberta or British Columbia do not quite over-fly the North Pole, they

The New Pearson Airport

After years of construction, enormous costs, confusing transfers and traffic re-routing, Toronto's new Pearson airport is open for business and ready to receive the world. Depending on traffic the airport is about 30 minutes' drive from central Toronto and has been built more or less on top of the old airport. There is still more work to do, but the now completed terminal is a beautiful and surprisingly efficient structure.

Some flights from the UK land at an older terminal, from which passengers will be taken to the new customs hall for some indeterminable amount of time. One negative feature is that you have to pay for baggage trolleys – you would think we have all paid enough tax and landing fees to deserve a little help with luggage.

Departures to Europe are extremely well run and efficient, so, unless there is a major storm, don't worry too much about getting there three full hours early for your flight. If check-in and security are all completed in 15 or 20 minutes, you will simply have more time to spend money on overpriced, barely edible food.

Getting from the airport to downtown Toronto is not too difficult, but it is pricey. Taxis cost around C$45 (£20) plus a tip. There is talk about extending Toronto's subway (underground) to the airport, but at this point it is just talk. Public buses and collective shuttles are also available for around half the price of a cab.

do cut across Iceland and Greenland. If daylight hours and weather permit, a flight to western Canada is worth every penny just for the views. Few people will ever have the chance to walk on Greenland or northern Canada's ice cap, so even viewing them from a height of 10,000 metres is a thrill. Crossing the Canadian north is humbling. For hours while in the air, you fly above a land dotted with thousands of lakes, and broken only rarely with the odd road or minor settlement. In winter the white is not blinding, but the ice is expansive and lonely.

Airport Codes

For what is probably some perfectly good reason, all airport codes in Canada begin with the letter 'Y'. Unlike more logical systems such as LHR, for London Heathrow, or DUB for Dublin, Toronto's Pearson airport is known as YYZ. Montreal's Pierre Trudeau airport, which is finally going through a refurbishment after the city's other gateway, Mirabel, flopped, has the code YUL. Vancouver's code bears some semblance to its name, YVR, while Calgary gets YYC. Perplexingly, Whitehorse has scored YXY.

Other Types of Transport

For obvious reasons the choice of land routes to Canada from the UK is extremely limited, but, once you arrive in Canada, overland or on-water travel may be required.

Up until the last 60 years or so, most Europeans crossing the Atlantic would board **ships**, usually destined for Montreal or perhaps Halifax, and then continue by **train**. Winnipeg boomed from the trainloads of people who passed through on their way to settlements farther west in the prairies. Trains were by far the most common form of long-distance transport, but in recent years aeroplanes and cars have virtually displaced all other forms of transportation.

It is possible to cruise to North America the luxurious way by spending six days aboard the *Queen Mary II*. Departing from Southampton once or twice a month through spring, summer and fall, the *Queen Mary II* arrives in New York, from where you would proceed north by air or land to Canada. Be aware that you will have to clear goods through customs twice if taking a US route.

Somewhat less romantic, but an alternative that the hardy may favour, is to travel on a ship belonging to one of the freight services that cross the Atlantic with passengers and cargo. Travel by freighter is somewhat slower than by air or cruise ship and takes 7–14 days, depending on the quality of the ship and ports of call. Ships offering passage generally have space for 10–12 passengers. All meals are included and facilities range from good to excellent. Costs vary and you should expect to pay at least £1,200 per person. A useful website for finding ships, pricing and schedules is offered at **www.thecruisepeople.co.uk.**

Travelling by sea is a good way to accompany your belongings – even the car with its steering wheel on the wrong side. More commonly, however, migrants who plan to move to Canada lock, stock and barrel will fly over and have their belongings shipped separately, or will sell everything and buy again when settled in their new country. With so many Canadians and Antipodeans spending time in Jolly Old, dozens of UK-based companies will ship goods anywhere around the world at competitive prices. You do not have to pay duty on personal belongings if moving to Canada, but should those belongings arrive unaccompanied, you will likely have to claim them from customs (which could be the port or local airport) after completing the required paperwork. Alcohol and tobacco are strictly controlled in Canada so they are *not* exempt from duty. Air freight is understandably much more expensive than shipping by sea, but also faster. When shipping by surface, size matters more than weight and a three-bedroom house of goods can cost thousands of pounds to ship.

Red Tape

Not only is Canada bureaucratic, but two distinct levels of government (federal and provincial) have a say in immigration and work. A new attitude of accountability at the federal level has simply increased bureaucracy, even though steps have been taken to speed up the immigration and visa process, due to a shortage of skilled workers. Consistent with national politics, Quebec maintains a totally distinct immigration policy, but each jurisdiction controls different aspects of Canada's red tape. The days of preferential treatment for Commonwealth citizens are long gone, so potential British migrants have to fill out the same paperwork as other foreign nationals.

Canada is not a corrupt country and most of the information you need can and in fact often must be found online (**www.canadainternational.gc.ca** or **www.cic.gc.ca**). The Canadian High Commission, Immigration, 38 Grosvenor Street, London W1K 4AA, has aggravatingly limited opening hours of 8–11am. Their website is **www.canada.org.uk** and this is really the only method by which to go through the immigration or visa process. Trying to call is virtually impossible and links through to a Canadian call centre. The Canadian visa office in London also processes applications from the Republic of Ireland.

A variety of visas allow extended stays in Canada. Once a permit has been granted, a few other internal steps need to be taken, in particular to obtain a social insurance number (needed for working and banking) and, for new immigrants, the recently introduced permanent resident card. This chapter will outline visa options for living in, working in and immigrating to Canada. Fortunately for British citizens, Canada allows dual citizenship – if you live in Canada long enough to meet the citizenship requirements you can gain a country without giving one up.

Canada is always reviewing aspects of its immigration policy, so the following information should be treated as an outline only, and may be subject to change – always refer back to the Canadian immigration site; **www.cic.gc.ca**. Furthermore, permission to work or live in Canada does not necessarily clear the way for newcomers to practise their profession. Engineers and medical professionals, specifically, have to take further steps to be licensed by their professions' governing bodies – and these restrictions operate both federally and provincially and may include taking exams. As all information has moved online, a simple search should reveal your specific professional association. Some professions are gradually making their qualifications national, removing barriers to inter-provincial movement.

Visas

British and Irish citizens may visit Canada as tourists for up to six months without a visa. If you are planning a non-working visit for longer than six months, it may prove easier to simply cross over to the United States from time to time. Alternatively, if you possess a tourist visa you must apply for an extension at least three weeks before it expires.

Arriving as a tourist is easy, although since 9/11 visitors and residents alike can expect longer lines and closer scrutiny. On entry into Canada you must have a valid passport and you will be required to fill out a customs declaration. Airlines are required to confirm the validity of passengers' travel documents, so expect to show your passport when you check in for your flight and before boarding the aircraft. Security personnel may also enquire about the reason for your trip and verify that you have sufficient funds, particularly if you have arrived on a one-way ticket, as well as ask for evidence of any onward journey.

Generally, a foreign national with a criminal record is not permitted to travel to Canada, except under certain circumstances. In order to be granted a visitor's permit, such travellers must demonstrate that they are rehabilitated, which means their single indictable offence occurred more than 10 years earlier. Rehabilitation may be applied for after five years and/or after a pardon. Although individuals with criminal records may be considered for entry or temporary residency on humanitarian grounds, it is unlikely that this would apply to UK citizens.

Medical Examinations

British, Irish and most European citizens do not need a medical examination before visiting Canada, unless they have lived for more than six consecutive months in certain designated countries within one year of going to Canada. As the list of countries is extensive, again refer to the **Citizenship and Canadian Immigration** site (**www.cic.gc.ca/english/visit/dcl.html**) if this might affect you. This site also provides a list of authorised doctors by country.

If you are planning on working in certain professions, however, such as teaching and medicine, you will need to pass a medical examination. A medical exam is also compulsory for those seeking to become permanent residents, and applicants may be turned down on medical grounds. Be aware that a medical exam and clearance may take more than three months to complete and costs over £150. Once you have passed a medical examination, it is valid for 12 months.

Use of a Representative

Some people who are planning to live or work in Canada may choose to appoint a paid or unpaid representative to act on their behalf. At any given time, only one person can represent you and you must complete and submit form **IMM 5476** (which can be downloaded or obtained from an immigration lawyer). A quick Internet search reveals the availability of a multitude of lawyers, members of the **Canadian Society of Immigration Consultants (CSIC)** and notaries from the **Chambre des Notaires du Québec** offering immigration-related services. Although they are able to help with various types of applications and can ensure the proper completion of forms, they cannot speed up the processing of applications – Canadian Immigration does not give preference to agencies or legal representatives. Unless your situation is complicated, it should be just as easy to work through the process on your own.

The Time to Process Visas

Different visas take varying periods of time to process. There is an active move to streamline the system, although the wait may last for a year or more – 80 per cent of European applications for permanent residency are processed within three years, although provincial nominees seem to make it through much faster. Student and specific work visas may be granted within days, whereas immigration applications seem to disappear for months. Although you can track your application status online, this doesn't shed too much light on the progress being made. At the time of writing this edition the Canadian government is actively debating the backlog of both immigration and refugee applications. Delays, application times and fees may well remain under revision.

Students

If planning to study for a short period (less than six months) you do not require a visa. This is particularly convenient for those doing a term abroad or who want to spend a short period of time learning French in Quebec. If you think you may want to continue your studies beyond the six-month period, you should obtain a student visa before arriving – otherwise you must leave Canada in order to apply.

In order to apply for a student visa you will first need to prove acceptance to a Canadian institution and the ability to cover your tuition and living costs. A student visa is not a work visa, but it allows for part-time, on-campus employment. Because education is a provincial matter in Canada, institutional regulations differ across the country. For a list of provincial and territorial departments of education, visit the webites of the **Council of Ministers of Education, Canada (www.cmec.ca)**, or the **Canadian Bureau for International Education (www.cbie.ca)**.

The process of applying to study in Canada can be reasonably efficient. Because foreign students pay considerably higher tuition fees than nationals, the various institutions compete actively to attract foreign students. Individual institutions set their own academic and language requirements. Quebec requires an additional certificate of acceptance and the educational institution should provide information about this process. Once you receive a letter of acceptance, you can download the appropriate visa application from the

Internet, or request it from the High Commission's visa department. Remember to fill out all paperwork in black ink.

To apply for the student visa, you will need:

- **a valid passport and two passport-size photos (with name and date of birth on the back).**
- **proof of financial independence (bank draft, four months of bank account records) and proof of payment of tuition fees.**
- **medical insurance.**
- **possibly a criminal records check.**
- **possibly a medical examination.**
- **a custodianship form if the applicant is younger than the age of majority (either 18 or 19, depending on the province).**
- **any documents not in English or French to be translated.**

Family members, including common-law partners, are permitted to live in Canada while you are studying. Age restrictions apply to accompanying offspring. Working is generally not permitted, unless the employment occurs within the institution or as part of the programme. A variety of hybrid study or work experience courses are offered at undergraduate and graduate levels, which may also let spouses find employment.

Needless to say, a myriad other possible rules and exemptions also exist. Many exemptions apply to students on development scholarships through the **Canadian International Development Agency (CIDA)** or on other forms of exchange. The majority of such exemptions and scholarships do not apply to citizens of wealthy, developed countries.

The principal application form for a study permit can be filed online, or downloaded from **www.cic.gc.ca**. To make sure that your application is complete, review and include document **IMM 5483**, which is a document checklist for a study permit. The fee for the application is C$125 (around £60).

After you have submitted the application, by mail or in person, you may expect at least one of the following responses: you may be invited to come for an interview; you may receive notification that the application has been declined; or you may receive a letter of introduction confirming the approval. When you give this letter to the immigration officer on your arrival in Canada, you will receive the study visa.

Student or Youth Temporary Work

Canada grants 12-month student/youth working holiday permits to British and Irish citizens. In the UK, the partnership is administered by **British Universities North American Campus** (**BUNAC**; 16 Bowling Green Lane, London EC1R 0QH, **t** (020) 7251 3472, **www. bunac.org**). In the Republic of Ireland the partnership is with **USIT** (**www.canada.usit.ie**) and applications must be made online. Both of these programmes are partnered with the Canadian **Student Work Abroad Programme (SWAP)** and are sponsored by the Canadian Federation of Students. Applicants must be between 18 and 35 years of age. Student programmes require that applicants be full-time students in their home countries, or have graduated or will be entering post-secondary education within 12 months. A student is defined as someone pursuing a degree or qualification in, at minimum, a two-year course. Numbers are restricted for student and non-student applicants. These programmes are available only for British and Irish citizens who reside in their respective countries. Working holiday visas for Europeans, Australians and New Zealanders have been negotiated independently with those countries and therefore have different application processes. Providing you meet the age qualification, have no dependants, are a resident in either the UK or Ireland and do not have a criminal record, these programmes offer the easiest way to live and work in Canada. Non-students can obtain a visa, but only once. With certain restrictions, qualifying students can receive temporary working visas more than once. Candidates must live in their home country during the application process.

The basic cost of the BUNAC programme is £180, and €379 for the USIT programme plus a €179 Canadian Government fee. These costs include visa expenses, as well as in-country orientation, but do not include the cost of flights, insurance or any medical exam required for specific employment.

In addition to the quite straightforward application form, you will need an official letter from your educational institution. Non-students must provide a personal reference letter. You will also need to have at least £500 in spending money, although more would be advisable, given the high costs associated with settlement in popular destinations such as ski resorts.

BUNAC also offers a Gap programme for British and Irish students aged between 18 and 20. The process is very similar to those outlined above, but is tailored to that particular age group.

Temporary Work

Most non-Canadians who wish to work in Canada will need a work permit. Some exceptions apply, particularly for the military (Canada has a military accord with the UK), business visitors, diplomatic personnel, performing artists, athletes, and several other professions A work permit does not represent an opportunity to immigrate or to obtain permanent residency.

Unquestionably the easiest way to obtain a work permit is to have a job already lined up – a job where the employer can demonstrate the need for your skills. **Human Resources and Skills Development Canada (HRSDC)** governs most employment issues. As a result of the North American Free Trade Agreement (which does not apply to the UK) some exemptions exist, but generally the

Case Study: Anthony McKenna, Ski Bum (Machinist)

Anthony, age 23, is from the north of Ireland and enjoyed a one-year work visa in British Columbia. A machinist by profession and a keen rugby player, Anthony came to Canada in search of the classic images of mountains, snow and the Great Outdoors. After working for several months on Vancouver Island, Anthony headed to Banff, in the Alberta Rockies, to work and ski for the winter, but ended up living in a ski resort in British Columbia.

How did you organise the visa?

I organised the one-year visa through BUNAC. Including insurance the process cost around £1,200. I flew into Vancouver where I received some help and advice from the SWAP office, which is partnered with BUNAC.

Could you tell me a little about your working experience?

I arrived in Vancouver in July 2004 and soon went over to Vancouver Island where I found a position on the local rugby team in Duncan, a community about 45 minutes north of Victoria. It was easy to make friends in Duncan and they quickly helped me to get settled and find work with a local company. Despite having an enjoyable experience I decided to escape the rain (as well as a life very similar to mine at home) and learn to snowboard.

As so many people do, I went to Banff but found that by late November most of the seasonal jobs had been taken, particularly by Australians. Through some contacts I was able to find work at a British Columbia ski resort. Unfortunately the snow quality has been poor this season, but the entire mountain has been ridable. At the resort I have worked in several positions and, while the pay is a low minimum wage, I have been able to live from my tips.

What advice would you offer anyone considering working in Canada?

The experience is absolutely worth it. British Columbia has exceeded my expectations and I am considering moving here permanently. The ski hill experience is excellent, particularly for someone from Ireland, but make sure to start applying for jobs as early as September.

My professional qualifications are not immediately recognised in Canada and I understand that rules differ even between provinces. Obviously for a working holiday I didn't mind, but to settle and make a decent wage it would be important to work out how to be licensed.

HRSDC will decide if your application contributes to the country's skill requirements and economic development. This chapter will address the issue of applying to immigrate as a skilled worker separately.

Needless to say, the application process involves several steps. British and Irish citizens do not need a temporary resident's visa and neither do British overseas dependants who have permission to re-enter the UK. A work permit is usually valid for a specific job and a specific period of time. Therefore, once you have received a job offer you will need:

• a completed application for work permit form (IMM 1295).

• a job offer letter or contract and HRSDC file number (Quebec Certificate of Acceptance), provided by the employer.

• proof of identity (passport).

• proof of funds.

• C$150 fee (non-refundable), paid by a bank draft in Canadian dollars and made payable to the Receiver General for Canada.

• a statutory common-law declaration (if applicable).

• any additional documents, such as medical papers.

Once again, if accepted, you will receive a letter to present on entry into Canada.

Immigration

Canada has six distinct immigration programmes. Details and forms are available online at the **Citizenship and Immigration Canada** website (**www.cic. gc.ca**) and applications are to be submitted to the Canadian High Commission visa office in London. After applying, you can expect to wait at least several months and up to a year for the paperwork to clear. If you are already in Canada when the paperwork comes through, you must physically leave the country in order to re-enter as a permanent resident.

Landed immigrant or permanent resident status does not translate immediately into **citizenship**. You have to live in Canada for at least three years before you may apply to become a citizen. Citizenship confers the ability to apply for a Canadian passport, to vote and to hold public office. For details on citizenship, once again visit **www.cic.gc.ca**.

Some people never bother with the citizenship step, but new rules now require that permanent residents who travel outside the country must have in their possession a government-issued **identity card** to show on their return; see p.149. Once you have achieved permanent residency status you are required to remain in Canada for at least two out of every five years, unless exempted for reasons such as working abroad for a Canadian company. If you do not fulfil the two-year minimum, your residency status may be revoked.

Unlike applicants for tourist and temporary visas, anyone wanting to immigrate to Canada must undergo a medical exam. Would-be immigrants also have to obtain original documents from universities and other educational institutions and from places of employment. You must also produce a copy of any police records.

Employing an **immigration consultant** will not hasten the process. The status of your application can be tracked online. If you are already in Canada and want to listen to a recorded message, call **t** 1-888 242 2100. But be warned, the message is lengthy and boring and when you try to connect to a person the line may be busy.

Skilled Worker Class Immigration

For the average British immigrant to Canada, this category may represent the most likely route of immigration. In order to qualify as a skilled worker, you must:

- **meet minimum work experience rules (one full year in a paid position).**
- **have enough funds to settle (this is calculated on a scale that is based on the number of people in the family); single individuals need about C$10,000 (£4,500) over and above the application and landed immigrant fees.**
- **score 67 out of 100 points from the six selection factors; this score has been reduced from 75 points everywhere except Quebec (although free movement is guaranteed within Canada); you can easily work out your score online. Do not bother trying to immigrate as a skilled worker if you do not have 67 points. The categories are:**
  - **education.**
  - **official language proficiency (points are awarded for both English and French).**
  - **work experience (this is complicated, with various evaluations for different professions).**
  - **age (it helps to be between 21 and 49).**
  - **arranged employment in Canada (find a job before you arrive).**
  - **adaptability (experience in Canada, family, spouse, and so on).**

If you plan to apply as a skilled worker, you can download all the necessary paperwork from the Citizenship and Immigration Canada website, but it is worth contacting the visa office in London for a complete package and checklist. If you complete the application improperly, the process starts all over again. The general fee structure for immigrating is as follows:

- **Right of Permanent Residence Fee: $490**
- **Skilled Worker/Provincial Nominees: $550**
- **Family Class (Principal Applicant): $475**
- **Sponsorship Application: $75 each**
- **Entrepreneur, Investor or Self-employed Person: $1,050**

Business Immigrants

The business immigrant category applies to those who will contribute to the economic prosperity and wellbeing of the country – essentially this means having enough financial resources to invest in the country and create jobs for Canadians. This division contains three sub-categories:

- **investors – people with a net worth of at least C\$800,000 (£400,000) and who are prepared to make an investment of C\$400,000 (£200,000).**
- **entrepreneurs – individuals with a net worth of C\$300,000 (£150,000) and who have experience and will own and manage businesses.**
- **self-employed – persons who intend, and have the ability, to develop their own work.**

The **investor** option is complicated. The C\$400,000 investment means the investor hands over the money and has it returned five years later with no interest. This option is used quite frequently, but only by people with large sums of cash that they don't care much about. A portion of the funds can be borrowed.

Entrepreneurs must demonstrate that they have managed and had a controlling interest in a business during at least two of the five years preceding their application. They must also intend, and be able, to manage and own a controlling interest (one-third) of a business in Canada and create at least one full-time job for someone who is not a family member.

The **self-employed** option is targeted towards a few industries – arts, athletics and farming. In other words, this is a fast-track method for attracting more Ben Johnsons. Should you want to take on farming, this could be the way to do it – but keep in mind that the option wouldn't be this easy by chance.

As with the skilled worker programme, there is a selection point system; however, applicants need only manage 35 out of 100 points in five categories. For more information, visit the website or contact the department directly at **www.cic.gc.ca**. Canada is keen to attract more investment, so this process at least appears to be a little less bureaucratic than some others.

Provincial Nomination

One way to circumvent the points system is to be granted provincial sponsorship. All provinces, except for two, and the Yukon Territory, have nomination programmes. The exception is Quebec. Each province mandates its own rules and highlighted industries, but if you can demonstrate a desire to move to that specific province and, ideally, find a local employer who wants or needs you, the province will grant a nomination that leads to an application for permanent residency. Provinces use the nomination system to attract migrants to specific regions or to encourage certain professionals. Because of the serious shortage of doctors in smaller towns, foreign medical professionals can request nominations in some provinces. Many South African doctors have made their way to the prairies, although permanent residency status has not allowed them to begin work immediately as medical practitioners: professional governing bodies have their own provincial and national standards, which involve exams and, of course, fees.

The different websites are linked through the Citizenship and Immigration Canada page and are also listed here:

- Alberta: **www.alberta-canada.com/pnp**
- British Columbia: **www.welcomebc.ca/en/index.html**
- Manitoba: **www.gov.mb.ca/labour/immigrate/index.html**
- New Brunswick: **www.gnb.ca/immigration**
- Newfoundland and Labrador: **www.gov.nf.ca/intrd//prov_nominee.htm**
- Nova Scotia: **www.gov.ns.ca/econ/nsnp**
- Ontario: **www.ontariomigration.ca**
- Prince Edward Island: **www.gov.pe.ca/immigration**
- Saskatchewan: **www.immigrationsask.gov.sk.ca**
- Yukon: **www.economicdevelopment.gov.yk.ca**

Family Class Immigration

The impetus for this form of immigration comes from within. Canadian citizens and permanent residents living in Canada may sponsor family members or common-law partners who are seeking to immigrate. Sponsorship requires a commitment that ranges from three years up to 10 years – three years for a spouse or partner and up to 10 years for their dependants. Somewhat different rules apply in Quebec and come into effect after the Canadian part of the process is completed. Applications for sponsorship must come from the Canadian citizen and not from the prospective immigrant.

This method of immigration provides an option for Canadians who would like to adopt from abroad. Family-class immigration may also be used for same-sex partnerships as long as the civil union took place in a legal Canadian jurisdiction.

Family-class immigration remains an option should you fall head over heels for a Canadian and want to live with your love happily ever after. However, this form of immigration does not necessarily offer a faster route than the skilled worker channel. Fiancé(e) status is not recognised, but common-law (opposite or same-sex) partnership is, so either marry or live together for at least one year, preferably in Canada.

Reasonable Accommodation

In 2007, Quebec's minority Liberal government set up a commission on 'reasonable accommodation' to look at the role of minority cultures and the individual in Quebec's society. Issues were raised around Jewish and Muslim diets, headscarves and the Sikh 'kirpan' as well as blood transfusions and honour killings. The term 'reasonable' features prominently in the 1982 Canadian Charter of Rights and Freedoms, primarily in describing government limitation. In unicultural Quebec, the issue was raised in terms of maintaining and defending the rights of individuals and principles considered essential in modern Quebec society. Unsurprisingly, the discussions revealed simmering issues of intolerance, including Quebec's long history of anti-Semitism. Conversely, the discussion brought light to issues that have proven important in Britain and Europe about the role of Islam and the rights of women in Western society. Such discussion would be hard to imagine in multicultural Ontario or BC and only time will tell which model of social development will prove more effective in maintaining social cohesion and individual rights.

Quebec is the only province in Canada where discussion of assimilation is as overt as in Europe. For many from the UK, Canada's diversity often comes as a surprise as does the reality that, overall, the modern face of Canadian society is quite cohesive. The reasons for this are many: space, economics and a culture of immigration – or the general lack of a sense of entitlement. As Canada continues to change, issues will certainly arise, as they logically will during harder economic times. A reality of the mosaic model can be a form of elective ghettoisation, where cultures can maintain much of their identity, including at times aspects that do not fit with Canadian ideas of individual rights.

Immigration in Quebec

The government of Quebec, with the agreement of the Canadian government, can approve skilled-worker immigration to that province without requiring the worker to go through the points system. In order to qualify through Quebec, you must meet Quebec's needs (*Est-ce que vous parlez français?*). Opting for this route means applying for a Quebec Certificate of Acceptance, before dealing with the national bureaucracy.

The Quebec immigration page is **www.immigration-quebec.gouv.qc.ca**.

On Arrival

Once you are legally in the country, you must follow a few more steps before you have satisfied fully all the requirements and are ready to work. These steps are not too arduous, but are required legally. For information about healthcare, social services and welfare, *see* Chapter 06, **Living in Canada**.

Get a Social Insurance Number

The social insurance number (**SIN**) is a nine-digit identification number that, once assigned, remains with citizens or permanent residents for life. It is issued for tax purposes, employment insurance (which provides income to a worker who later becomes unemployed), government pensions and other government services. You need to supply this number to your employer and to those providing banking and other financial services. Visitors with temporary visas receive a number that begins with a 9; it will have an expiry date.

On arrival in Canada you should be given the necessary SIN application paperwork. If not, you can get the forms from a local government office, post office, or online (**www.sdc.gc.ca**). As only original documents can be used as proof of visa status, it is worth applying in person if at all possible. There are government offices in most cities, which can be tracked down either through the above website or by looking in the government blue pages at the front of the local telephone book. Should you choose to apply by mail, you will have to send all original supporting documentation (permanent resident card, landing papers, passport, and so on). When the SIN card is mailed back, all personal documents will also be returned to you, but the government office takes no responsibility for the documents. Send applications to **Social Insurance Registration**, PO Box 7000, Bathurst, New Brunswick E2A 4T1.

For first-time applicants there is no fee for a SIN card. The government assumes nothing remains after you have paid all the other immigration costs. Replacement cards incur a nominal C$10 fee. Because your social insurance number can be used fraudulently if it falls into the wrong hands, it is important to take care of the card and to report its loss or theft. Although the number is required for employment, banking and government services, it does not need to be shown for purchases or other daily transactions.

Get a Permanent Resident Card

Canada introduced these identity cards at the end of 2003 in response to 9/11. Nevertheless, Canada, along with Britain, Ireland and the USA, does not require citizens to carry identity cards with them at all times. While permanent residents do not need to have the cards on hand constantly, they will need them whenever they leave Canada. Without the card, returning residents may run the risk of not being permitted to board flights to Canada.

New residents receive a card automatically when residency is granted, but permanent residents already in Canada must apply for the card. The process takes several months and costs C$50. For information about the permanent resident card, visit **www.cic.gc.ca/english/pr-card/index.html**.

Professional Organisations

Specific professional bodies in Canada govern the various professions at federal and provincial levels. Healthcare, teaching and engineering organisations maintain their own professional standards and take responsibility for examinations and their certification process. If you intend to work in one of these fields, it is essential that you research the qualification process before you arrive in Canada. Fortunately, Canada usually accepts the qualifications of most British professionals. Even moving within Canada can be bureaucratic: provincial regulations differ and if, for example, you are required to show academic records, you need to produce originals and not copies of those used for immigration purposes. This is also true of police reports and work history.

Useful Addresses

For Canadian High Commission and embassy addresses in the UK, *see* p.260.

- **British High Commission in Canada**, British High Commission, 80 Elgin Street, Ottawa, Ontario K1P 5K7, **t** (613) 237 1530, **generalenquiries@ britainincanada.org, www.britishhighcommission.gov.uk,** or Google "Britain in Canada".

- **British Consulate-General in Toronto**, 777 Bay Street, Suite 2800, Toronto, Ontario M5G 2G2, **t** (416) 593 1290, **f** (416) 593 1229, **toronto@britain incanada.org**.

- **British Consulate-General in Montreal**, 1000 De La Gauchetière Street West, Suite 4200, Montreal, Quebec H3B 4W5, **t** (514) 866 5863, **f** (514) 866 0202, **montreal@britainincanada.org**.

- **British Consulate-General in Vancouver**, 1111 Melville Street, Suite 800, Vancouver, British Columbia V6E 3V6, **t** (604) 683 4421, **f** (604) 681 0693, **vancouver@britainincanada.org**.

- **Trade Office in Calgary**, Suite 700, 205 5th Ave SW, Calgary, Alberta T2P 2V7, **t** (403) 705 1755 , **f** (403) 538 0121, **calgary@britainincanada.org**.

- **Embassy of Ireland**, 130 Albert St, Ottawa, Ontario K1P 5G4, **t** (613) 233 6281.

- **Honorary Consulate, Quebec City**, British Consulate, Le Complexe St-Amable, 700-1150 Claire-Fontaine, Quebec City, Quebec G1R 5G4, **t** (418) 521 3000, **f** (418) 521 3099.

Living in Canada

Finding a Home

Buying

Canadians love their houses and place a high value on home ownership. It is estimated that 70 per cent of Canadians own their homes. Even Francophone Quebecers are bucking that province's tradition and have begun to buy, instead of renting. The ability to own land and a home is fundamental to the New World ideal, and this has long been one of the great attractions of North America.

When compared to similar urban markets, Canadian housing is quite affordable, but prices are rising. Vancouver is expensive by most people's standards, but alongside comparable international cities such as Sydney or San Francisco, Vancouver prices seem more reasonable. Unlike homeowners in the United States, Canadians cannot write off mortgage interest against tax but, on the other hand, Canadians pay no tax on capital gains when they sell their primary residence.

As long as you have patience, funds and a few ideas, finding a home in Canada can be an enjoyable experience. Homes across the country are extremely varied in style and location, but where you decide to live is as important as the sort of home you choose. Many people in Britain can only dream of owning a home that sits on a few acres of land, whereas you can achieve such a dream in many parts of Canada.

Cities have 'better' and 'worse' areas in terms of property values and ease of getting to work, but rarely does an area represent a threat to personal safety. Choosing a neighbourhood in which to live involves evaluating services, lifestyle and proximity to work and friends, as much as image and value. Expansive cities result in long drives and commuting times must always be considered. Except around Toronto, roads are not as clogged as in Britain, but winter driving can sometimes be hazardous and distances staggering. Weather and bridges also have an effect, especially for those driving at peak times in Montreal and Vancouver. Canadians think little of driving long distances, but the old real estate rule of location, location, location still applies.

Although a home in Canada may not always be an investment, cost governs any decision to buy. Property is regional by nature, and local economies and prices vary substantially. Within the confines of a real estate region, most middle-class accommodation falls within a predictable price range. Modernity or character can add value to property and define the neighbourhood. Vancouver's ultra-modern glass towers rank among the most expensive dwellings in Canada, whereas established neighbourhoods in other cities can represent better value for money. Suburbia dominates most Canadian communities and, as a result, services have spread outwards and rendered city centres less convenient for basic shopping. With families in older areas ageing, and property values increasing, younger families have migrated further out and bought newer, more modern homes. Facilities, such as schools, have followed.

An interesting trend back towards the centre of cities is slowly taking place, with apartment and townhouse construction increasing in those areas. Traditionally, apartments have been associated with renting; however, their new incarnation as condominiums, or condos, along with either price or location competitiveness, has encouraged movement towards higher-density living. Overall Canadians still opt for private, detached houses, but traffic volumes and smaller families are creating a shift in the market. Central Toronto and Montreal have numerous new high-density developments and, as older row houses are fixed up, their values increase. Even in booming suburban Alberta, higher-density developments are creeping into central Calgary and Edmonton and attracting life and services into the once extremely quiet city cores.

The Housing Market

The last decade has been good for the construction industry. House construction has boomed and prices have shot up in many regions of the country. Low interest rates and a strong economy have resulted in capital flowing into property. Greater Vancouver, which experienced a lull after the Hong Kong investment boom subsided, has again witnessed substantial price increases, with Vancouver claiming the highest average house prices – detached houses in desirable areas easily top C$1 million. Continuing through 2007 there were double-digit price rises in booming western markets, while Toronto has seen a modest decline in some areas. In February 2008, the national average for a home was around C$313,000, or roughly £155,000. These are some of the average city or provincial house prices in 2008:

- **Calgary: C$415,017**
- **Edmonton: C$338,347**
- **Halifax: C$223,579**
- **Manitoba: C$173,809**
- **Montreal: C$315,358 (older data)**
- **New Brunswick: C$143,207**
- **Newfoundland: C$151,244**
- **Ottawa: C$283,199**
- **Prince Edward Island: C$131,594**
- **Saskatchewan: C$209,702**
- **Toronto: C$382,048**
- **Vancouver: C$623,517**
- **Victoria: C$487,696**

Source: Canadian Real Estate Association, 2008 (**www.crea.ca**)

These figures include condominiums, bungalows and two-storey houses. Within each category, prices vary. Average condo prices are lower than house prices. Economic uncertainty in the United States will affect the Canadian economy, but a housing deficit in some markets and lower interest rates should continue to encourage the market.

Average house prices are important, but so is the ability to pay, whatever the cost. A Royal Bank of Canada study released in March 2008 reports that housing affordability in Canada is at its lowest since 1990. As opposed to recession and the high interest rates of the late 1980s, current affordability has been eroded by steadily increasing house values. Alberta's extremely hot market has begun to soften, but Vancouver, already the most expensive city, expects to see continued price increases. Vancouverites currently spend nearly 70 per cent of their income on home ownership costs as opposed to around 40 per cent in Saskatchewan, though this has increased from below 30 per cent in under two years. To the east, affordability is 30–35 per cent of household income.

Types of Homes

The 'average' Canadian home is very different from that in Britain. Unattached dwellings are far more common than terraces and most domestic properties come with some yard (garden) area. Needless to say, climate has dictated construction styles since the arrival of the first settlers and insulation is essential. Except where rock or high-water levels prevent digging, Canadian homes are usually built with basements. Building codes are provincial, but, in general, foundations must descend below the winter frost line. For most houses this means **foundations** that are at least four feet below ground level and, more typically, as much as 8–10 feet deep. This type of construction prevents the frost heaves associated with the freeze and thaw of the seasons. **Basement space** created by the deep foundations can virtually double the size of a house, so that a typical Canadian bungalow will have as much floor space underground as it has at ground level. Basement areas obviously have limited natural light, but small windows allow some connection to the outside world.

Almost all homes have **central heating**, **double- or triple-pane windows** and various forms of **insulation**. Canadians tend to keep their homes warm and, in addition to furnace heating, some houses feature under-floor heating and even **air-conditioning** for use during the hot summer months. Wood-burning fireplaces, installed for their appearance rather than for utilitarian purposes, are still common, but are gradually giving way to gas – not quite the same ambiance, but much cleaner. The only simple, non-insulated properties are found in a few of the warmer parts of British Columbia or as cottages that the owners use less frequently during winter.

Construction in the far north is unique, if not terribly attractive, as climate dictates that most **services**, including water and sewerage, are located above ground. Permafrost makes digging difficult and the melt caused by warming can destroy foundations. Water is pumped continuously through pipes to prevent them from freezing and houses are built propped above ground level to protect the ice layer. Foundations shift as the ground warms and moves, and northerners grow accustomed to their doors sticking each spring.

Different **regions** of the country have reasonably distinct styles of architecture. In very general terms, brick has been used most extensively in central Canada, whereas western and Atlantic Canadian homes are framed in wood. Wood-framed houses are less substantial than those of brick but wood framing allows the addition of good insulating materials and opens the way to interesting architectural designs. Housing in Montreal, Toronto and other eastern cities includes rows of classic Georgian-Victorian red and grey brick houses, but in the west only the Gastown section of Vancouver features that style. Ontario's thousands of working-class bungalows have evolved from the row house style and tend to be brick one- and two-storey homes built during and since the 1950s. Loyalist houses, similar to the large wooden structures of New England, are also found in the east.

Quebec contains a predictable mix of styles. Typical French mansard roofs cap Victorian bay windows. The oldest country homes reflect the province's roots in Normandy and Brittany. Roofs in Quebec City and other parts of the east are equipped with ladders so that, during winter, home-owners can climb up and chip off the ice. A country style of house, constructed mostly of wood and developed in Quebec, is aptly named the Québécoise. Scottish brick, used as ballast in ships sailing from Europe to pick up cargoes of lumber, is found in many buildings.

British Columbia has the greatest range of architectural styles. A milder coastal climate and an artistic culture have contributed to the construction of some very interesting homes. Beautiful log cabins are found throughout the interior of British Columbia, as are the most basic of prefabricated units used to provide 'instant housing' for residents of mining and lumber towns. It is not unusual in any part of Canada to see a house transported on the back of a large truck. Drainage is very important in this high-rainfall area.

House sizes have increased in recent years, no doubt keeping pace with growing waistlines and wealth. In prosperous, high-growth parts of the country new subdivisions have developed at a staggering pace and, while these areas may look desperately sterile, trees will grow and community-centred services will develop. As many families own two or more cars, the majority of new houses include double or even triple garages. Density and a lack of space limit this feature in central Vancouver, Toronto and Montreal, but most apartments include one underground parking space.

A large **garage** may seem a little excessive over summer, but after one winter of scraping ice from windscreens most Canadians appreciate the protection that a garage provides. Integrated into most new homes, these car-sheltering structures often dominate the front of a property. House measurements do not include the attached garage space.

Modern neighbourhoods cater to the vehicle culture. Older parts of cities frequently feature back alleys, which provide access to external garages, but most new areas do not include alleys. Garages in these areas are at the front of the house and face the street. Developers use the land gained by the elimination of alleys to extend back gardens or cram in more houses. Almost all neighbourhoods include some parkland, along with schools and shopping areas. Public transport in the form of buses arrives quite quickly to new housing developments, but few have a rail service.

External styles of housing are changing, but the basic ideal of two or three bedrooms, a kitchen, multiple bathrooms (at least two) and a basement has remained fairly constant. Space allows for large, modern appliances and most homes have a washing machine and a clothes dryer (wet washing freezes outside in the winter). Tile and hardwood flooring is slowly replacing more functional surfaces and granite counters have become popular in more expensive kitchens. Not everyone chooses to move into new developments; many prefer to purchase older homes in more convenient locations. Less time and money spent on commuting can compensate for the expenses involved in upgrading an older-area house. In looking for a home, external appearance is important, but the inside is what really counts.

The Process of Buying and Selling Homes

Some Canadians move often; work, needs and profit keep the housing market busy and, as long as the money is there, changing homes is not very difficult. The vast majority of house purchases and sales happen with the help of (and pressure from) a real estate agent. If buying while still in the UK or soon after arrival in Canada, you will almost certainly require the services of an agent. The help they offer should compensate somewhat for what seem to be exorbitant fees. On the upside, buyers do not feel the pinch quite as strongly because sellers pay the commissions (which will be included in the price).

The basic steps when purchasing property in Canada include deciding where you want to live and what you can afford, securing financing (if required), researching homes, contacting an agent, looking, looking, looking, making an offer (with possession dates and any special requests or provisions), running everything through a lawyer and finally moving in. None of this differs very much from the UK and it can happen extremely quickly if wanted. If the property is under construction, as many currently are, expect delays. If the home is new, the federal goods and services tax (5 per cent) must be paid. Some provinces levy an additional tax of 1 or 2 per cent.

Estate Agents

Cities are large, so you may use the real estate agent as a guide to areas, general values and desirable neighbourhoods, but you should have at least some idea about where you may want to live. To this end, consider renting for the first six months or year (*see* p.163) in order to become better acquainted with the community. The Internet has become an outstanding source of information and allows you to research properties, contact an agent and view pictures of homes – all from a great distance. Perhaps the most useful site is the national **Multiple Listing Service** (**MLS**; **www.mls.ca**). Although this site does not contain every house for sale in the country, it is extensive and there is no pressure in just looking. MLS also offers advice on buying, selling and contacting agents.

Real estate agencies, as with so much else in Canada, fall under provincial jurisdiction, and the business is further broken down to a local board level. From a consumer's point of view, services are virtually the same across the country. Quebec's estate agents operate in a slightly different manner, in part because of that province's different legal system.

The national body representing the vast majority of agents is the **Canadian Real Estate Association** (**CREA**; **www.crea.ca**). CREA's mandate is to represent the industry nationally, but it also owns the MLS trademark and manages the largest listing service. The website provides an interesting breakdown of average prices in the various markets. Use CREA's site to find information on local real estate boards and to gain a better understanding of fees, rights and obligations. CREA also runs a website for commercial properties at **www.icx.ca**. Essentially, realtors are governed by local rules and the consumer has some recourse through the provincial boards. Alberta is the only province with a self-governing real estate board. All other provinces administer their own real estate boards, although some may ultimately adopt the Alberta model.

Realtors are required by their profession and by law to pass a written examination, usually after completion of a course of study that ranges from three months to one year. Realtors are salespeople who are obliged to represent their clients. They must disclose who they represent, which is relevant because realtors are permitted to represent both the purchaser and the seller in a transaction – great news for the realtor, who then keeps the entire commission. From either a buyer's or seller's point of view, a realtor should be an advocate for acquiring the best possible price. Agents who represent both parties may choose to abrogate any role in price negotiation and simply present offers and counter-offers.

In addition to negotiating sales and taking care of most of the piles of paperwork, a real estate agent should offer you current, solid advice on the local market, discuss your needs and organise viewings. Although their role is governed by law, realtors are not lawyers or notaries (who may replace a lawyer for real estate transactions in some provinces). They fill a front-end function – advertising, guiding and negotiating. Keep in mind that a realtor is almost always keen to complete the transaction, so expect enthusiastic support for the finalising of any deal.

Another important fact to keep in mind is that realtor fees are not set in stone and are negotiable. This does not mean they are happy to negotiate, and some present their fees as an absolute. As a general rule, realtors in Canada use a '7/3' fee structure – 7 per cent on the first C$100,000, and 3 per cent on everything else. Therefore, the sale of a house for C$300,000 (the national average) requires the seller to pay C$13,000 in real estate fees. Realtors divide the money earned between the buyer's and the seller's agents. Although a percentage may go the realtor's team or office, the proceeds pay for advertising, professional dues and whatever other costs are incurred. Some realtors now work on a 6/3 fee schedule while others have moved to a flat 5 per cent fee. All of this is negotiable and competition is increasing. When selling, ask your realtor what other incentives she or he may offer to increase traffic.

British Columbia and Alberta realtors now face competition from a **One Percent Realty** firm (**www.onepercentrealty.com**). The cost structure is not that simple, because the company charges a C$5,000 minimum and the seller covers advertising costs. But with listings on MLS and other local listing ser-vices, properties still enjoy broad publicity. It is difficult to assess whether other agents steer their clients away from homes listed through One Percent Realty.

Either way, if you list a home for sale with an agent, you will be locked into that arrangement for some period of time (usually around 90 days). If the property does not sell in that period, you can choose to list the home with another agent, pull it from the market, or try and sell it by yourself. When buying, you may well choose to contract a realtor as your agent or simply call realtors representing properties for sale. Increasingly, realtors are asking buyers to sign some sort of agreement, but, if you don't, you are under no obligation to any one person. The purchaser, who is the driver of any deal, may feel more comfortable developing a relationship with an individual realtor. As the buyer, you are paying the commission by way of the purchase price, but you do not pay any fees directly. If a property is listed with an agent, you may as well enjoy the service.

Although a good agent should guide you through the entire process, you, as the buyer, have the responsibility to conduct some individual research and understand what you want and can afford. It is easy to ask someone to show you around million-dollar homes, but if your budget limits you to a quarter of that price, the commission-based realtor will go hungry. An agent's usefulness centres on helping you gain access to properties, communicating with other realtors and creating several degrees of separation from the seller.

Selling Privately

More and more homeowners are dispensing with the services of agents as they try to sell privately. This is not as simple as it sounds, but it may be worth the effort. With a private sale, the buyer and seller hope to save thousands by coming to a mutual agreement on price and by filing paperwork themselves. There is really no way to avoid involving either a lawyer or notary in the process, however, unless you have a very thorough understanding of the entire process.

A small but important percentage of properties in Canada are sold privately. Traditional real estate agents can present a myriad reasons as to why one should not go this route, but the strongest argument against it has long been the difficulty of bringing together buyers and sellers. With realtors listing around 80 per cent of Canadian homes, their network clearly remains the largest. Furthermore, as some property transactions take place over long distances (from the UK for example), the process of connecting with lawyers, mortgage brokers and home inspection services can be daunting. Also, some private sellers simply put out a sign at the front of their house, which eliminates any potential buyer who lives thousands of kilometres away.

The Internet has facilitated private selling by creating an affordable and efficient way to bring together the two parties. Numerous listing services now exist in Canada (be careful not to end up on a US site) and all of them claim to be doing fantastic business. When purchasing your first property in Canada, you may decide to check out some of these sites. If you are already in Canada, pursuing this course may be comparatively easy, but, if you are still in the UK, make sure that you have all the finances organised and have obtained the services of a lawyer within the provincial jurisdiction before you purchase privately. A few of the sites advertising private sales include:

- **www.bchomesellers.com**
- **www.bytheowner.com**
- **www.canadahomesforsale.ca**
- **www.forsalebyowner.ca**
- **www.forsalebyownercanada.ca** or **www.fsboc.com**
- **www.homesell.com**
- **www.welist.com**

The presence of many more websites than these leads one to wonder how much further an already small portion of the market can be divided. If you choose to purchase privately it is still recommended that you look closely at similarly priced residences in the area. People selling privately hope to save the commissions but rarely want to list for less. For the buyer, the final cost may well be the same while the seller may find that the property takes much longer to sell, which incurs other maintenance costs.

Negotiating

Negotiating is an important element of the entire real estate market. If realtors had complete control over the market, most would choose to price properties so that they would sell for the list price as quickly as possible. In reality, most sellers hope to make as much money as possible and most buyers want to save a little, so some back-and-forth bargaining can be expected. Negotiable items include price, possession dates and even finishing. In Canada, the seller generally keeps all chattels – things that are movable, whereas fixed items, including appliances, remain in the sold house. Window coverings, microwaves, built-to-fit furniture and similar items may or may not stay.

If you are in the market for a new property, particularly one at the planning stage or under construction, there may be less room to haggle on price, but the buyer may be able to make structural changes or upgrade furnishings. New or used, the market is driven by current trends. Recent years have favoured sellers in many regions as house buyers offered bids above the original list price. The market has generally avoided the frenzied buying seen in other countries.

Lawyers' Fees

Either before or during the offer to buy, you should have a lawyer lined up. As part of your offer you will be expected to pay a token sum as evidence of good faith (the amount varies according to the offer). These funds go into a trust until the offer is finalised. If you should withdraw your final offer for any reason not listed as a condition, you could lose this money. This sum will be added to your down-payment. The ability to secure financing is commonly listed as a condition of purchase and may be an easy way to withdraw from a transaction. Other conditions include the results of the home inspection, a title search (proof the sellers own the home) and anything else agreed to by both parties.

In addition to other expenses, your costs include lawyer's fees. While those costs may seem extraordinarily high for a relatively common purchase, the fees charged should cover several items, including the title transfer. Basic lawyer's fees range from C$400 to C$500, and you can expect to pay another C$500 to C$800 in additional costs that your lawyer will manage. Notaries are a little less expensive, but operate in only a few jurisdictions. Your realtor should provide you with all this information.

After you have found a home, agreed on a price, secured a mortgage, contracted a lawyer and made the realtor very happy, the process of taking possession can be quite efficient. The lawyer should make sure all the funds are transferred at appropriate times and will supply you with countless papers to sign – often only in black ink. The standard advice is to read every document, but a good lawyer should go through these documents with you.

Home Inspection

Unless the seller can provide a current report, the buyer is almost always advised to engage the services of a home inspection company. In British Columbia the structural assessment may evaluate the risk of leaks or the stability of the land. Often, the buyer may include a statement making the offer to purchase subject to the results of the home inspection. If an inspector indicates that significant structural work (over C$2,000) is needed, the deal may be forfeited or rewritten. Inspections cost several hundred dollars, but are worth the expense. When contacting an inspection service, find out what the company inspects, as some do not test appliances or look at a building's structure. An inspection of your own home from time to time may be useful in order to gauge its state and that of its constituent parts, such as the furnace and expensive appliances.

Mortgages

Benefiting from the worldwide decline in interest rates, Canadians are now more indebted than ever before. Interest rates took a nosedive after 9/11 and are once again falling with the sub-prime crisis in the USA, although banks are tightening their lending requirements. Recent increases in the value of the Canadian dollar against the US greenback have encouraged the Bank of Canada to lower rates, despite a strong domestic economy. Low rates, along with unstable stock markets, have encouraged borrowing for real estate. Canadians, like the British, now find themselves with more expensive homes and record levels of debt, but because of this debt the Central Bank is loath to drive rates up quickly, so people continue to borrow to buy increasingly expensive homes.

If you are working – and therefore already established in Canada – and have a solid down-payment, it is not very difficult to secure a mortgage. Mortgage brokers will help you find the best deal and the lending institution will often pay the broker's commission. Another option is to saunter into any bank and ask to talk to someone about mortgages. Although banking ranks as one of Canada's largest industries, bank employees are relaxed and friendly and will take the time to discuss your needs.

Banks or other lending institutions will lend up to 75 per cent of the value of the property you intend to purchase. So, once you have established the maximum amount that the bank is willing to let you borrow, you are pre-approved and can look for homes up to that value. The figure that banks generally use for mortgage affordability is 32 per cent of household income. This means that household expenses should not exceed more than one-third of the pre-tax income generated by the individual or couple who intend to buy, although allowances are made in expensive markets such as Vancouver. People in a salaried position, with three years of tax returns, pay slips and good credit, qualify easily. The 20 per cent down-payment offsets what little risk there is for the bank. The situation becomes more complicated for immigrants, seasonal workers, the self-employed and those without the 20 per cent deposit.

It should not be too difficult for anyone coming from the UK to secure a mortgage provided you can prove current employment in Canada and demonstrate a history of gainful employment in the UK. Make sure you maintain your UK bank accounts and credit cards, otherwise you may have to start developing a credit rating all over again. The larger the down-payment, the easier it will be to secure a mortgage. You may even be able to obtain a mortgage to start a business (for example, to purchase a hotel). Banks are interested in your ability to repay, and if you can demonstrate financial stability the banker may be willing to display generosity when it comes to interpreting financial statements.

Acquiring a first mortgage is often the most difficult part of the process and for young Canadians, or Canadians in more marginal situations, saving for the 20 per cent down-payment can be almost impossible. This comes as no surprise to many residents of the UK and Ireland who often wonder how young people can possibly get into a first home. Although 100 per cent mortgages have existed for years in the UK and from 2008 are now in fact becoming limited, they are new to Canadians, who have generally put at least 5 per cent down. A mortgage-loan-insurance provider then guarantees the gap between 5 per cent and the required 20 per cent. The best-known provider in Canada is the **Canada Mortgage and Housing Corporation** (**CMHC**; **www.cmhc.ca**). This crown corporation's original purpose was to help with Depression and wartime housing shortages. In the 1950s the programme expanded to 'help Canadians access a wide choice of quality, affordable homes, while making vibrant, healthy communities and cities a reality across the country'. The mortgage broker or banker will apply for CMHC support (or a guarantee from another institution) on your behalf. Fees apply but they are added to the mortgage and are not expected up-front – which is really the point of a mortgage in the first place.

Another option that may be available for people with mortgage difficulties is to assume an already existing mortgage. This could be a useful alternative if you are not short of cash but the banks won't lend you the money because you lack employment status or credit history. In assuming a mortgage, you take on the seller's debt and pay out the equity. This option becomes even more enticing if the seller is willing to incur the fees or if the original mortgage has an excellent rate of interest.

A wide variety of mortgages is available, and banks spend great sums telling the public that they have the right product for every individual. There are 'cash-back' plans, air miles plans, fixed rates, variable rates and plain old bad rates. During the last few years some variable-rate mortgages have had an interest rate below prime. Recently the flexibility in mortgage rates has decreased and major banks are only reluctantly lowering rates in line with the national prime rate. Interest on fixed-rate mortgages depends on the length of the term and can be several points above prime. *See* 'Money and Banking', p.177, for a list of Canada's major financial institutions.

While mortgage terms vary, banks use 25 years as the base for the overall length of a mortgage. Contracted terms with a bank can run between six months and 10 years and must be renegotiated on maturity. Locked-in periods guarantee rates and/or cost, but incur fees if the property is sold prematurely. The fee is usually equivalent to three months' interest. Locked-in terms also limit the holder's ability to pay off the mortgage too quickly. Be aware that open mortgages exist, particularly among variable-rate mortgages, and they allow you to increase payments and sell with no restrictions. The two catches are interest-rate fluctuations (which can also help) and fixed monthly payments – your rate may be 5 per cent, but your monthly cost could be equivalent to 7 or 8 per cent. The extra money is applied to the principal.

Mortgage interest cannot be written off against tax in Canada unless the property is an investment, in which case tax is paid on the income generated. You owe no tax when you sell your primary residence, but capital gains on investment properties are taxable. You will pay a sales tax when you buy a new home, and all home-owners pay municipal (or council) taxes.

Renting

Most Canadians would rather own than rent, and even in Quebec, where the ownership sentiment has traditionally been weaker, there is still a move towards purchasing a home. Statistics indicate that 70 to 80 per cent of Canadians rate owning a home as their highest investment priority. Culturally, Canadians value home-ownership. That noted, renting may sometimes be the best option, and a few brave souls continue to argue that their money is best invested elsewhere. Of course, buying requires that you have the money and stability to do so and, while a strong push towards the purchasing of both primary residences and investment properties has driven prices up, rental costs have not risen as dramatically. Many investors have bought properties to rent, but with more home-owners than ever before, rental vacancies are on the rise. Nearly 5 per cent of the rental properties in Greater Toronto are currently vacant – a figure that was less than 1 per cent a few years ago. This trend applies to most parts of the country other than Quebec.

More apartments than houses are available for rent, although basement suites are common, particularly around universities and colleges. Rents are almost always calculated monthly and therefore are paid in 12 **instalments**. As a result, February is the most expensive month on a cost-per-day analysis but, overall, renters do better paying by the month, rather than weekly.

Average **rental rates** in Canada tend to hover around C$1,200 (£600) per month. As with all averages, this figure is not particularly revealing, but it demonstrates what you can expect to pay for a two-bedroom flat in urban Canada. Furnished or executive suites can cost three times that price, and basic rooms or basements in shared houses cost considerably less. Central Vancouver's rates are high, in line with property values. A one-bedroom flat with a water view will cost more than C$1,500 per month and a two-bedroom apartment at least C$2,000 monthly.

Before you rent, establish whether the rental cost includes **utilities**. There is no fixed rule, but generally large, managed buildings include heat and electricity in the price, whereas privately owned units may not.

Most rental agreements require you to sign a contract stating that you will stay for a **fixed length of time**. Proprietors always prefer a year, but six-month contracts are common. Generally at the end of the term the contract automatically shifts to month by month and the owner may raise the rental price. Thirty days' notice before vacating a property is standard and the renter must ensure the place is thoroughly cleaned and the carpets shampooed.

A **damage deposit** of between 50 and 100 per cent of one month's rent is generally required at the time of signing. This deposit will be returned when you leave, subject to a property inspection. Each province has specific rules that govern renting, and **rental contracts** can be downloaded from the Internet. It is always worth signing a contract to limit the risk of conflicts. Tenants must maintain the property in good condition and adhere to bylaws and other specific rules. For their part, landlords are responsible for maintenance and structural upkeep.

When looking for a place to rent, the **local newspaper** is the best place to start. Buy a local map and phone a few places. This old-fashioned method should be comparatively efficient. **Rental agencies** exist, but not to the same extent as in the UK. The good news is that the owner usually pays the fees when you rent through an agency. Most cities have large, privately owned buildings dedicated to rentals. All have offices and it is easy to telephone and find out about availability. The phone call route also applies to private residences, although it may be easier to find larger, furnished houses through an agency.

In order to rent, you will usually be asked for **proof of finances** – pay slips, money in the bank and/or a credit check. Make sure you have the damage deposit and the first month's rent. You may also be asked to provide **personal references**, although those in the UK are not likely to be contacted. As a broad generalisation, British (or Irish) nationality will work in your favour in such relationships. The exception could be around ski resort areas (Banff, Whistler) where the robust Commonwealth culture, with extensive partying and other activities, is not conducive to good home maintenance.

Home Insurance

It is essential that you insure your household contents and your home itself. After obscene increases following 9/11, prices have now become more realistic.

If you buy or rent an apartment or condominium, a group plan will probably cover the insurance on your unit's exterior, but not your personal belongings. In rare circumstances, townhouse units may be individually insured as 'bare land condos', which creates a far more complicated situation and is therefore generally avoided. Houses should be insured inside and out, as well as covered for specific threats where necessary. **Earthquake insurance**, for example, is essential around Vancouver. In some areas, owners should consider taking out flood insurance.

Basic household insurance usually covers damage from fire and other causes. Contents insurance usually covers belongings up to a certain value and you may purchase household and contents insurance as a package. People will often buy coverage of C$25,000, C$50,000, or even C$100,000, in case of theft or loss. Rates vary according to location, security (a discount may apply if you have an alarm system), goods and the market. To avoid possible disputes later, it is worth photographing valuable items such as jewellery. If such possessions should be lost, you may need an appraisal certificate in order to recoup the entire value.

The insurance industry is massive and plans are written with profits in mind. It is, therefore, extremely important to understand a policy's exclusions, the deductible (the original sum they will not pay) and the effect a claim will have on rates.

Home Utilities and Services

Needless to say, once you have bought or rented a place, you will incur numerous additional and ongoing costs. Utility costs are generally reasonably priced in Canada by world standards, but the furnace will run 24 hours a day during long, cold winters. Furnaces should be cleaned every two or three years.

Although home utilities may seem complicated when viewed nationally, in reality they are rather straightforward, as each jurisdiction operates with limited competition. Most utilities at one time were provincial Crown corporations, but many have now been sold, separated or chopped up into various different companies. Some companies focus more on utility distribution, while others deal with the production side.

Led by Alberta and Ontario, the Canadian utilities sector has undergone partial deregulation. The desperate power blackouts experienced in California, cost overruns in other parts of the USA and the Enron scandal have tested the public's interest in privatisation. Nonetheless, the utility industry has permitted competition, which includes some involvement by provincial and municipal interests. For example, EPCOR, a corporation owned by the City of Edmonton, is one of Alberta's primary producers and distributors of gas, electricity and water. Hydro-Quebec ranks as one of the largest Crown corporations in the country and one of the world's largest hydroelectric energy producers.

From a consumer's point of view, most people will use the service provider already connected to their property until such time as a much better deal presents itself. Utility industries rely on the existing infrastructure, so, no matter what name appears on the bill, the electricity, gas or water will continue to travel to your home through the original channel. When buying a property, you will probably continue with the service that is already in place. New developments usually make some provision for utility infrastructure.

Electricity

Hydroelectric production is a disproportionately large contributor to electricity production in Canada, contributing about 60 per cent of total manufactured electricity. Hydro dominates in Quebec, British Columbia and Manitoba and remains important in Ontario. Fossil fuels (coal) are widely used elsewhere to power steam turbines and are of significant importance to heavy industry in Alberta. Nuclear power, used widely in Ontario, may slowly be returning to favour.

Although electricity is not usually the principal source of heat in Canadian homes, it is used in some large buildings and in warmer climates, such as Vancouver, where constant, regulated heat is not as necessary. As in Britain, electricity powers appliances, lights, computers and so forth, but at a lower voltage. Canada's system operates at 110 volts – enough for a good shock, but rarely death. British hairdryers and toasters will generally not work so are not even worth bringing. Canadian ones will burn out in Britain.

Sockets accept either a two- or a three-pronged plug and have no on/off switch as in the UK. Generally, Canadians worry far less than the British about leaving lights on and equipment running. In winter, heating systems run 24 hours a day and lights often stay on. Even large business towers will leave lights on through the night, although this practice is gradually losing support.

Should you wish to delve into the intricacies of the Canadian electrical industry, visit the website for the **Canadian Electricity Association** at **www. canelect.ca**. Local services vary throughout the country.

Natural Gas

Most Canadians use natural gas to heat their houses. Electricity comes second and oil is used in some homes, particularly in the north. Canada's natural gas reserves are massive and new sources continue to be discovered. Gas is not widely used for home cooking but it is the main fuel source for furnaces.

The overwhelming majority of Canadian homes have furnace systems and even many large buildings use boilers for heating. Homes are well insulated, with furnace ducts routed throughout the structure. Generally, furnaces are located in house basements and should be serviced from time to time. Hot-water tanks, holding anywhere from 45 to 100 gallons of water and set to maintain the water at a regular temperature, are also heated by gas. If you run a bath, shower and dishwasher all at the same time, it is possible to use up the hot water and then have to wait for the tank to reheat. In homes with a simpler plumbing system, turning on two or more taps at the same time will interrupt flow – and a shower can become scalding hot if cold water is run elsewhere in the house. A less dangerous situation occurs when a hot tap siphons warm water from the shower.

Gas fireplaces have become common, replacing traditional wood fires. The burning of wood is not banned, but is losing favour because of cost. Coal fires are almost never seen. Although gas fires are more ornamental than practical, fireplaces with a built-in fan can generate a good amount of heat (but that uses both gas and electricity).

If you found reading about the electrical industry fascinating, you may want to move on to the site for the **Canadian Gas Association** (**www.cga.ca**). As with electricity providers, local delivery varies from province to province and within each province.

Air-conditioning

One of the coldest countries on earth also has very hot summers, and in the humid central regions many homes and most hotel rooms use built-in air conditioners. Although cooling systems feature less prominently in the west and in the Atlantic provinces, their popularity is increasing. Toronto, Montreal and Winnipeg can swelter through temperatures that climb above 40°C. The heat on its own can be oppressive, but humidity takes the greatest toll.

Further west, southern Alberta experiences almost no humidity and the heat and cold become much more tolerable. The old prairie joke states 'It's a dry cold', which somehow makes minus 30°C more bearable. To combat stinging eyes and cracking skin, Albertans use great quantities of 'artificial tears' and moisturiser. Upper-end homes have humidifiers installed with the heating system. Another alternative involves placing small portable humidifiers in various rooms or even boiling water on the stove.

Heating Costs and Billing

The cost of basic heating depends on a number of factors but overall is not terribly expensive. Recent spikes in resource prices have driven costs up, and cold winters result in the furnace running constantly.

If you leave the house for a few days in winter, don't turn the heat off, only down, or pipes may freeze and burst.

Consumers pay bills monthly and metering may differ between jurisdictions. Costs usually drop dramatically during the warmer months, unless air-conditioning units drain large quantities of electricity. Therefore, as an extremely general outline, electricity and gas for an average-sized two-storey home cost around C$200 per month – more in winter, and conceivably much less at other times of the year. Local billing will often cover water as well. Private companies offer 'locked in' assured pricing, arguing that the consumer will benefit from cost assurance – much like a fixed rather than variable mortgage.

Water and Sewage

For the most part Canada has clean, safe and palatable water. Given that the country has the world's largest reserves of fresh water, it is surprising to discover a thriving bottled-water industry. Interestingly, when petrol (gas) exceeds C$1 (45 pence) a litre, people become outraged, yet they are willing to spend over C$2 for bottled water that may not be any cleaner than city tap water – and the plastic bottle will probably end up in a landfill site.

Municipalities handle water sanitation and purification. Some communities meter all consumption while others charge flat monthly fees. Usually, billing for water use is incorporated into the gas, electricity or municipal tax bill. Water rates are generally quite low, which may account for extremely high water usage levels in Canada.

Municipalities maintain reserve systems that sometimes run low during times of drought and, although rare, water restrictions are applied from time to time. Restrictions do not extend to limiting showers, but may apply to lawn-sprinkler use during dry periods. Despite heavy rainfall on the west coast, Vancouver Island has relatively frequent water shortages because the island has no permanent ice pack. Prairie farmers maintain small reserves for their own use, as droughts are common in parts of the prairies. Atlantic Canada has drier weather in the summer, but rainfall (descending as snow) frequency is similar to that in Britain.

Most water sanitation systems remain in good condition, although the authorities invoke water-boiling precautions from time to time. Walkerton, Ontario, a community northwest of Toronto, experienced widespread illness and seven deaths when *E. coli* contaminated the local water supply. This outbreak, which resulted from negligence 'and possibly weak provincial regulations, became an election issue in the province. Canadians take clean drinking water for granted and use water without hesitation.

Water bills include the cost of sewage maintenance. Sewage treatment is generally very good and modern, though it has been late in coming to many communities – even those as large as Halifax and Victoria. Fortunately, the amount of raw sewage dumped directly into the oceans or lakes has been decreasing, but some direct contamination continues. In 2006, the Sierra Legal Defence Fund, now Ecojustice, stated that Ontario has the best standards for drinking water, followed by Quebec, Alberta and Nova Scotia. Ecojustice gives the federal government an 'F' for enacting binding national regulations.

Garbage

Rubbish collection is another municipal responsibility, with home-owners billed through local taxes. Kerbside collection generally takes place once or twice a week, depending on the municipality. By some measures, Canadians produce more waste per capita than anyone else on earth. Recycling efforts are increasing and some municipalities include recycling pick-ups with the regular rubbish collection. Still, much work remains if garbage-generation is to be substantially reduced. From time to time the issue makes the national media, but just as quickly fades away. Canada is spacious and an 'out of sight, out of mind' mentality applies as waste quickly disappears into far-off landfills. Halifax is a global leader in separating organic waste and processing refuse.

Interestingly, Canadians are a very clean, civic-minded people. You rarely see litter, or even graffiti, and, while Canadians from a young age accept the need to place litter into receptacles, they rarely take stock of just how much rubbish they generate.

Snow Removal

Unlike in the UK, little stops when the snow falls. If life were to grind to a halt every time snow fell in Canada, the country would cease to function. Except in the most extreme conditions, highways and city streets remain open throughout winter and business carries on as usual. Municipalities are responsible for clearing city streets, businesses clear the area around their premises, and the federal and provincial governments take care of highways.

Residents must clear snow from pathways in front of their homes and have been fined for not doing so. After a good snowfall the great tradition of shovelling drives and footpaths takes place – and a disproportionate number of heart attacks occur because of the exertion. Snow in the prairies is relatively easy to clear because it is light and dry, but the wet flakes that fall in their trillions further east are thick and heavy. Atlantic Canada can receive upwards of a full metre of snow in as little as two days. In St John's they truck snow to the bay and dump it as there is simply not enough a space to pile it along streets.

Every Canadian home (other than those on the west coast) has a snow shovel somewhere. Owners of homes with long driveways may invest in a snow-blowing machine. A device for chipping ice often proves useful, as does a little salt to prevent too much ice forming on pathways. Apartment-dwellers will probably have their paths cleared, as will those living in townhouse complexes; some provision for snow removal is probably included in the maintenance fees.

Bills and Taxes

In conclusion, home-owners in Canada incur several ongoing, unavoidable costs. Services are modern, and mostly efficient, despite an uneasy relationship with Mother Nature. From a national perspective, the provision of services can appear complicated, but locally residents do not need to make too many choices. Costs for gas and electricity have been rising, but remain affordable by world standards. Canadians live in well-insulated, warm homes where a fire is more of an aesthetic extra than a necessity.

Municipal taxes, which cover other costs and are based on the home's value, can be paid monthly, in semi-annual instalments or annually. As a general rule, municipalities set taxes at around 1 per cent of a property's assessed value.

Communications and Entertainment

Canadians are well connected to the outside world. Telephone services, the Internet and to a lesser extent postal services all work well. Alexander Graham Bell is buried in Canada and the fibre-optics giant Nortel Networks topped the Toronto Stock Exchange until the company experienced a dramatic decline in profits. Almost every home has at least one television set and a telephone, and a majority have computers. With the exception of mobile phones, costs for communications services are not outrageous, and competition has done a good job in lowering prices.

Telephone

It is not too surprising that in a country as large as Canada the telephone has become extremely popular. Isolated populations and a mobile workforce have encouraged the development of a telecommunications infrastructure. Mobile (cell) phones do not carry the same social cachet that they do in Britain and Canadians are well down the user list, but the devices continue to grow in popularity. Most homes use **fixed landlines**, but, as mobile phone costs decrease, more people are opting to install lines only for their Internet connection. The installation of a landline is easy, as most houses are already wired and you will just pay a connection charge of C$55 or so; the phone can be connected remotely. If there is no line, it will cost you another C$100, but service is prompt.

As with almost everything else in Canada, telephone companies began as provincial entities, but the entire industry is going through a major overhaul. Saskatchewan and Manitoba still have provincially owned telephone companies, but elsewhere in the country the private industry is busy expanding and merging. Service is divided somewhat regionally between **Bell**, dating back to 1880, **Telus** (which began in Alberta), and now **Shaw** and other **digital providers**. Bell dominates in both Ontario and Quebec and is involved throughout the Atlantic provinces where **Aliant** is the largest provider. In the North, **Northwestel** provides most of the services. Telus began in Alberta as a government-run telephone service, was privatised and eventually took over the British Columbia service. As Bell's largest competitor, Telus seeks to expand east, but it has had labour disputes and accusations of poor service. Conversely, Saskatchewan's wholly government-owned service remains popular in that province and the company has even found contracts internationally.

Free-market competition has spawned a plethora of long-distance service providers. With patience and time, you can find excellent deals for calling overseas – costs that are equal to or even lower than a long-distance call within a province. Local calls from a fixed line are free in Canada. Monthly line-rental rates range between C$25 and C$40, depending on the number of extra services you add, such as caller display. Increased competition is driving prices down, but some areas do not yet have the infrastructure that is needed for real choice. **Public telephones** are distributed widely and are becoming increasingly easy to use. Older machines accept only quarters, dimes and nickels (25-, 10- and 5-cent pieces), which is fine for local 35-cent calls, but difficult for long-distance calls, which may require more than 15 quarters for the first few minutes. Newer phones accept phone cards and even credit cards. The most useful phone cards in terms of cost are not terribly efficient, but offer excellent value for money. As in the UK, use of these cards involves first phoning a free number (1-800, 1-888, or something similar), selecting a language, typing in a secret pin number and eventually making the call.

Directory enquiries is t 411. *See* pp.248–9 for regional telephone codes.

Mobile Phones

Canada has a variety of mobile phone operators including **Fido**, **Bell Canada**, **Telus** and **Rogers Cellular**, and service is steadily improving, but remains expensive by world standards. Understandably, large areas remain without cellular coverage because of long distances and limited population. **Text messaging** exists, but is not used to the same fanatical degree as in the UK. Irritatingly, you pay when you receive a call, as well as when you make one. Different offers, such as free local calling or no long-distance calls, are available, but minutes register whenever the mobile phone is used.

Mobile telephones are expensive if purchased independently, but are greatly discounted or even free when acquired as part of a contract. Contracts last for one to three years, involve a credit check and are becoming less expensive to break. Fortunately, you can change your actual service package (number of minutes, long distance, and so on) within the contract. Pay-as-you-go options are also available, but prove much more expensive. Number portability has recently arrived in Canada, so it is now possible to change service provider while keeping your existing number. More competition should be arriving in the market and will hopefully lead to better pricing and rate plans.

Some mobile phones from the UK work in Canada, but not necessarily in all parts of the country. Partnership contracts and infrastructure have slowed this process, but worldwide phones are becoming more common. A British phone will work in Canada if the UK provider has a partnership with Rogers. It is worth noting that innovation and change are common in this industry, with much of it led by the larger US market. Mobile phone prices should continue to decline, with more options becoming available.

Fax

Facsimiles in Canada virtually mirror those in the UK and continue to be used for documents too important to send by e-mail but not quite worthy of posting. Some legal documents must be signed in black ink, presumably for faxing purposes. Most businesses have fax machines, but they are less common in homes. If you need only to send a fax from time to time, most business-supply companies, as well as some post offices, offer fax services. Many computers can also be used as fax machines. Scanners and high-speed cable have made a dial-up fax less of a necessity in the home.

Post

Under no circumstances should you complain about the Royal Mail, once you have enjoyed the services of Canada Post. Slow, disorganised, costly, but with very well-paid employees, Canada Post stands as an institutional tribute to union-driven inefficiency. Canada may be larger than Britain, so sorting and distribution may take a little longer, but Australia's postal system fares much better and it covers only a slightly smaller area. Some say service has improved, but gifts posted overseas for Christmas still have to be sent off early in November, and sometimes there are postal strikes.

Delivery comes, at most, once a day and never at weekends. Delivery times vary, as do the service hours of postal outlets. Fortunately franchise outlets at some locations remain open Saturday and Sunday. Residents in well-established areas receive direct delivery of mail to their own letterboxes, but almost all newer developments have group boxes located somewhere near the end of the street. These boxes, which have individual keyed slots for each unit, are not too inconvenient and may speed up the process – they even come equipped with a larger box for oversized packages.

Postcodes

Canadian postcodes are six digits long, with a combination of letters and numbers. Each province has a standard first letter, but the letters do not correlate with the provincial name. British Columbia codes begin with 'V', Alberta 'T', Newfoundland 'P', and so on. The two-letter provincial abbreviations used in postal addresses are more logical:

- **Alberta: AB**
- **British Columbia: BC**
- **Manitoba: MB**
- **New Brunswick: NB**
- **Newfoundland and Labrador: NL**
- **Northwest Territories: NT**
- **Nova Scotia: NS**
- **Nunavut: NU**
- **Ontario: ON**
- **Prince Edward Island: PE**
- **Quebec: QC**
- **Saskatchewan: SK**
- **Yukon: YK**

Alternatives to the Post and Receiving Mail from Abroad

To some extent, postal use has undergone an important transformation as e-mail has replaced letter writing. In younger circles, it is not considered impolite to e-mail a Christmas card or birthday greeting. Logically, the electronic age, in conjunction with fax and courier services, should have taken some pressure off Canada Post. But the advent of large-scale Internet shopping has again increased the demand for traditional postal services.

Canadians purchase many items from abroad – particularly from the United States. Large Internet merchants, such as eBay and Amazon, have Canadian divisions, with products priced in Canadian dollars. In the end, however, the majority of items for sale are not in Canada and therefore have to pass through Canadian customs on their way to your house.

According to the Canada–US Free Trade Agreement and NAFTA, goods manufactured in Canada, the USA and Mexico (with some exceptions) may flow more or less freely. Therefore, if you buy a product from a US site, all you should owe after paying the purchase price is sales tax – 5 per cent nationally and whatever percentage your province of residence levies. If a courier service, such as DHL or Federal Express, delivers the goods, the driver may just collect the extra tax at your door. Canada Post will leave a notice, which you can use to claim the package and pay the tax at your local outlet. If the package comes from a non-NAFTA country, you may need to prove the amount paid to customs, which *may* involve a trip to the local airport.

Goods from the USA face a double-handling hurdle – the US Postal Service as well as Canada Post. Functioning in but one language, the US postal corporation competes with Canada Post for snail-like service. Send two different, equal-sized packages from one country to the other on the same day and the odds are slim that they will arrive together. Fortunately they should eventually reach their final destination – possibly even in one piece.

Not surprisingly, private delivery services do well in Canada and throughout North America. All the expected players, FedEx, UPS and DHL, compete with Canada Post. In the downtown areas of larger cities, bicycle couriers weave in and out of traffic year-round, carrying documents between businesses. Some smaller communities not served by the large delivery firms have home-grown delivery companies that ply routes to larger centres.

Canada Post Costs

Basic postage for mail sent from Canada to the UK is comparable to that for the reverse trip. A letter sent by air costs around C$1.60. Pricing for packages depends on size and weight, and it is not worth guessing, because if the post-age paid is just a penny short, the package will be unceremoniously returned. Surface mail is much slower, with delivery sometimes taking several months. Airmail can cross the Atlantic in as few as four days (but don't count on it).

Canada Post has implemented a variety of express post services that guarantee various delivery speeds for hefty surcharges. Additional services, such as registered mail and tracking mail, are available and explained online at **www.canadapost.ca**.

The Internet

Per capita Internet usage in Canada is slightly higher than in the UK and currently ranks 13th in the world, and Canada has the second most Internet service providers (ISPs) after the USA. The Internet has become an integral part of both business and private society. Primary schools come equipped with computer laboratories and one rarely meets someone who has no online connection at home or at work. Governments offer a high percentage of their services online and telephone information services will often direct you to a web address. In many instances, the Internet represents the easiest way to obtain information and will regularly prove faster than trying to speak with a human by telephone. Without question, however, an age gap remains within the usage figures, and constant references to e-mail and web addresses must seem quite foreign to retirees who missed the Internet wave.

Monthly Internet costs are slightly lower than in the UK, and Internet cafés are decreasing in number correlating with an increase in laptop usage. As familiarity with the Internet has expanded and computer prices fallen, it has become easy to own and maintain a home computer. High-speed cable connections, in some instances tied into television cable services, mean computers can be left running and connected all day long. Dial-up connections and separate broadband lines are also becoming less common. Service provision is competitive and has reached all but the most isolated corners of the country.

Laptops have been fully integrated into business and an increasing number of wireless sites are now available. Signing on to US networks is one challenge Canadian business people face when south of the border: Canadian postcodes do not always fit the American system and can result in blocked access.

Television

Canadians like their televisions, but the sheer number of channels limits the extent to which conversations focus on 'last night's programme'. The vast majority of homes have **cable** access, which easily offers more than 50 channels. **Satellite** dishes proliferate in rural settings. Within a mere century, once-isolated homesteads can now enjoy Mexican soap operas or the latest hits from Bollywood – all in the comfort of the living room.

Digital television is gaining in popularity and offers a middle road between the 30- or 40-channel option on cable and hundreds of choices with satellite. Digital providers are also actively promoting pay-per-view programming.

The United States produces the great bulk of television programming and local service providers use American broadcast systems, and add on the Canadian channels. As a result, not all channels are available everywhere and less-than-relevant local US news programmes can be seen in far-flung parts of Canada. For example, a viewer who is desperately interested in Detroit's morning traffic problems may watch the scene on a television in across-the-river Windsor and in more distant Banff, but not in Calgary.

Television service is affordable or, at least, is considered enough of a priority for every home to have it. There is **no television licence** to pay for. Televisions from the UK cannot be used on the Canadian system, just as PAL video cassettes will not work in Canadian machines. Some multi-region DVD machines can play both European (region 2) and North American (region 1) discs, whereas older ones also have regional restrictions.

See also **Canada Today**, pp.105–107.

Time Zones

Canada functions with five and a half distinct time zones and most regions also use daylight saving. Only Russia, with seven time zones, has more. Continental USA is divided into three, with another two for Alaska and Hawaii.

The origin of the Greenwich Meantime system comes from Canada and was developed by Sir Sanford Fleming of the Canadian Pacific Railway. Dealing with transcontinental railway construction and particularly schedules was difficult, as each region operated an ad hoc time system based on what was thought to be noon. In 1878 Fleming proposed a regulated division of 24 time zones measured from the royal observatory in Greenwich. In 1883 the proposal was adopted and with some adjustments remains in use worldwide today.

Living with different time zones affects many aspects of life in Canada. 'Blackouts' are imposed during elections as polls close at 8pm, meaning that British Columbia could know the results before voting (in the USA there are no blackouts, which can influence voting in the west). National news broadcasts and sporting events are aired to try and serve all markets, and as the major stock exchange is in Toronto (and New York), brokers have an early start in the west or finish their day late in the east.

Money and Banking

Currency

The national currency is the Canadian dollar, which trades and floats openly. The dollar, like all other currencies, is measured against its US counterpart and has recently risen in value after several years of weakness. This has had mixed

Loonie Bucks

Canadian money is a colourful affair whose value shifts significantly in relation to the US reserve currency. In making a move from paper, the Canadian mint had to design new coins. The one-dollar coin is gold in colour and shows the Queen on one side and a bird, the loon, on the reverse side. Rather than becoming a 'buck' or some other familiar moniker, the new dollar was quickly embraced as the loonie. Several years hence a two-toned two-dollar coin replaced its note and illustrates an image of a polar bear – so what cute name did Canadians develop? Polars, perhaps? No, with an eye to consistency, or complacency, the new coin quickly became a twoonie. These terms are used frequently and discount loonie and twoonie stores can be found.

The one cent coin has retained the British 'penny' designation (though may soon be eliminated), five cents is a 'nickel', 10 cents is a 'dime' and 25 cents a 'quarter'. Notes come in denominations of 5, 10, 20, 50 and 100 dollars. Several different designs are in circulation, but all remain legal tender.

repercussions for an economy so dependent on exporting south. Businesses never have trouble making change, but different waves of counterfeiting have led some shops to refuse particular denominations from time to time.

The Bank of Canada

The Bank of Canada prints the nation's money, controls its flow and sets interest rates. Although the federal government appoints the head of the central bank (Mark Carney in 2008), the bank remains independent from parliament. As a result, interest rates cannot be manipulated according to political whims. The Bank of Canada follows a strict policy of inflation prevention, which through the 1990s kept interest rates reasonably high. Although greatly reduced from the 17 per cent and 18 per cent of the early 1980s, Canadian interest rates have been relatively high when compared with those in other developed countries. As a consequence, inflation has remained low, but systemic unemployment has only recently begun to drop to around 6 per cent from years at nearly 10 per cent.

Although Canadian interest rates closely follow those of the USA, the trend is changing. A stronger currency and low inflation has given the Bank of Canada a slightly freer hand in setting policy.

Other Canadian Banks

Canada's banking industry is extremely important to the economy. The Canadian industry includes 14 domestic banks, 33 foreign bank subsidiaries and 20 foreign bank branches. However, the six largest Canadian banks control over 90 per cent of the assets in the industry. As in the UK, the large banks have branches everywhere and from a consumer's perspective there is little difference between them. Nevertheless, it is always worth maintaining an account with one of the big banks simply for ease of access (for UK addresses of Canadian banks, *see* pp.261–2). The largest banks in order of market size are:

- **Royal Bank of Canada** (RBC; **www.royalbank.com**)
- **Bank of Montreal** (BMO; **www.bmo.com**)
- **Canadian Imperial Bank of Commerce** (CIBC; **www.cibc.com**)
- **Toronto Dominion Bank** (TD; **www.td.com**)
- **Scotiabank** (formerly the Bank of Nova Scotia; **www.scotiabank.com**)
- **National Bank of Canada** (based in Montreal; **www.nbc.ca**)

With the exception of the National Bank, all of these corporations have a highly visible presence throughout the country. Each represents an amalgamation of smaller banks and trust companies, and if the federal government would allow it (a no-go area according to the official government position), the banks would likely merge into two, or perhaps three, mega-banks.

The capitalisation of Canadian banks has fallen somewhat in world terms, but the industry is nevertheless extremely profitable and stable. Canadian banking is liberal and all the main companies maintain a presence offshore in places like the Caribbean and the Channel Islands. Scotiabank's investment in one of Argentina's largest banks took a major hit during that country's banking crisis and Canadian banks have been hurt by the US sub-prime mortgage débâcle, but, for the most part, the international endeavours have been rewarding.

Overall, banking in Canada provides a more pleasant experience than in the UK. It is possible to shake a bank teller's hand and, except on certain days, the queues are not too long. ATMs (Automatic Teller Machines) or ABMs (Automatic Banking Machines) are everywhere. Canada has the highest number per capita of cash machines in the world and most, for a fee, will accept cards from different institutions. Machines are not exposed to the open street as in the UK, but are usually inside buildings or through doors, which offers some degree of shelter (and safety). Machines dispense C\$20 and C\$50 notes and accept deposits. Most banking services can be accessed online and you can pay bills from the comfort of your personal computer. The large banks all have free phone numbers and, after a little waiting and a few recorded messages, you can speak to a human being. Once you have an established history with a bank, much can be done over the phone, but first meet a personal banker at what will become your local branch.

On the downside, Canadian banks charge fees for almost everything, so it is worth discussing accounts thoroughly. A typical account may have a monthly fee, an overdraft fee or allow a limited number of withdrawals before fees kick in. The large Dutch firm ING has stormed into the Canadian market offering free online banking, so this may lead to a reduction in customer banking fees.

Many different types of **accounts** exist, but generally most people have a chequing account, a savings account and at least one credit card. You can open a high-interest longer-term account that in reality pays very little. Major banks offer US dollar accounts but it is easy to convert Canadian currency to US dollars. Opening a bank account is simple, particularly if you have a social insurance number (*see* p.149) and some other form of identification.

Credit Cards

Credit cards are used and accepted everywhere. The debit system, using a bank card, is called **Interac** in Canada and is available almost everywhere. The hybrid credit/debit cards that are common in the UK are not seen in Canada.

The credit card culture is widespread and, despite horrendous interest rates, Canadians carry an alarming amount of debt on their cards. A good credit rating means you can acquire a card with a high limit very quickly. Most cards offer added bonuses such as air miles or reduced petrol costs; some even have a cash-back feature and many offer insurance. Fees come with the cards offering bigger bonuses, but it is worth looking into credit cards that earn free flights or cost discounts. People with poor credit ratings will find it hard to obtain a card, but people with no credit history – an issue that new immigrants sometimes face, *see* box, pp.76–7 – may be able to get a low-balance card in order to build a history. Some larger shops also offer credit cards for use only in their outlets and this may be a way to build up a better credit rating – or fall further into debt.

The Rate of Exchange

The rate of exchange against sterling also floats, and over the last 10 years British visitors have found Canada to be proportionately affordable. One pound will generally buy C$2 (down from several years at C$2.20). It is not difficult to transfer money to Canada, but if you are carrying more than C$10,000 dollars in whatever form when entering Canada, it must be declared.

Before converting sterling to Canadian dollars, it is well worth tracking the rate of exchange for some time and doing the conversion in Canada. On depositing UK funds into a Canadian bank where you already have an account you will not pay, or should not pay, any commission. The rate of exchange will be slightly lower than the internationally posted amount, but it will be better than the rates offered in the UK. Be aware that several rates exist, so talk to the branch manager, particularly if you are setting up a lot of services, and you may be offered a preferential rate.

Responses vary and, while some tellers may be most helpful, others will stare blankly at foreign currency. Foreign cheques may face the same reaction – if you have a good record with a local branch, the person helping you may not insist on putting a hold on personal cheques, but if you are not a known customer a personal UK cheque can be held for up to 21 days before the funds are released into your account. The two solutions to this problem involve either bringing your funds across in a certified bank draft or writing a series of smaller cheques that will not raise concerns. Electronic transfers are also possible, but costly.

Other Investment Options

Beyond just basic banking services, financial institutions present Canadians with a wide variety of investment options. Recent legislation has permitted significant crossovers within the financial services industry so that now banks offer insurance and individuals can manage their own investment. Traditional brokerage companies still exist, although many have become subsidiaries of larger banks. During the NASDAQ-driven tech bubble, many investors went online, and made their own trades for a fixed fee structure. After massive losses and corrections in the industry it would be interesting to know how many people have returned to the guidance of a traditional broker. Certainly many investors have shifted out of the stock market and into real estate.

That noted, Canadians tend to be investors and the country's largest market is in Toronto – the Toronto Stock Exchange (TSX). The Montreal exchange is fusing with the TSX, and Vancouver and Calgary have other lesser exchanges. Winnipeg has Canada's most important commodities exchange. Over the years, several insider trading problems have arisen in Vancouver and Calgary, but generally the Canadian financial sector is modern, efficient and transparent. Trading commissions vary and many major companies list in both Toronto and New York. Tax-sheltered retirement-savings plans encourage Canadians to invest within their own country, but many wealthy Canadians keep funds sheltered offshore.

Shopping

Canada adheres firmly to the North American shopping model. Shopping centres (malls), large retail outlets and enormous grocery stores are ubiquitous. Automobile dealerships pop up everywhere and televisions inundate viewers with advertising. More positively, service is friendly, prices generally reasonable and the environment trusting. Security is becoming more common but, just as in the case of banking, the consumer is not treated as a potential threat but as a customer.

Traditionalist Europeans may scoff at the mall culture and it is true that large shopping centres lack the quaint appeal of small-town shops lining the local high street, but an extreme climate breeds functionality. At minus 30°C, Edmonton's massive mall or Montreal's underground city become oddly appealing. Culturally, Canadians are an outdoor-orientated people who enjoy skating, skiing and cycling, but they want their shopping to be designed around comfort and efficiency. Moreover, although 80 per cent of Canadians are now urban, the homesteading tradition meant long trips several times a year in order to purchase supplies. In more recent times, people can do their shopping daily but, with large houses and huge refrigerators, people tend to stock up.

In many families both parents work outside the home, so weekends (except for Sundays in Nova Scotia) become the time for purchasing provisions. Giant US box stores have moved into the Canadian market and, if their number is any indication, they are doing quite well. Wal-Mart is perhaps the best known of the US companies and its opening of a store in the Yukon town of Whitehorse indicates a change to smaller markets. Northern towns have always had small general stores that carried every product imaginable, but Wal-Mart's entry changes the local dynamic and lowers consumer prices. Dog mushers living out in the bush can now buy feed at a fraction of the former price, but at what cost to the local community?

Canada's oldest corporation, the Hudson's Bay Company, has withdrawn from the fur business but continues to maintain an important presence in the economy. Large HBC stores figure prominently in most city centres. The classic, semi-ornate sandstone structures, which predate the glass towers of today, remain in many city centres, although some now sit empty or are being converted to other services.

Canada's retail sector, an important part of the economy, employs large numbers of people at low wages. Staff in clothing and shoe stores will regularly earn only the minimum wage (from C$8+ an hour, depending on the province). Commission and bonus systems are also common, and the exuberance shown by a salesperson makes it easy to tell which shops use this form of motivation. However, service in Canada is generally excellent and workers are friendly and outgoing just because they are that way. Cynical British visitors may take the broad smile and friendly 'hello' as false, or 'American', but it is genuine. Canadians use 'please', 'thank you' and notably 'you're welcome' frequently – and conversely a rude customer is not always right! There is still a human element to business in Canada. As a visitor with an accent you will be treated well and servers will show a genuine interest. Although cities are large and modern, a small-town sense of building relations and being friendly prevails.

Many shops have generous returns policies and feelings will not be hurt if you try something on but do not buy it. If you return goods, you will receive either a refund or a credit towards something else. Obviously time limits apply when returning products, but generally retail outlets settle such issues in the customer's favour.

Although bartering is not common, it does exist. House sales usually involve some back-and-forth negotiation and you should try hard not to pay full price for a new or used car. If purchasing household appliances or other larger ticket items, it is also worth trying for a deal. Use the Internet to compare prices. Trying to negotiate with a shop attendant, however, will be futile unless the person works on commission. Still, when shopping for most consumer goods in Canada, it is rarely necessary to pay the full retail price. Shops offer discounts and sales constantly, with the biggest events taking place on Boxing Day. Canadians line up by the thousands on 26 December, race into shops and consume like mad after the respite of the previous day.

Many companies have climbed onto the membership bandwagon and offer and even sell discount, club and credit cards. Credit cards (Visa, MasterCard and to a lesser extent American Express) are accepted almost everywhere. Signing up for a shop-specific membership can be annoying, but you will receive good discounts on everything from groceries to furniture. In return, retailers get to track your shopping patterns and at the same time build loyalty.

Groceries

There are food stores everywhere and a few names will seem familiar to British newcomers. Safeway has stores across Canada, as do a variety of other large chains. Small corner stores, handy for picking up items after hours, are much more expensive. Milk and bread are no longer delivered to the door. Regular supermarkets have faced stiff competition from even larger superstores, but there appears to be a place for both in the market.

Food outlets fall into one of five broad categories: small corner stores or speciality shops, regular supermarkets, fresh and speciality markets (such as farmers' markets), superstores and even larger warehouse stores. Individual shopping preferences will be based on convenience, price and, perhaps, quality.

Without doubt, food shopping in Canada has its generic aspect, but some regional variations do exist. Fish features prominently on the coasts and Ukrainian and European sausages are found in parts of the prairies. Cheese is much more expensive than in the UK because of production and importation rules. Overall, however, groceries tend to cost less in Canada than in the UK. Fruits and vegetables can vary considerably in cost and quality from season to season and fresh juice is expensive, despite the fact that Canadians are the highest per capita juice consumers in the world.

Also worth noting is the fact that, except for Quebec where grocery stores stock beer and wine, alcohol is not sold in grocery stores. Consumers of beer, wine and spirits buy their supplies in separate shops, which may be government-owned or private, depending on the province. The product is highly taxed so bring as much as you can (which is one bottle of spirits or two bottles of wine) when you fly over.

Clothing

Canadians care about their appearance, but not to the extent that some Europeans do. Harsh winters require good jackets and footwear while fancy

---

The Metric System

Canada converted to the metric system in the early 1970s, though some imperial measures are still commonly used in daily life. Interestingly, while the metric system has always been used in France, French Canadians functioned with miles and inches for much of their history, having to translate terms from English. Measurements of distance and speed in Canada is entirely metric, as are temperatures, but weights are often given in pounds (never stones), and drinks are served by the ounce.

---

miniskirts just look silly at −30°C. Most well-known brands of clothing are available but tastes vary across the country. It is still possible to finds guys walking around in a pair of old jeans and lumberjack shirt.

Montreal is the country's most fashionable city and Vancouver its most relaxed in style, but not necessarily in terms of cost. Stores carry seasonal clothing for obvious reasons and it is often difficult, yet financially rewarding, to purchase garb outside the relevant season. Jackets, gloves and mittens, toques (winter hats) and boots are more widely available than in the UK and, without doing an item-by-item comparison, prices tend to be better.

Of the nationwide chains, either the Bay or Sears usually anchor one end of a shopping mall. Eaton's was formerly a big player but succumbed to some poor business management and was bought out by Sears. Overall, the Bay carries a slightly higher-end inventory. Budget outlets, such as Zellers and Wal-Mart, also carry clothing that is functional, if not always sturdy. Marks & Spencer has withdrawn from the Canadian market. Upper-end retailers, such as Holt Renfrew, usually locate in the principal business district of each city, and furs can still be purchased (and even worn) throughout the country.

Shopping malls and strip malls (a row of shops with external entrances and a parking lot in front) all offer a broad range of clothing and footwear. So many Canadians live in durable and fashionable outdoor sporting attire that it is gradually developing into a national image. Mountain Equipment Co-op (MEC), a not-for-profit retailer, now has shops in most major cities and its label can be found on untold trousers (pants), jackets and backpacks all over the country. To identify a Canadian backpacker (if their pack for some odd reason does not sport a maple leaf), look for the MEC logo. Other outdoor-activity and work-clothing shops compete in the same market and, while non-utility apparel is common, stylish comfort forms a national theme.

Appliances

There is no point in bringing major appliances from the UK. The electrical system in Canada has half the voltage and sizes are different. Most homes are sold or let with the appliances included so you may not even have to shop for them. All major chain stores and outlet shops sell electrical appliances and it may be worth haggling about price. Local newspapers and 'bargain finder' papers frequently list used appliances for sale. Most homes have a clothes dryer, as well as a washing machine, and dishwashers are extremely common.

Furniture and Household Items

If new is not too important, it is possible to furnish a home entirely with second-hand furniture very affordably. Weekend garage sales (similar to car boot sales) are easy to find, and some dedicated bargain-hunters spend their weekends poking through other people's unwanted belongings.

Furniture and home shops offering new goods for sale are everywhere and cater to most price ranges. IKEA and similar outlets have done well by filling Canadians' new and strikingly large homes with their products. Interestingly, while certain shops will maintain a reputation for having upper- or lower-end stock, actual prices may not necessarily reflect that reputation, so for larger-ticket items it is worth shopping around.

Even more shops offer special credit or 'no money down' arrangements, but make sure you read the contract and understand the associated costs – and your ability to pay when the bill does come. Many Canadians seriously damage their credit rating by failing to live up to their obligations on such debts.

Antiques and custom items from the UK may be worth bringing, as they will be hard to find in Canada, but for more modern goods the cost of transportation may not be worth the effort.

Online Shopping

After a period of trepidation and learning, Canadians are now happy and willing to purchase directly from the Internet. As a result, major Canadian retailers have gone online, which makes price comparisons much easier. Goods may also be purchased from abroad, but this involves waiting for postal delivery and possibly dealing with customs (see 'Post', pp.172–4). Internet purchases are secure and major firms accept credit cards directly, while other service businesses, such as eBay, will lead you through safe-pay options.

Shopping Hours

Canada is not quite a 24-hour retailing country (except online) but it is moving in that direction. Despite a 2004 referendum in which roughly 55 per cent of Nova Scotians rejected Sunday shopping, in 2006 the province bowed to pressure, allowing all businesses to open on Sundays. A few restrictions apply in parts of Atlantic Canada, but Sunday is no longer an official day of rest. Shop hours increase towards Christmas, but as a rule shops are open Sat–Wed 9–6, Thurs–Fri 9–9. Store hours adapt to the local market, with some retailers remaining open as long as possible. A few drugstores (chemists) never close, and even the odd furniture shop will hold 24-hour sales for promotion purposes.

Cross-border Shopping

Back in the days of a strong Canadian dollar, hordes of bargain-hunting Canadians poured across major border crossings to buy cheaper products in the United States. In the 1990s, the weaker Canadian currency (which the government quietly let slide) stemmed much of this flow and in some cases reversed it. During this same period Canadian cigarettes that had been exported tax-free to the USA were smuggled back into Canada and sold illegally, all in an effort to escape the country's high taxation on the product. This smuggling occurred at such rates that the government was forced to reduce tobacco taxes for a period of time.

The overall cost of living is once again higher in Canada than in the United States, and the huge American consumer market leads to levels of competition that are not as common in Canada. As the US dollar weakens, Canadians are again venturing south to buy but, since free trade, price differences are not likely to be as large. Moreover, not all items cross the border easily. Border crossing times are a serious disincentive to shopping in the USA, yet for Canadians living close to the border the wait can be worth the effort – but of course one must evaluate the economic cost to Canada of avoiding taxes at home. Automobile and book prices have received the most attention due to the recent strength of the Loonie. Books often have printed a Canadian and US price, with the former being up to 40 per cent higher! Automobiles are even more aggravating, with prices in Canada regularly thousands of dollars higher. Importing a car from the USA is difficult but not impossible, and Canadians will continue to look south until the integrated industry adjusts costs.

Queuing and Etiquette

Canadians have little problem lining up on the few occasions they need to. Although not prone to striking up conversations as readily as Americans tend to do when waiting in line, Canadians respect personal space and everyone's turn. Of course there will be exceptions, and with broad ethnic diversity misunderstandings can occur, but for the most part complaints are made quietly and courtesy is considered important. Doors are held open and, while Canadian society does not have the structured formality of speech found in Latin countries, it is important to say hello and thank you.

As a shopper you are welcome to walk in and out of shops in the British or American style but you can sometimes wait quite a while to receive service. Feel free to chat with salespeople and certainly treat them as equals – in this mostly classless society, they are.

GST and PST

The GST (currently 5 per cent) is Canada's much-maligned federal goods and services tax. The provincial equivalent of the GST is the PST (from 4–12 per cent), and all provinces, except Alberta, charge it in one way or another. Needless to say, Albertans were the most vocal opponents of the GST's introduction. Provincial sales taxes are generally applied to a large range of goods and services.

All provinces, except Quebec and Prince Edward Island, charge this tax on the selling price of the item before GST is applied. GST is likewise charged on the selling price of the item before PST is applied, which prevents GST from being charged on PST. Quebec and Prince Edward Island base their provincial sales tax on the total of the selling price plus GST – tax on tax. The provinces of Newfoundland and Labrador, Nova Scotia and New Brunswick now charge a 'harmonised sales tax', or HST. Instead of charging a provincial retail sales tax as well as the GST, they charge only the HST at a rate of 15 per cent. All three territories (**Yukon**, **Northwest** and **Nunavut**) impose only the federal GST.

The following general rates of provincial sales taxes apply to most purchases:

- **Alberta: no PST**
- **British Columbia: 7 per cent**
- **Manitoba: 7 per cent**
- **New Brunswick: 13 per cent HST**
- **Newfoundland and Labrador: 13 per cent HST**
- **Nova Scotia: 13 per cent HST**
- **Ontario: 8 per cent**
- **Prince Edward Island: 15.5 per cent; adjusted HST**
- **Quebec: 7.5 per cent**
- **Saskatchewan: 5 per cent**

The shock with all these taxes is not so much the amounts, but the fact that they are added after the list price. A little annoyance on small purchases becomes a significant price augmentation on high-priced items such as automobiles. Houses are taxed separately; while GST is charged on new construction, rebates help somewhat.

Although not openly discussed, many tradespeople will offer to leave off the GST and PST if you choose to pay cash. This informal economy is illegal and may leave you with no guarantees of quality or warranties on products or services.

Life in Cafés, Bars and Restaurants

Eating and drinking out occupies a central position in the Canadian way of life, but the local pub or café does not hold the same place in society as in Britain or Europe. Canadians frequent certain establishments, but not in any sort of fiercely loyal manner. Irish- and British-style pubs are common and good places to hear those accents, but they do not have quite the same feel.

Cafés, Bars and Discos

Because of restrictive alcohol regulations, not all establishments serve beer, wine or spirits. Cafés – whether posh or not – serve coffee, tea and a wide selection of juices. They also have food – anything from sandwiches and bagels (fabulous in Montreal) to doughnuts, which are all but a national institution. Frequent coffee shop visitors develop a degree of loyalty for particular locales and small-town coffee shops are ideal places for older farmers and workers to discuss the weather. A few coffee shops offer table service, but for the most part they function with counter service.

Establishments that serve alcohol tend to open later in the day and, while Canadians are good drinkers, there is little encouragement to begin imbibing in the morning. All pubs and bars have table service, which may mean it is the bartender who comes to your table. It is very important to remember to tip the server, even if purchasing directly from the bar.

Rather than paying for each round, it is customary to run a tab or bill and pay when leaving. A few clear social rules apply when it comes to paying. Groups of friends may simply divide the bill evenly, whereas others will calculate exactly what they consumed – this becomes complicated when factoring in taxes and tips. No one will refuse your offer to pay the bill and in some social settings people just take turns paying.

The term 'disco' is not used very often, although it is understood. Dancing establishments are usually referred to simply as bars or nightclubs. Dedicated nightclubs will often charge an entrance fee, whereas other bars will simply morph into a place for dancing as the evening progresses. Some bars impose cover charges for a band or special event. Dress codes are sometimes enforced, particularly in image-conscious places like Montreal, but overall going dancing is not quite the same event as in Europe. 'Clubbing' has developed in some areas, but not as a distinct cultural element. Much Music, Canada's own dedicated music-video channel located in Toronto, espouses a clubbing-style culture and raves are reported from time to time, but the majority seem happy enough with the regular dance bars.

In the west, country bars and nightclubs compete and draw large crowds. During Calgary's Stampede the whole city goes western and locals two-step to popular western tunes. Beer tents are set up across the city and serving hours are extended. Kitchener, Ontario, a city outside Toronto, celebrates its German roots each year with Oktoberfest. Indeed, most communities have at least some sort of festival that involves drinking and chatting up the opposite (or same) sex. As a dangerously broad generalisation, Canadians are liberal romantically, but it is up to you to find when and where!

Alcohol-licensing hours vary across the country and bars will generally remain open until two or three in the morning. The dancing action begins at around 11pm (or even earlier in smaller places) by which time queues will have formed outside the premises, so you must dress to stay warm as well as to look good. Because of the crowds, running a tab is much less common in clubs and you will be expected to pay for drinks as they arrive. Servers in nightclubs can earn a small fortune from tips on every drink sold.

Speciality bars serving cocktails or martinis come and go. They are generally in the downtown business districts or in better hotels. The more proletarian 'lounge' exists throughout Canada.

Restaurants

The restaurant industry in Canada is huge and the variety impressive. Most restaurants also include a bar or lounge section where you can enjoy a drink while waiting for your table. Dress codes are rarely enforced, but it is quite obvious what attire is expected. Very few restaurants require men to wear ties, but jeans and running shoes will be out of place at more refined establishments. Rural Canadians from a farming tradition eat fairly early – 5 or 6pm – and restaurants will fill up around 7pm.

Large chains of restaurants specialising in steaks, pizza or seafood are spread throughout Canada while fairly diverse local restaurants sprout up at any time. Newcomers from Britain will be surprised by the sheer number of Japanese restaurants, which increases as one moves west. Sushi in Vancouver can be as affordable as American fast food and is arguably more common.

Service tends to match the style of the establishment. Fine dining restaurants offer fine service, although in Canada a relaxed friendliness exists between server and patron. In less formal but just as expensive restaurants, meal sizes are large and the service outgoing and entertaining (or annoying). Servers

Tipping and Tax

Canada is a tipping society and the restaurant industry receives the most obvious net gain from this system. Staff in restaurants are only paid the minimum wage (roughly C$8.50 per hour) but can earn enough to raise a family. Although people within the industry always try to push the percentage up, the standard amount of a tip is between 10 per cent and 20 per cent of the bill. Tips are even given if purchasing from the bar, but fortunately bars and pubs all have table service. In addition to this sum – which in effect is given as standard – sales tax is also added. There is a federal goods and services tax (GST) of 5 per cent, which shows up on most products, as well as a provincial sales tax everywhere but in Alberta; see p.185. Some places even add a liquor tax, so that a C$20 meal and C$5 beer could well end up costing over C$32.

As a simple guideline for tipping, if service is adequate, triple the GST.

gather around to sing happy birthday when the occasion warrants it and drinks come quickly. People drink coffee right through dinner and more beer is consumed than wine. Rye (Canadian whiskey), mixed with ginger ale or cola, is also a perfectly acceptable accompaniment to a meal, as are other 'highballs' (similar mixed drinks) or cocktails. The 'Bloody Caesar', a vodka-based drink, has gained broad appeal and was invented in Calgary.

It is becoming more common to order a bottle of wine with a meal, but this has traditionally been regarded as a splurge because restaurants price wine well above its actual cost. House wines, served in carafes or by the litre, represent the most economical option. A gradual trend towards bringing your own wine is developing, but corkage costs are high and the general population is not familiar with this practice.

See also **Getting to Know Canada**, 'Food and Drink', pp.19–26.

Transport

For obvious reasons, transport is extremely important to a country like Canada. A large land mass, spread-out clusters of population and a harsh climate all have an impact on the movement of people and goods. The construction of a transcontinental railway line unified the country in the late 1800s and currently two rail companies cross the entire country. Large trucks move goods in all directions and two seasons apply to the roads – winter time, and construction time.

Public Transport

Canada has limited public transport networks, but they do function. Adolescents drive from the age of 16 and it is not uncommon for students to drive their own cars to high school. That cultural reality, combined with a comparatively small but well-dispersed population, has reduced the emphasis on a public transportation infrastructure. Toronto has a good system of trams (streetcars) and a few subway lines, but only Montreal can claim a truly extensive metro system. Vancouver, with its bridges, mountains and earthquakes, has the above-ground SkyTrain, which connects with buses and ferries. By 2010 when the Olympics arrive, Vancouver will have a train to the airport and a generally expanded public service. Calgary and Edmonton (the most car-dependent large city in Canada) both have limited Light Rail Transit (LRT) trains, which for the most part run above ground because of high water-table levels. Public transport services in other municipalities are limited to bus and perhaps ferry (used on rivers, lakes and oceans) services. Commuter trains, including some double-decker trains on a few routes, make their way into the three largest cities.

Local bus services vary according to the volume of passengers, time of day and routes, but generally are not too frequent or particularly direct. It takes some time to figure out bus routes, but fortunately phone and online trip-planning services exist for all public systems. Bus fares range from C$1 (in smaller areas) to around C$2.50 per ride. The fare includes connecting trips, so remember to ask the driver for a transfer ticket. Tickets have expiry times, usually around two hours from the time of purchase. In some cities tickets are good for one-way journeys only, but in others the ticket remains active for the return journey providing the return takes place within the allotted period of time. If paying with cash, you will need the exact amount, or else have to pay more than the fare, as bus drivers do not give back change.

If you plan to use public transport regularly, several money-saving options are available. Monthly passes or books of prepaid tickets are the most common of these. Seniors (over 60 or 65 in some jurisdictions), the disabled and students qualify for discounted passes.

Taxis

The taxi experience in Canada is not always pleasant. Prices are high and service is, at best, inconsistent. Toronto cab companies have introduced a code of ethics that, among other things, requires the driver to speak and understand English and know the city's major routes and destinations. This is not always the case in other cities. It can be annoying to arrive at a city's airport and find the taxi driver has so little local knowledge that you have to provide directions to your destination.

More positively, airport taxis have more-or-less predetermined prices so you shouldn't worry too much about being taken on a grand tour.

For the most part, you can recognise taxis by a light on the roof and the word 'taxi' written on the vehicle's side. They are not all one colour or one style of vehicle. Taxis are available for hire if their light is on.

When travelling with several people, it can sometimes be worth hiring a limousine, not only to experience the fun, but because limousines will carry as many as 10 passengers.

Intercity Travel

Coaches

Bus services ply routes between cities and to smaller destinations but a cross-country trip by bus is not recommended – you would be settling in for several days. **Greyhound** operates nationally and many different companies function regionally. Interestingly, costs are often only slightly lower than the cost of an air ticket between major centres. However, coach travel delivers you right to a city's centre and can be safer than driving your own car on winter roads.

Trains

VIA Rail (**www.viarail.ca**) runs train services in Canada, and for many British visitors the 'iron horse' forms an integral part of the romantic image of Canada. Train services in the west have been greatly reduced, but, in the main Ontario–Quebec population corridor, train travel remains an option. While a trip across Canada in the famous 'Canadian' is enjoyable, keep in mind that the majestic mountainous segment takes up a relatively small part of the journey and flying is far less expensive. The well-promoted Rocky Mountaineer takes travellers through the mountains in relative luxury, but has difficulty staying on schedule and isn't necessarily worth the cost.

Train travel in central Canada is worth serious consideration. A second-class VIA Rail seat is far more comfortable than a cramped aeroplane seat, and train stations are well located in central areas. Prices are competitive with flying and a journey out of Toronto by train can be far more enjoyable than the same trip by car during rush hour.

Planes

The airline industry has long straddled a difficult divide in Canada. Vast distances are ideal for flying, but small populations make profitability difficult. Furthermore, the partial government management of Air Canada and a long history of bailouts have led to a mixed picture.

Low-cost carriers have entered the market and prices have fallen dramatically. Even with Air Canada, domestic one-way flights now cost half the price of a return trip and the airline has removed restrictions such as staying over a weekend.

For a list of Canadian airlines *see* **First Steps**, 'Internal Airlines', pp.132–3.

Private Vehicles

Canadians love cars and, despite their faults, the country depends on private transportation. Car ownership is higher than in the UK, but lower than in the USA. Trucks often outnumber cars in rural Canada and a family of four may own four vehicles. Automobiles are big-ticket items, but you can buy a car for a surprisingly small outlay of capital. Used cars are sold and resold until they eventually rust away, while competition among new car dealers keeps prices competitive.

Needless to say, Canadians, like everyone else on the North American continent, **drive on the right**, but this was not always the case. In Canada's younger days, both British Columbia and Atlantic Canada set out their road systems in the same fashion as in the UK. Newfoundlanders continued to drive on the left until 1947. The other provinces made the switch in the 1920s. In Nova Scotia, 1923 became known as 'the year of free beef' because it was too hard to retrain the dim-witted oxen to pull on the right, so they were sent for slaughter.

Canada has converted its signage to **metric** (miles are also shown in a few areas with heavy US traffic). Highway **speed limits** are generally 100kph or 110kph. The police usually ignore cars travelling 10kph faster than that, but from time to time they enforce 'zero tolerance' policies. Signs indicating speed cameras outnumber the actual number of cameras but, once caught, you will get a speeding ticket in the post. Quebec uses aerial surveillance to catch speeders, but the warning signs are written in French only – indeed, except for a few bilingual municipalities, all road signs in Quebec are in French; stop signs in Quebec use the word *'Arrêt'*, and not 'Stop' as in France. New Brunswick and parts of Ontario and Manitoba, as well as the national parks, use bilingual signs.

Overall, Canada has very good **roads**, particularly when you consider the person-to-territory ratio. Road maintenance represents a significant government expense, especially in rural areas where vehicles are few and far between. **Traffic jams** are common in the big cities, and particularly around Toronto, but in the mountain parks cars will also inch along during 'bear jams'.

The risks associated with **winter driving** cannot be understated, and every year numerous accidents occur after the first snowfall. Snow accumulations in Atlantic Canada can virtually bury cars, and in Newfoundland poor visibility makes the thousands of moose all that much harder to see. The police rarely close highways completely, but winter storms can slow traffic to a crawl. Drivers in rural areas carry chains and even emergency provisions in case of a breakdown. All new cars come equipped with full-time running lights and drivers must keep their **headlights on at all times** in the north. In bumper-to-bumper traffic, the lights may seem unnecessary, but on open roads and at twilight, cars become much less visible.

Typically, motorists are polite and **pedestrians almost always have the right of way**. Unless a corner has traffic lights, you should stop for anyone standing there and looking ready to cross.

For driving information, road reports and general information go to the **Canadian Automobile Association** website (**www.caa.ca**). Its main page will use your postcode information to link you through to the relevant provincial pages.

Registration, Licensing and Insurance

Vehicles are registered and insured provincially and if moving province you usually have a grace period of three months before you must change plates, insurance and your licence. Plates do not stay with the car as in Britain, but are given to you after you have obtained insurance and paid the car registration fee. While some people may then cancel their insurance, the system helps to ensure that all drivers at least get third-party liability insurance.

Fuel Prices

For the first time in history, in 2004 the price of petrol (gas) edged up above a dollar per litre in a few parts of the country and there was outrage. Not too long before that, gas cost less than 60 cents (roughly 26 pence) per litre. This is always very entertaining to the British, who are accustomed to paying well over double the Canadian average for fuel. Nevertheless, Canadians cover huge distances and, as in the UK, the majority of the price goes to the government as tax. Whenever there is a hint of crisis in the oil-producing world, prices increase within days, yet surprisingly they take significantly longer to drop when the issue is resolved. The lowest prices in the country are still currently around the C$1 per litre mark.

You must re-register your vehicle each year and a dated sticker attached to a corner of the licence plate proves you have paid the fee (around C$50). Registration is similar to the UK's road tax, but is of course administered provincially. Most provinces call for front and back licence plates, but Quebec and Alberta only require rear plates.

Insurance costs are high and, whether public or private, operate on a sliding scale that takes into account the driver's age, record and the vehicle itself. After an accident it can take years to return to the highest rating, and therefore the lowest charges, so you may consider paying the cost of minor damage yourself. As elsewhere, repair costs bear no correlation to the value of the automobile – rebuilding a C$20,000 car piece by piece easily costs twice the original value. And while on the subject of gouging, provincial governments have begun to step in and force insurance companies to re-evaluate some of their charges after unconscionable post-9/11 price increases.

Provincial automobile insurers are privatised in those provinces that have privatised most other services, but remain public in provinces where the government has hung on to a variety of services. There is debate about which system is better, but in provinces with a privatised system make sure you shop around before signing on with a company.

If, as a newcomer from the UK, you cannot demonstrate a clean driving history, you will end up paying the highest rates, so make sure you obtain all relevant documentation from your local insurer before moving to Canada. Even then, it is unlikely that you will receive the best rates, but it should help. Once in Canada and fully insured, do not give up your insurance for any lengthy period of time. If you travel out of the country, try to keep your name on someone's insurance or just suspend, not cancel your own, otherwise the insurers will argue they have no proof of your driving record and will drop you down several levels.

Fee structures vary greatly, but overall you should expect to pay at least as much as you do in the UK. Newly insured drivers can be forced to pay more than C$2,000 a year, although experienced drivers with good records may get away with as little as C$750. The law requires that you purchase third-party liability insurance, but additional coverage is recommended. Obviously, coverage for theft or damage is a good idea, as is some sort of coverage for if you hit an animal (deer, moose and elk are all too commonly struck) or slide off the road in poor weather conditions.

Authorities will accept your UK or international **driving licence**, but not if you are resident in the country. Therefore, once settled, you will need to obtain a local licence, which involves paying a fee and may require you to take a driving test. Licences remain valid for five years, include a photo and specify the category of vehicle the licence applies to. You may be surprised to find the label 'probationary' on your first Canadian licence, which could cause problems when you try to hire a vehicle in other countries.

Canada has no national equivalent of the **MOT** and Alberta has no MOT at all – some of the cars on the road in that province would not make it out of the garage in the UK. British Columbia implements the strictest emissions controls in the country and each province has its own regulations. For information on emissions standards, contact the Registrar of Imported Vehicles, 405 The West Mall, Suite 400, Toronto, ON M9C 5K7, **t** 888 848 8240. Although the rules are not clearly defined, insurance companies may require a vehicle inspection for cars older than 10 years before they will provide coverage.

Buying a Car

Never an enjoyable pastime, buying a new or used car in Canada is much like the process in the UK. Prices are not fixed (despite what you may be told) and, even more aggravatingly, the ticket price excludes all sorts of charges such as delivery and tax. The Internet has helped shoppers compare prices, but always be prepared for a much harder-sell environment than you would normally find in Canada. Used cars are sold on lots and privately and many used-car salespeople live up to their brash reputations. No tax applies to cars sold privately.

Hours not Miles

The British tend to talk in actual distances, despite horrendous traffic congestion, whereas Canadians talk in time. Thinking nothing of regularly driving a couple of hundred kilometres, Canadians rate distance in hours. Quebec City is three hours from Montreal, which in turn is two hours from Ottawa and six hours from Toronto. Toronto is over 30 hours from Winnipeg, and so on.

Except in genuinely congested areas around the three largest cities, the main hindrance to progress on the road is weather. Summer driving is fast, with cars rolling along happily at 110 or 120kph, but in winter ice and blowing snow can lead to road closures and serious accidents. Therefore Calgary is normally 10 hours from Vancouver, but in winter the journey may take up to 15 hours.

Conglomerations of car and truck dealerships result in unattractive 'car malls', which blight the architectural landscape. Newspapers come filled with advertisements, while trader magazines cater to those selling privately. When the time arrives for you to buy a car, you will have no shortage of choices.

As buying a vehicle in a different province from where you live will create some problems, it is worth purchasing the vehicle in your intended home province. Although the absence of a provincial sales tax means lower automobile prices in Alberta, the local PST will be extracted when you register the vehicle in a different province. In some provinces used cars may have to pass stricter engine inspections, so perceived savings may well be lost. Nevertheless, you certainly can change provinces and take your car, but unless you are studying or on a temporary contract you will need to obtain a new insurance policy, licence plates and driving permit after your move.

Alternative Transport

Dogsleds and canoes remain iconic symbols of Canada and some still use them for travel today. Dogsled races are popular in many communities and Yukon and Alaska co-host the annual Yukon Quest race, which is considered to be even tougher than the famous Iditarod. Many enjoy canoeing, and in cottage areas some use canoes to travel between properties. The more common power boats roar around waterways after the ice has melted.

Snowmobiles continue to be the main form of transport in some northern towns. As no parts of Nunavut have road access and summer muskeg is virtually impassable, snowmobiles make perfect sense.

Crime and the Police

Canada is a safe country with crime rates similar to those in northern Europe. A high perception of safety helps to lower crime-related rhetoric, although the media and politicians do their best to create fear. Cities have rough areas, but generally not major 'no-go' areas, and the majority of Canadians do not fear walking at night. Gun crime is lower per capita in Canada than in the United States or the UK.

Interestingly, crime rates in Canada have declined steadily in recent years, with the lowest rates found in Newfoundland. For a myriad social and economic reasons, Regina, Saskatchewan has the highest crime rate of any capital in the country. At the time of writing, Quebec City has gone for over a year without a single murder. Only in terms of petty crime do Canadian statistics reach those of the United States (the country it is most often compared to) and it is thought this is partly because Canadians are more likely to report minor crimes.

The controversial American documentary film maker, Michael Moore, took his cameras north of the border in *Bowling for Columbine* in order to demonstrate the lack of paranoia in Canadian society. Bravely, he opened people's unlocked doors in Toronto and talked to gun-owners about why they do not shoot each other. Clearly, Moore's film had a specific agenda and, sadly, Canadians do lock their doors and install alarms, but for the most part his point was well taken. Canada is generally a law-abiding society and is far less militarised than the USA or even Britain. Despite numerous exceptions, an overall trusting nature pervades social and economic interaction in Canada. Although it is becoming less common, people leave their cars running unattended and unlocked in cold weather with little fear of theft. You can continue to carry your wallet in your back pocket and wear jewellery in public.

Most transgressions occur on the roads, where speeding, illegal lane changes and the like are as common as elsewhere – most people agree with the rules, but actively break them anyway. Driving while under the influence of alcohol continues to claim lives across Canada despite active campaigns against it. Traffic police are strict and fines high. When driving through Ontario you often see large signs that clearly state the amount of the fine for the various over-the-limit speeds.

Gun ownership is relatively high (although much lower than in the United States), and gun murder rates are much lower. As part of its attempt to control weapons, the federal government introduced a gun registration programme, which turned out to be an unmitigated disaster. Handguns and automatic weapons are tightly controlled, but hunting rifles remain common in rural areas (where more gun accidents per capita occur than in cities). The federal government's poorly managed and poorly promoted attempt to force gun-owners to license their weapons raised the ire of rural voters, who refused to comply. Poll after poll shows that the majority of Canadians favour gun control, so it may be concluded that the failure of the registration programme was political in nature.

Like Britain, Canada does not impose the death penalty, and the last execution took place in 1962. From time to time, populist, conservative politicians raise the idea of holding a referendum on the subject, but it receives limited debate and support. As with the gun issue, the influence of American broadcasts on the Canadian media scene has led to a percentage of the population taking their populist cues from south of the border.

An alarming increase in gang-related activities has raised crime rates in large cities and poorer areas. Smaller cities such as Winnipeg have serious gang problems, but these rarely affect the general population. Gang members tend to be immigrant or refugee youth or those simply marginalised from society. While gang violence is by no means confined to any one ethnic group, it is interesting to look at the historic development of Vietnamese gangs. Many

The Mounties

The world-famous Royal Canadian Mounted Police (RCMP) continue to be an important police force in Canada and have rightly maintained their excellent reputation. Trained in Regina, Saskatchewan, they only wear the red uniforms for ceremonial duties as it turned out they were a bit of a giveaway in undercover operations. In addition to secret service and detective duties, the Mounties remain the main police force in western and northern Canada. The eastern provinces have provincial police forces and therefore the RCMP is federal in those jurisdictions.

Formed in 1873 to police the newly constituted Canadian Northwest, the Mounties earned their famous reputation of 'always getting their man' during the mad Klondike gold rush at the end of the 1800s. Despite the wild expanses of the Yukon, geography only permitted limited access into and out of the territory. Thanks to good governance and classic Canadian tax collection, the rush to Dawson City was a relatively orderly one and, although a few murders were committed, every single perpetrator was caught and tried.

The Mounties are generally well respected and continue to be known for being impeccably honest. In traditional Canadian fashion, rules are always followed, and it is likely be a Mountie who gives you a ticket for illegally crossing the street at 2am when no one else is around.

Vietnamese moved to Canada as refugees during and after the war in that country. Generally, Canadian society welcomed the newcomers who, in turn, brought with them the fantastic work ethic associated with immigration. Many young people also brought memories of violence and war. It is easy to understand how some Vietnamese youth, often living with distant relatives and put into schools where they barely spoke the language, became attracted to gang culture. The same pattern occurs among some Somali youth. It is important to note that if gang violence were not discussed in the media, the majority of Canadians would have no idea it was happening.

Motorcycle gangs, most notably the Hell's Angels, have had a strong presence in Canada and particularly in Quebec. They are typically involved in drugs, prostitution (which remains illegal) and other unsavoury activities, and turf wars have broken out in Montreal and led to innocent people being harmed. It appears that gradually the police have been winning this battle, and several gang leaders now enjoy free food and accommodation.

Canadian prisons hold a disproportionately high number of First Nations people and, while native society is becoming healthier, huge problems continue to exist. Institutional racism, social breakdown and substance-abuse problems are all to blame, but slowly the issues are being addressed inside and outside native society. While there are recurrent accusations of policing impropriety, Canadians place a lot of faith in their police service. In fact, they demonstrate reasonably high levels of trust in most public institutions, although faith in government is waning.

Policing takes place at several levels and includes municipal, provincial and federal police forces. The famous 'Mounties' continue to be the principal law enforcement body in smaller towns throughout the west and north.

To contact the police in an emergency, call **t** 911.

Health and Emergencies

Canadians continue to be extremely proud of their healthcare system, which is one of the last purely public systems in the world. Using up huge portions of provincial budgets, the system is provincially administered, but governed by the federal Canada Health Act. An increasing number of allied health services (such as physical therapy) have been partially privatised, whereas all hospital services remain public. Wait times in emergency and for some surgeries have reached crisis levels in certain jurisdictions. Because of federal government cutbacks, the provinces pay more than 80 per cent of healthcare costs, and each province manages services in a slightly different way. Through a series of 13 different internal agreements, 'a reasonable standard' of healthcare is assured to all Canadians throughout the country.

You become eligible for healthcare **only once you are a permanent resident**, or are sponsored by a local employer; before that, or if you are on a foreign student visa, you will need private medical insurance. Regardless of which province you find yourself in, you then have to sign on to the local healthcare system (look for 'Ministry of Health' in the blue pages of your local phone book). You will receive a **healthcare card** and a number, which you will need whenever you seek medical care. Acquiring the card usually involves visiting a provincial health office. Some provinces require residents to pay **healthcare premiums** while others take the costs directly out of provincial taxes. The premiums, essentially insurance premiums, are means-tested and have a maximum cap – employers often cover these costs as part of a benefits package.

Both British Columbia and Alberta charge separately for healthcare coverage, but individuals have no choice when it comes to insurers and Alberta plans to phase out fees. Anybody without a provincial healthcare card has to pay the full cost of services. Many employers will include the provincial insurance costs in their benefits packages, while low-income earners do not have to pay premiums. Dental treatment is not covered.

Reciprocal agreements throughout the country mean that all provinces except Quebec will accept each other's healthcare cards. Out-of-province visitors to Quebec must pay directly for medical services and then make a claim in their home province. Quebecers outside their province have to do the same and make a claim for out-of-province medical expenses in Quebec. Provincial coverage is extended to Canadians travelling outside the country for short periods, but the amounts paid will not cover serious emergencies, so travel insurance is recommended.

Those moving within Canada usually enjoy a three-month overlap between the provincial healthcare systems (except for Quebec). You must apply for coverage in the new jurisdiction within three months of arrival, which is the length of time that the previous province extends its coverage. When moving to Canada, in theory cover begins immediately providing your visa or landing papers are in order. You must apply for coverage within three months of arrival. Should you require medical attention before that, you may have to pay for the service, but you will receive reimbursement when your card is issued.

While the overwhelming majority of Canadians support national healthcare, it is in fact a bit of a myth that the system is entirely public. No programmes cover pharmaceuticals (at least for now) and, despite what the US media say, drug costs remain high. **Blue Cross (www.bluecross.ca)**, a government-recognised, not-for-profit organisation, is the best-known source of additional medical coverage, which can be offered by your employer or obtained privately.

The medical system does not cover **dental services** and, if your employer or Blue Cross is not there to help, costs may be prohibitive. While expensive, dental services are good and widely available, however. If you have no dental insurance, it is worth trying to negotiate costs with service providers. Moreover, not all **rehabilitation** services are covered either, so you may have to pay for physiotherapy after that fall while skiing. Furthermore, the public system does contain private elements. Some cosmetic surgery clinics have sprung up around the country, sucking out fat and augmenting chests. The Canada Health Act does not cover such services and the patient pays all costs but those same clinic doctors will treat medical conditions, like skin cancer, under the public system.

Canadian **hospitals** tend not to be quite as institutional as those in the UK. Children's hospitals make an effort to create a more comfortable environment for the kids and many healthcare providers do not wear uniforms. Waiting times in emergency and for some surgeries have reached crisis levels in certain jurisdictions, reflecting staffing shortages, heavy bureaucracy and shifting populations. At both hospital and clinical level many communities suffer from a shortage of physicians. The reasons for this situation are many and include the draw of higher wages south of the border. Canada provides excellent medical training and, while wages are certainly above Canadian averages, medical professionals can earn much more in the private US system. Small towns experience the greatest shortages, as do poorer provinces.

Although signing up with a **general practitioner** is a recommended step, many family doctors are simply not taking new patients. Canadians are not tied to one doctor or practice, but it helps if you can build a history with an individual physician. Fortunately, walk-in clinics and hospital emergency rooms mean you can see a doctor if you need to.

SARS

Toronto had a particularly difficult time in spring 2003 when several people were infected by the Severe Acute Respiratory Syndrome (SARS). Spreading from Asia, SARS was seen as a potential worldwide epidemic, which threatened millions. As the first Western city to encounter SARS infections, Toronto received a great deal of publicity as the world suddenly noticed how quickly such illnesses could travel. The depiction of Torontonians living in fear and walking around their city with surgical masks was exaggerated, but the health crisis was real. In the end over 40 people in the Toronto area died of SARS, and aspects of the economy such as tourism and filming were greatly disrupted. Tourism has recovered; former prime minister Jean Chrétien likes to take some of the credit after spending millions to bring the Rolling Stones to Toronto to encourage people to visit again.

Despite all the problems with the healthcare system, it generally works well. Canadians consider healthcare to be part of their national identity and believe that, despite high costs, there are no truly better models to learn from.

Canada as a whole has become heavily involved in **medical research**, with individual universities specialising in different fields. Researchers compete but, as neither the education nor medical systems are private, information is shared quite openly. The **pharmaceutical industry** in Canada is large and profitable, with a strong presence in Quebec and Ontario. Importantly, pharmaceuticals are not necessarily covered outside of hospitals and costs can be prohibitive, and continue to increase.

Emergencies

The important telephone number to know in all parts of Canada is **t** 911. That number, the equivalent of 999 in the UK, puts callers through to a dispatch officer who will direct the call to the police, ambulance or the fire department. The 911 number should not be overused and is not necessarily confidential. A move, currently under way, would implement a 211 number nationally to provide confidential 'vital community and human service information'.

When healthcare emergencies occur, ambulance service is not always covered. Some jurisdictions provide ambulance service and include a fixed cost to the patient – in Ontario this amounts to C$45 if a physician deems the service to be necessary. The province covers some other medically necessary services, but in other cases the patient may be handed the entire bill – if this should happen, play dead.

Once you have reached the hospital, an emergency room filled to capacity occasionally leads to a denial of service. More commonly, you can expect a long wait, with priority extended to those experiencing chest pains and to other immediate issues. Emergency-room response times vary greatly across the country and depend on many factors. For more minor issues, it may be just as easy and more efficient to go to a medical walk-in clinic, many of which have extended opening hours.

For emergencies that are not specifically medical, the response usually comes from either the police or the fire service. With wood forming such a large component of construction materials and the problems that result from winter cold, fire-related issues usually receive a prompt response. Not uncommonly, fire alarms go off accidentally during very cold spells, leading to the evacuation of buildings. Strict fire codes apply to all properties and larger structures have sprinkler systems installed.

Burst pipes, flooded basements and other household emergencies require the services of a plumber or electrician, as the case may be. Your insurance company should cover serious damage, but do not expect immediate payment or prompt reconstruction work.

At the preventative healthcare level, various governments have declared war on smoking and have implemented virtual bans in several provinces. Health education features prominently in schools, but their reduced levels of physical activity have undoubtedly contributed to children's obesity. As part of an attempt to reform healthcare systems, governments are looking more closely at primary healthcare and prevention. Recently the government of Ontario eliminated 'junk food' from provincial schools, and some members of parliament are pushing to follow Denmark's lead by banning trans-fats.

Social Services and Welfare Benefits

Canadians continue to see their country as a welfare state, but this is more myth than reality. British visitors are sometimes shocked by the level of homelessness – something that was virtually unknown in Canada 20 years ago. Government welfare services do exist, but they are less generous and more complicated than in the past. All levels of government administer services and support, which vary by province. The 'dole' as known in the UK is far more complicated in Canada, with varying levels of payments and qualification rules.

A single, healthy and employable person must actively look for employment and rarely goes more than 60 days without finding some sort of work. Those who return frequently for 'income support', as welfare is now known, may suffer from undiagnosed disabilities such as foetal alcohol syndrome. Benefits vary by province and according to individual needs. A single, employable man or woman might receive around C$400 a month in financial support (less in Alberta and New Brunswick and much more in Newfoundland and the north), in addition to job training and employment services. People with short- and long-term disabilities, children and others with definite needs qualify for other levels of support.

In a general sense, people living in Canada are not left completely 'out in the cold'. The federal government is generally most concerned with First Nations, Inuit and veterans. Provinces provide direct financial support to general residents through a complicated mix of systems that include cash payments and rent support and the aid of social workers. Cities have been most directly burdened by increasing numbers of homeless as well as individuals in high-risk lifestyles, by providing policing and supporting shelters and food banks. Studies have supported the need for greater preventative healthcare and social programmes, but recent political trends have limited the role of government in social policy.

Abuses of the system undoubtedly occur. Those Canadians who have never required government aid probably view the entire system as quite foreign, but others have learned to take advantage of it. It is all but impossible to quantify these people as a percentage, but it is likely a reasonably small minority. As hospitals remain purely public, patients who need some other form of social support often disproportionately burden emergency wards; a day in hospital is often more expensive than a full month's rent.

Many of even the federal and provincial services available lean heavily on volunteers. Volunteer and religious organisations do significant work, at both the local and national levels, by running shelters, food banks and support groups. Because volunteer organisations respond to local needs, they sometimes represent the most effective option for dealing with particular issues. The drug-related problems of Vancouver's downtown eastside receive a fair amount of media coverage. With help from city, provincial and federal governments, outreach organisations manage many of the support services for the area's residents – often volunteer workers are those who have experienced the same problems.

Government Services

All working Canadians pay into an **'employment insurance' (EI)** fund, which is a federal programme designed to support people who become unemployed through no fault of their own – those who are laid off or whose seasonal work comes to an end. Currently, stricter rules and lower unemployment rates have led to the government taking in far more in EI payments than it pays out, resulting in calls for premium reductions.

The EI programme was developed from a previous 'unemployment insurance' programme, which apparently sent the wrong message. In its various incarnations, EI has been very useful to seasonal workers, such as people in the fishing industry, who have no work at certain times of the year. It also provides maternity support and financial support for those unable to work due to injury, illness or compassionate leave. EI benefits may also extend to people looking for work after leaving prison. EI requires applicants to have worked a pre-set number of hours or days based on where they live and the local employment market. *See* **Working in Canada**, p.234. By design, the EI programme is not long-term, although workers in certain industries will receive financial support year after year. Separate programmes deal with longer-term unemployment and permanent disabilities. Online information about most federal government services can be found on the **Human Resources and Skills Development Canada** website (**HRSDC**; **www. hrsdc.gc.ca**).

The extent of federal services is wide-ranging and includes support for seniors (*see* 'Retirement and Pensions', pp.203–206), former members of the armed forces and aboriginal people. Long-term disability programmes fall under federal management, as do aspects of career planning and job training. The provinces run other employment training programmes, often with federal support. Each province manages employment centres, which provide help for the recently unemployed and those returning to the workforce. Most communities will have some sort of government **employment centre** with a jobs database and trained staff. Many of those looking for work make use of these centres as a first step.

Beyond purely employment issues, all levels of government employ social workers and personnel for the sometimes-difficult tasks related to child safety and other social services. Hospitals employ social workers and they also work with the police on matters involving domestic issues. In the words of one social administrator, 'Help is there, but normally you must ask for it.'

One major difficulty for child welfare is the age of majority, which is either 18 or 19, depending on the province. Much of the support infrastructure for at-risk children or those in abusive situations who have become wards of the state is removed once they become 'adults'. While some former wards do indeed go on and do well, many remain in marginal situations.

Provincial aid programmes vary and some were cut back dramatically through the 1990s. British Columbia has long been a logical destination for drifters – for climatic reasons, if nothing else – but the province also provided generous welfare support. Many of those services have now been cut back, some rightly so, but young people begging on the streets have become a common sight in Vancouver and Victoria.

More specific social spending occurs around certain social groups and environments. The issue of financial and social support for aboriginal people tends to be a 'hot topic' that is discussed frequently. Some Inuit communities along the coast of Labrador received international attention when various reports revealed shockingly high levels of substance abuse and suicide. Several years on and hundreds of millions of dollars later, little has changed, except that many 'consultants' have earned good wages.

Recent political and economic swings have indicated a move back towards social spending after a lengthy period of austerity. Government programmes that were once virtually bankrupt are now in much better financial shape, thanks in part to balanced budgets and lower levels of unemployment, which means fewer people draw benefits. Restructured programmes have become more difficult to access and this has undoubtedly reduced abuses, but perhaps left behind some of those in need. A gradual return to greater social spending appears to be under way.

Overall, Canada has low levels of poverty, but rates for children living in poverty are higher than the developed-world average. The governing Liberals have promised on various occasions to eliminate child poverty in Canada, but have failed to do so.

Retirement and Pensions

At one time Canadians had very high levels of personal savings, but it appears that the cultural disposition towards conservative investing has faded. Disillusionment with stock markets and notable increases in housing costs may have contributed to this swing, which may also owe something to even higher levels of economic confidence and, therefore, a diminished sense of having to save for a rainy day.

To some extent, working Canadians can count on fairly solid government support in their retirement, but those who plan to depend solely on government pensions after 65 must learn to budget well. Aside from earning or inheriting huge sums of money, the average citizen has four ways to prepare financially for retirement, which are discussed below. One additional approach to free up some cash involves downsizing the family home. The capital thus liberated is automatically tax-sheltered, as Canadians do not pay capital gains tax on profits made from the sale of a primary residence.

UK Pensions

A UK state pension is normally payable in Canada, but **you will not get annual increases in the benefit** once you have ceased to be normally resident in the UK. This means that your pension will stay at the same rate as when you left the UK, or when you first qualified for the pension if you were already living in Canada at the time. After 20 years, even with minimal inflation, you could be seriously less well off than when you first retired, and than if you had stayed in the UK where the pension is index-linked.

HM Revenue & Customs can provide retirement pension forecasts for people who are outside the UK or are about to go outside the UK (if the person is not within four months of UK retirement pension age).

If you have paid National Insurance contributions in the UK, the Inland Revenue will usually send you a claim form about four months before you reach UK state pension age. You will usually be paid straight into your bank or building society account in the UK or your bank account abroad, if you have one. Or, if you wish, you can choose to have your pension paid by payable orders sent straight to you by post. Payment is made every four or 13 weeks in arrears.

- **Department of Work and Pensions (UK), www.thepensionservice.gov.uk.**
- **HM Revenue & Customs (UK), www.hmrc.gov.uk.**

The Canada Pension Plan

Dating back to the mid-1960s, the Canada Pension Plan (CPP) underpins the national government's structure for securing dependable retirement income for Canadians. The plan exists in all parts of Canada, except Quebec, where the provincial government manages its own Quebec Pension Plan (QPP).

Contributions to both plans are compulsory, and Canadians who have contributed for the required minimum number of years can begin to draw the pension any time after reaching 60. The scheme is based on a retirement age of 65 and drawing it before then results in a 0.5 per cent monthly decrease for each month it is taken early. Starting to draw it later (which must happen by age 70) results in a 0.5 per cent monthly increase for each month it is taken late.

CPP amounts change yearly as the fund is indexed against inflation, but currently the maximum amounts paid is around C$864 per month. Contributions are based on average national wages, again a number that fluctuates, but which is around C$40,000. All salaried employees, plus their employers, must contribute to the plan. Self-employed individuals must pay the full calculated amount. In order to receive the highest pay level at retirement, you would have to contribute from age 18 to 65; however, a certain number of drop-out periods (for education, child-raising and so on) are calculated into the equation. Amounts paid are set on a sliding scale according to the number of years and amount of contributions.

The fear that with an ageing population and poor returns on investments the CPP would cease to be universal or would require higher levels of contributions has now waned. Some reforms in 1998 and strong investment returns appear to have restored financial order. Some more financially independent-minded Canadians and politicians have argued for the ability to opt out of CPP and to manage their own retirement financing, but this does not appear to be in the works.

Benefits can be transferred to spouses and, now, to same-sex partners. The system allows families to continue receiving pension support, even if the primary contributor has died. Payments to those families come as either a lump sum or in instalments. Provisions apply in the case of divorce (if no one re-marries) and to common-law relationships.

You will find information about CPP on the HRSDC web page (**www.hrsdc. gc.ca**) and on **www.servicecanada.ca**.

Old Age Security

For seniors who have never worked, old age security (OAS) and the guaranteed income supplement (GIS) offer a lifeline, but the funds are available to all Canadians over age 65. Currently OAS payments, which are indexed against inflation, are around C$500 per month. When there is no other income, GIS will increase that amount.

In order to receive OAS payments, you must have lived in Canada for at least 10 years – 40 years for the full amount. For tax purposes, OAS is added into gross income (as is CPP) so it is, in essence, taxed back from seniors who have high monthly incomes. Seniors whose income exceeds C$50,000 annually will keep little of the OAS payments, and it is probably pointless for those bringing in more than C$70,000 to even apply.

Private and Employer Pensions

Canada does not require private employers to provide pension plans, but the provinces place strict controls on the plans of those who do. When considering a move to Canada, take into account the quality of a company's pension plan. Long considered one of the bonuses of public service, government employee pensions are generally excellent, although civil service jobs are not as secure as they once were.

Whether public or private, pension schemes come in various forms and are based on the number of years of contributions, which basically relates back to how long you stay with the job. In most cases, new employees begin contributing immediately but do not become vested for a period of time – on average two years. With some plans, employers match employee contributions, but more generous companies will cover all the costs. Stock-option schemes, where a company offers employees its shares at discounted prices, are also very common. This investment option certainly helps to build loyalty, but has hurt employees when share prices have dropped dramatically, as was the case, for example, with Nortel Networks.

If the employer does not fully manage the pension programme, the employee may purchase a private fund at retirement or after leaving the job. In some cases, funds may be carried over to a new job. If, as an employee, you have not stayed long enough in the position to become vested, you may withdraw your own contributions, but will lose those from the employer.

Registered Retirement Savings Plan

The Registered Retirement Savings Plan (RRSP) forms a fundamental part of Canadians' retirement plans and is a government-regulated, tax-sheltered programme. RRSP contributions must be made by the end of February each year and count as a deduction against the previous year's taxes. The tax year matches the calendar year and in most cases returns must be filed by 30 April – or sooner if possible.

RRSP savings are not tax-free, but rather tax-deferred. Limits on individual contributions are based on the taxpayer's previous year's tax return and reach a maximum of 18 per cent of income – actual dollar amounts are increasing: C$20,000 in 2008, C$21,000 in 2009 and up to C$22,000 in 2010. The government-issued 'Notice of Assessment', which confirms the previous year's assessment, also gives the RRSP deduction limit for the current year. This means you must work for at least one year before you are able to contribute.

Because contributions to an RRSP come off your *pre-tax* income, they reduce your taxable income. The saved money is then registered and may grow, unimpeded by tax, until such time as it is de-registered (withdrawn). You may remove money from your RRSP at any time, but must add the withdrawal amount to your gross taxable income. Locked-in pensions can be transferred to locked-in RRSPs, and this offers a way to protect us from ourselves while regulating the amount that may be taken out.

The idea behind the RRSP system is to encourage people to save for retirement and allow them to defer tax on that money until such time as their income is reduced and they enter a lower tax bracket. You are now permitted to contribute to your RRSP until 31 December of your 71st year, at which point you must begin withdrawing funds. Obviously, contributors should not take the money out in one lump sum, but should withdraw a certain amount each year. One of the most common ways of doing this is with a **Registered Retirement Income Fund (RRIF)**. The RRIF ensures that you withdraw at least the minimum amount, while allowing the other funds to grow sheltered from tax. If you are worried about running out of money, you may choose to move your funds to a **Life Investment Fund (LIF)**, which sets a maximum on annual withdrawals.

RRSPs fall in and out of fashion and you do need to have the money in order to invest it. Financial institutions love RRSPs and each year a boom in investing takes place towards the end of February as working Canadians scrounge and borrow in order to contribute. A variety of regulations govern RRSP investments, including much more relaxed Canadian-content thresholds. The reality with such investments is that they do not always grow and corrections in the market can be particularly damaging to seniors on fixed incomes. In recent years, Canadians have put a little less of their money into RRSPs and more into real estate. From time to time the government allows individuals to borrow from their own RRSPs, without penalty, to help them to enter the housing market.

Education

Levels of education in Canada are very high and education is valued culturally. In an advanced economy that cannot compete with cheap labour, the focus has turned to achievements in management, innovation and intelligent resource extraction. A percentage will always 'drop out', but terminating one's schooling at age 16 happens far less frequently than in the UK and is widely seen as a poor choice. Funding remains an issue within the various education systems and costs have risen dramatically at the post-secondary level.

Overall, the Canadian education system differs markedly from that in the UK. Outside Quebec, the classroom grades number from 1 to 12. Until very recently Ontario, punishingly, had a grade 13. Regular education in Quebec, which goes only to grade 11, is followed by two or three years at a *collège d'enseignement général et professionnel* (CEGEP). Grades (or years) are generally split between two or three levels of schools – elementary, junior high (intermediate or middle school) and high school. In certain districts the middle schools do not exist, and in really small communities one's entire education may take place in the same room.

Because education is a provincial matter, Canada has no national department of education, but the federal government is partially involved in funding post-secondary institutions. Compulsory education varies, but generally includes kindergarten through high school. Required schooling begins between the ages of 5 and 7, while high school finishes at around age 18 – the equivalent of grade 12.

Students in the public system do not wear uniforms and they receive, overall, a very broad education. Even at the university level, most students follow some course of general studies before specialising in a discipline. This breadth of teaching varies significantly, but, generally, Canadian schooling embraces exposure to many disciplines and activities. At the early levels British students tend to be more proficient academically, although by high school Canadian children score just as well.

The provincial nature of education means that standardised testing is also provincial, even though qualifications are accepted throughout the country. Globally, Canadian students fare quite well, with Alberta's students ranking among the highest in the world – this achievement may be partly due to the province's wealth and also to a professional workforce that values education. 83 per cent of Canadians have completed high school and over 40 per cent have gone to either college or university – the highest percentage in the world.

School Boards

The provinces set education standards, and school boards, which may also be called districts or, in New Brunswick, district education councils, administer public schools. Nationally, Canada has over 250 boards, which are represented by the **Canadian School Boards Association (www.cdnsba.org)**.

The vast majority of Canadian students fall within the public system and each school board faces its own special challenges. Toronto and Vancouver have many issues associated with immigration and diversity, whereas boards in northern and rural regions may have to deal with huge distances and a shortage of resources. Locally elected trustees run school boards.

Private and Independent Schools

Canada does have many private schools, but they fill a far less important role in general society than in the UK. A few élite schools are scattered across the country and the young of wealthier families may attend them, but private schools are just as likely to be religious in design, or even focused on students with challenges. Private and independent schools remain governed by provincial curricula and must meet provincial standards and prepare students for higher education. Several provinces direct some funding away from the public system to private institutions. For a list of independent schools, contact the **Canadian Association of Independent Schools**, PO Box 820, Lakefield, ON KoL 2Ho, **t** (416) 780 1779, **www.cais.ca**.

For a variety of reasons, among them the formidable influence of the US media, English Canada does not have even one celebrity lifestyle magazine. As a result, the social élite receive less attention than in other countries and few Canadians would know very much about their education. Great distances and provincial standards mean that even private schools tend to respond to local issues, rather than national status. Upper Canada College, located in Toronto, is perhaps the best-known private school in English Canada, but even so it is hard to imagine students flying from St John's or Regina to board there.

Religious Education

In many provinces, a parallel Catholic school board exists alongside the secular public system. This is not the case in British Columbia or any longer in Newfoundland and Labrador since a 1997 referendum. Interestingly, the Catholic system dates back to pre-confederation and issues with Quebec, which has now restructured its school system along linguistic lines.

Provincial Catholic school systems are not private and citizens can choose where their taxes go. Catholic schools cannot refuse non-Catholic students and must comply with provincial education standards, which includes teaching about evolution. Other private religious schools are located throughout the country. Some are entirely private – and exist up to the post-secondary level. Some religious communities, such as the Hutterites, may fall under the jurisdiction of the local school board, and basic schooling will take place in English and follow the regular curriculum. The reality in such communities is that religious teaching takes place in all other aspects of daily life.

Home Schooling

The choice to educate children at home has become increasingly more popular in the United States and is permitted in Canada. In order to take over education responsibilities, parents must meet the education standards of the province or territory. Home schooling is popular among some religious communities and with those who have become disillusioned with the broader education system, but is also used by families who may be travelling for an extended period of time.

Special Needs Schooling

The various provinces offer a variety of services, in both the public and private school system, for students with disabilities and challenges. Although national and provincial laws protect the rights of all Canadians with challenges, it is well worth looking around for different programmes within the school system. Philosophies and ideas for assisting and integrating students with unique needs differ according to regions and specific schools and therefore parents should take the time to compare. Severely challenged students often attend separate schools or divisions within schools, but for those whose disability is less severe, schools may pursue a policy of integration. Integration programmes take various forms and may result in students being accompanied by special aides, or in modifications to the school's infrastructure.

Just as programmes have been developed for students at the lower end of the curve, there is some provision for 'gifted' students and students with behavioural problems. A degree of streamlining begins in middle school, and most school boards offer either programmes or separate schools for accelerated study. Equally, some schools and programmes have a definite focus – towards the arts, vocations, academia or behavioural modification.

Language Immersion

Language will always be an issue in Canada. From politics to education to immigration, bilingualism shows up everywhere. Depending on where you live in Canada, you may rarely encounter the other national language in your daily life, but at an administrative level both official languages are used and sometimes confused. In addition to English and French, many other languages are spoken and recognised in Canada. Internally, Canada's First Nations students receive education in their own languages, at least to a level where trained instructors are available. In the new territory of Nunavut, much of the education takes place in Inuktitut and the territory is gradually developing more texts and standards. Older immigrant groups have maintained some schooling in their own languages and it is always surprising to find people born and raised in Canada yet who speak English with a distinct 'foreign' accent.

The majority of new immigrants to Canada do not come from either the English- or French-speaking world, and therefore English as a second language (ESL), or its French equivalent, must be incorporated into school systems. Over 40 per cent of students in the Toronto school system do not speak English at home – Toronto's schools have the highest immigrant population in the world. While the benefits of this diversity are obvious, schools must devote a significant amount of their resources towards creating a reasonably level playing field in terms of education. Fortunately, for younger children a new language comes quickly, but at higher levels the adaptation process may be much more difficult.

In addition to choosing between the secular and Catholic school systems, parents have some other choices to make. To support national bilingualism, all English-speaking provinces have **immersion schools** where instruction is almost entirely in French. The immersion process has not been perfect, but it has resulted in thousands of English Canadian students developing a proficiency in French. After 12 or more years in the system, many students have not managed to lose their rather strong accents, but they do come away with high levels of comprehension. A small percentage of students in immersion experience problems with phonics and mix the two languages – they spell English words with French phonetics and vice-versa. Some jurisdictions offer various forms of later immersion, with French schooling beginning at age 9 or 12. This may be an option for immigrant families, or for those who want to ensure a child's firm grounding in English.

The linguistic reality in Quebec means that the province is faced with teaching English as a second language. In an effort to protect the French language, immigrants to the province are required to educate their children in French. Whether openly admitted or not, this legislation was aimed at Montreal's traditionally large English-speaking community and, perhaps to a lesser extent, at other minority communities in the province. If you were born and educated in the province in a language other than French, your children may be educated in that language, but if not, French is the primary option (although English is taught as a second language).

The immersion system has prospered in English Canada and expanded beyond French. The most important up-and-coming language is Spanish, so some parents are choosing to educate their children in that language. Of course, some children end up in an immersion programme simply because the bilingual school is the closest to home.

Funding and Costs

Provincial taxation funds the public school system. Public education is a right and no one may be refused schooling; attendance is compulsory. Despite the funding, some costs are passed on to parents. Every school will levy certain fees each year for certain activities and materials. These costs are not consistent and in most cases a provision exists for families with limited resources.

Although independent schools may qualify for some funding, the excess costs are made up through tuition fees. Direct costs to a parent with a child in the public school system may add up to several hundred dollars per year, whereas private schools may cost thousands.

Funding for public education often comes second to healthcare as a percentage of provincial expenditures and includes significant infrastructure, teacher and employee wages, teaching materials and even transport – the classic yellow school bus.

School Hours and Holidays

Local school districts set their own hours of operation and annual schedules according to provincial guidelines. It is very difficult to generalise about school hours across the country as they vary according to local realities and necessities. Children in Canada often start their school day earlier and therefore finish earlier than in Britain. In most parts of the country kids are at school by 8 or 8.30am and will finish their day by 3 or perhaps 4pm, although after-school activities such as sports may keep children at school much later. The lunch break usually lasts an hour, and younger children enjoy a couple of play breaks.

As both parents often work outside the home, the early starts are a good way to get the whole family going, but parents often have to make some arrangements for their children after school. By high school, when classes often end earlier in the afternoon, students are left to their own devices, which in many cases involves going to a paid job. Younger students may attend a planned activity or go to some form of day care.

With a few exceptions, the Canadian school year begins in early September and carries on through June. During that time several professional days (when students do not go to school), a few statutory holidays and breaks at Christmas and Easter interrupt the school year. As working Canadians have limited holiday time (often two or three weeks annually), many parents will enrol their children into summer camps and activities during the long break at the end of the school year.

Teachers and School Structures

Canadian teachers form an important political voice and their unions hold significant sway in most provinces. When compared to other public service employees with similar levels of education, teachers in Canada are quite well compensated for their commitment. Teacher strikes are not unheard-of and teachers' unions frequently act as vocal advocates for greater funding and, of course, public education.

All teachers have university qualifications, with many completing all or part of another degree before moving into a faculty of education. Competition for acceptance into education faculties is strong and would-be teachers require high grades. Many move on to complete postgraduate degrees in education. Teachers may teach in a different province from the one where they gained their qualifications but they have to be accepted into the other province's professional body (which always involves a cost).

Individuals trained as teachers in the UK will generally be able to have their professional credentials accepted in Canada. This process involves providing original transcripts and perhaps even passing some sort of test. The board of the provincial governing body makes the decision about accepting the individual.

Within a particular school, teachers will be employed to cover certain subjects and it is generally accepted that most teachers will also participate in some form of extra-curricular activities, such as coaching sports. During contract disputes, teachers may choose to 'work to rule', meaning they will fulfil only minimum working requirements.

Each school's structure includes a principal, an assistant principal and a variety of departmental heads, although this will depend on size and need. In addition to teachers and administrative staff, schools often enjoy the help of volunteers from the local community.

Choosing a School

If you are moving within Canada or from the UK to Canada, your children are entitled to a public education. Immigrants may have to show proof of residency. Despite the variety of alternative and private school options, the majority of students will attend the school closest to where they live. Occasionally, schools may fill beyond capacity, but essentially they cannot refuse students. Finding a 'good school' often becomes a factor when choosing an area of a city in which to live. As younger families have moved out to the suburbs, new schools have opened up and older ones have closed down or been revamped.

It is worth talking to other parents in the area to evaluate the local school(s) and you should visit the schools themselves. Your children may be more advanced in some subjects and behind in others, but the school system will ideally insert them in at their age level. School activities play a significant role, so if your child has specific interests or is very active, a school's location may be important.

Post-secondary Education

Individual provincial and territorial governments have the responsibility for post-secondary education in Canada, at both university and college levels, and they provide most of the funding. Additional financial support comes from the federal government, research grants, and student tuition fees. Tuition fees remain a hot topic of debate and large fee increases have occurred during the last 15 years. Fees that were once below C$1,000 dollars a year can now run into the thousands.

Virtually all post-secondary institutions in Canada have the authority, by charter or local legislation, to grant academic credentials. Generally speaking, public universities perform the degree-granting function – offering under-graduate degrees (bachelor's) and graduate degrees (master's degrees and doctorates). Colleges offer vocationally orientated programmes of study that lead to certificates and diplomas, while some grant a few applied-arts degrees that are the equivalent of, or lead to, university-level qualifications. The expansion of the degree-granting abilities of some colleges or the linking of certain courses to university transfer programmes has taken some pressure off overcrowded universities. Even at high school level, some courses are now being designed for application at university level.

In general, the post-secondary school year begins in September and continues to the end of April or early May, although some institutions operate year-round with four semesters, including two shorter ones over spring and summer.

A regular undergraduate university degree in Canada takes roughly four years, based on the September to May programme, with additional time factored in for apprenticeships and work placements (required for engineers and medical professionals). Students can apply to universities anywhere in the country, but will pay lower tuition fees if they remain in their own province.

Every province in Canada has at least one university and often several. While different schools specialise in certain fields and, without question, some schools have achieved a slightly more prestigious reputation, socio-economic ranking plays a very small part in the public-provincial system. The tendency in Britain and the USA to hold the élite universities in higher esteem does not really exist in Canada. The national magazine, *Maclean's*, does an annual ranking of Canadian universities that is taken quite seriously – it regularly highlights several universities (McGill in Montreal, the University of Toronto, University of Western Ontario and the University of Alberta in Edmonton, for example) as having high levels of education, but most universities become known for particular disciplines. Moreover, many Canadians will choose a university on the basis of location and cost, rather than reputation.

Colleges abound and offer a wide variety of course work that ranges anywhere from vocational training to special-interest studies. Many colleges, like universities, are public, although private institutions are increasing in number. Some private colleges have a distinctly religious basis whereas others focus on a specific discipline – both Vancouver and Toronto, for example, have well-known private film schools.

Admittance to University or College

Cost, competition and desire have made it increasingly more difficult to gain admittance to a university and, in some cases, college. For Canadian students carrying on from high school, high marks have become the most important element in their application.

As the high school system has a degree of streaming, it is important for students intending to go to university to pursue the highest levels in each stream. This is not as important for those students who plan to attend a college that places less emphasis on the academic route.

Once accepted into a university or college, students must maintain a specific grade-point average and may need to achieve certain scores in order to move on to different faculties. With the exception of certain disciplines, students are first accepted into the Faculty of General Education, from which they may apply to other faculties after the completion of certain courses.

Students from Quebec leave high school and carry on to CEGEP before university. The CEGEP system directs students towards either a vocational or a university route. Students pursuing the latter may earn some credits toward the university degree.

Any movement between universities within Canada and internationally tends to be complicated and bureaucratic. The transfer of credits is generally permitted, even between some non-Canadian institutions, but you might not receive the full equivalent of time studied. If you have already completed an undergraduate degree, you are welcome to apply to a different institution for graduate studies – in fact it is often recommended that you do so.

The Government of Canada actively recruits foreign students to come and study in Canada (*see* **Red Tape**, 'Students', pp.140–41). If considering a permanent move you will find tuition fees are lower for permanent residents.

In order to pay for university, many students seek government-backed loans as well as part-time jobs and scholarships. The rate of fee increases may slow somewhat in coming years, but there is little evidence that university education will become more affordable. To this end, students may remain closer to home where the bank of mum and dad can help. All institutions provide information about financial assistance.

Recreational Courses

Despite shockingly short holidays, many Canadians are active and embrace the outdoors – a good idea given the nature of the country's environment. Some studies show that people on the west coast are the most active in the country, while disturbing trends toward increased obesity suggest an increasingly sedentary culture. Nonetheless, cities and towns have developed walking and cycling trails and, even at −30°C, you will see hardy people out jogging. With mountains, lakes, an endless coastline, public skating rinks and community fitness centres, recreational opportunities abound, and no one says you have to be good to participate.

If you are looking for recreational courses, begin by enquiring at a local university. Outdoor education programmes almost always offer, to the general public, courses designed to make nature more accessible. Community courses, managed or supported by the municipality or the local education board, provide instruction in any number of activities. For the most part, prices are not prohibitive and courses take place in the evenings or on weekends. As you drive around a city you may see signs saying 'learn to cross-country ski' or 'learn to skate'. Local community centres will host different programmes and will often maintain a local skating rink. Indoor swimming pools are common and the local pool will offer swimming instruction. Curling clubs are very popular in Canada, especially in prairie towns, and although competition may be fierce, the environment is friendly and introductory courses are always available.

Families where both parents work outside the home (which is the majority) can take advantage of a wide variety of summertime recreational courses that are at least partly designed to entertain children out of school. Local school boards or city recreational departments offer such courses. Day and summer camps form the foundation of Canadian society, with children often spending several weeks 'at camp' in the summer learning to canoe and swim.

Taking Your Pet

Pet ownership rates in Canada match those in Britain and other Western countries. Rural regions, with boundless distances to run, things to sniff and other animals to meet, will thrill any dog. While cats are also common, they are not as obvious as their canine cousins. In addition to the usual risks from people and automobiles, domestic cats can have trouble defending themselves from wild animals. Many people choose to keep their cats in the house and sometimes leave them unaccompanied for long periods in small apartments.

Pet-owners are responsible for their animals' actions, and towns and cities have become progressively stricter about cleaning up faeces. In the winter some dog owners may be tempted to bury the evidence in the snow, which leads to much disgust once the snow melts in spring. Communities have off-leash areas, but otherwise dogs should be walked on a lead.

The **National Animal Health Program** is the governing body responsible for the importation of animals and animal products, including pets. As an agricultural nation, Canada has strict rules to maintain its environmental integrity. Surprisingly, a fairly long list of creatures may enter Canada without a plant protection permit, among them tarantulas and scorpions – neither of which would fare particularly well should they escape into the snow. According to the **Canadian Food Inspection Agency (www.inspection.gc.ca)**, the fact that Britain is a non-rabies country bodes well if you want to bring Spot with you to your new home – although the flight will be very hard on him. Be aware that the cost of transporting animals may well work out to be more expensive than your own air fare. Not only is there also the price of the flight, but also vets' fees for microchipping, vaccinations and blood tests, import permits and possibly insurance. At this time, Canada does not insist on quarantine for cats or dogs coming from countries where rabies is not prevalent, although it would be a good idea to come with proof of vaccination. **Jets4Pets, t** 0845 408 0298, **www.jets4pets. com**, can arrange all aspects of getting your animal to Canada, except for those elements that must be dealt with by your vet.

As a signatory to the Convention on International Trade in Endangered Species (CITES), more exotic pets may raise a greater concern. Turtles and their eggs require an importation permit, as do many reptiles and amphibious creatures. The importation permit, in many cases, will only be granted to zoos or research laboratories. Beyond the general classification as pets, products made from endangered species are also restricted, so leave the alligator boots at home.

It is always advisable to confirm animal regulations before coming to Canada. Birds from Asia cannot be brought into the country because of avian flu. Under no circumstances may you bring your pet primate, unless you are coming from the United States. Gorillas, monkeys and their many cousins may only come into zoos, so have your husband shave his back and hands before leaving for Canada.

Working in Canada

From a national perspective, Canada's working environment is diverse and offers many opportunities. However, huge distances mean employment is highly regional. The affluent banking community of Toronto differs markedly from the resource industry towns further north in Ontario.

As is the case throughout the developed world, a great majority of Canadians work in service industries, but those services reflect the local economic environment. Almost all communities feature the same predictable fast-food restaurants, but the clientele is home-grown and style and presentation reflect the local area.

When measured against the cost of living, wages are reasonable in Canada, but many employees manage only two weeks off during the first few years in a job, and, while theoretically the working week may be 37 or 38 hours, some professionals put in much more time than that on the job.

This chapter will take a broad look at the labour market and Canada's working environment, but it must be noted that significant regional and professional variations exist. As a nation, Canada walks an interesting line between New World capitalism and Nordic-style socialism, although the capitalist model has dominated for the last 20 years. Government is a major employer and union workers enjoy guaranteed high wages and comfortable working conditions in important sectors. Other sectors have minimum wages and limited workers' organisation. Canada's impressive supply of natural resources has created impressive wealth, and kept people in smaller and diverse communities contributing and participating.

Business Etiquette

British people should find the Canadian business environment friendly and accessible. Canadians pay little heed to class distinctions and most people are generally pleasant and respectful in their business interactions. For the most part, civility rules when it comes to doing business. In recent years a noticeable shift to the use of first names has taken place in many business relationships but within the business or professional setting, doctors are still accorded the title of Dr, followed by the last name. Secretaries and support staff may or may not use the more formal Mr, Ms or Miss, depending on the specific corporate culture in which they work. Although a structured European or Latin style of relationships does not really exist, the harder-sell style sometimes associated with the United States has not taken hold. A common mistake newcomers make is to believe that the Canadian business environment mirrors that of the USA, and this is simply not the case.

Canadians see themselves as polite and, while it is easy to exaggerate a national ethos, business relationships tend to be cordial and the human element is not forgotten. Loud arguments are rare and it is not acceptable to be openly rude or too pushy. Car salespeople may be the brashest group in the business market, but they are an exception and it would be interesting to know if the least couth among them earns a very good living. The real-estate sales culture also possesses some of that 'go get 'em' pushiness, but overall the sales environment is not terribly aggressive.

As in other developed economies and in smaller communities, a belief persists that it is important to build relationships and that reputation matters. During a boom, as experienced in oil-rich Alberta, tradespeople are worth their weight in gold and customers may have to wait for long periods, but generally verbal agreements are respected and all are expected to fulfil any obligations. People in service industries are often not well paid and the service can reflect this reality. Servers in restaurants and bars earn gratuities – generally 15 per cent – and therefore, despite earning only minimum wage, the take-home pay can be significantly higher. Table and bar service is polite and friendly but not subservient. There is not a clear relationship between quality of service and the tip expected, although this was presumably the original idea behind tipping.

Canadians are not emotionally demonstrative (outside the hockey arena) and a handshake continues to be the normal greeting between both men and women. The presence of so many minority communities has caused the Latin kiss on the cheek to catch on in a few areas, and in Quebec the kissing of both cheeks is appropriate in familiar environments.

Condescending to women, by calling them 'sweetheart' or anything similar, is likely to receive a frosty reception and in extreme instances may elicit legal reprisals. Although certain industries maintain a gender bias, the divisions are breaking down, so, for example, it would not be a good idea to joke about women drivers when around coaches or large lorries. A mistake commonly made in Canada, as well as in the UK, is to assume that a woman in the medical profession must be a nurse. Without doubt, the majority of nurses are female, but medical schools produce more women graduates than men, which results in increasingly more women doctors. These gender issues are relevant in the Canadian business and professional environment. Men still earn more, are greatly over-represented in politics and remain the 'head of the household' in a declining number of conservative and religious families but, overall, Canadians at least think of women as having equal rights and opportunities and therefore treat them as equals in the working environment.

In business settings, greetings do not have the same degree of formality found in southern Europe. A little polite conversation about the weather or last night's hockey game is fine and enjoyable, but it is perfectly acceptable to 'get down to business' quickly. Tradespeople who come to your house should give their name and that of the company they work for – obviously a security measure. You are not required to offer coffee or refreshments to people working in your home, although it is perfectly acceptable to do so.

Dress

The 'downtown' professional dress code is a jacket and tie for men and conservative dress for women. In resource-based communities and smaller towns, only a few professionals will dress in this manner. Male school teachers will not necessarily wear a tie, but the principal will. Generally, front-line banking staff do not bother with formal business dress, but managers, stockbrokers and analysts will. Hotel managers wear business suits and the staff uniform worn by employees generally includes a tie. Bureaucrats and other government employees, even at the upper management level, may not necessarily don formal wear, but dress codes do vary between departments. The now-important and ever-expanding information technology world seems to live by its own standards, though its managers and consultants know when it is appropriate to dress up.

Tattoos are currently very trendy all across Canada, and not limited to any particular economic or professional group, although most of those who sport tattoos belong to a younger age group. Servers in restaurants and bars will happily expose their midriffs and body art, but such displays are not appropriate in a professional environment. Some employers have moved to a 'casual Fridays' policy, which allows employees to dress down once a week. If the local hockey team is doing extraordinarily well, some people will wear the team's jersey to work, and in Calgary the entire city goes western during Stampede week. Otherwise, jeans are not considered appropriate business attire. Dress codes reflect local culture, but generally are quite predictable in Canada. Few bankers wander about in city-style pinstripe suits, but the higher-end banking and legal professionals do favour a degree of formality.

Western Canadians believe their business style is more relaxed than that in central Canada. Calgary has a lot of big money and, although the city is growing rapidly, the pace and style of business remain slower than in Toronto or Montreal. People on the west coast adopt an even more relaxed appearance; while it is possible to spot the odd British gentleman emerging from a tower in Vancouver, comfortable west coast clothing holds sway.

Not all medical professionals wear uniforms and the traditional 'scrubs' come in any number of colours. Engineers, field workers and those involved in resource industries dress much more for climate and comfort than for appearance.

Where Business Takes Place

Canadian cities have large, impressive downtown cores that feature skyscrapers and, sometimes, interesting architecture. Head offices and banks locate in these central areas, while industry and manufacturing takes place in industrial districts or on the outskirts of communities. Some business clubs exist, but the private club culture is less significant than in the UK. The various chambers of commerce and associations such as Rotary perform important roles as community participants.

Business lunches and breakfasts occur frequently, but do not revolve around the pub. It may be fine to have a pint or a glass of wine during a sales lunch, but alcohol figures less prominently in the professional environment – if unsure, wait for direction from the client. A lot of business, particularly sales, takes place on golf courses and even at ski hills during winter. Golf has become extremely popular, and corporate golf tournaments are often just an excuse to give away promotional merchandise. It has been said that the person making the sale should not win the round of golf. The sporting culture tends to be less competitive than in the UK. It is acceptable to be an average golfer or skier but it is never appropriate to laugh at or comment on poor performance.

The Labour Market

When viewed as a whole, the Canadian labour market appears to be broad and diverse. However, the country's size and its regional make-up create a labour environment that varies greatly from one region to the next. Great differences among the provinces affect everything, from unemployment to taxation to basic industries, and while Canadians will pick up and move across the country, such an undertaking is far more complicated than driving from Cardiff to Edinburgh for a new job.

That noted, the labour situation in Canada does show certain broad consistencies. On the positive side, the division of labour between men and women is fairly equal and constantly improving. Unemployment rates have declined steadily and are at record lows in some parts of western Canada. Recent government budgets have reduced personal taxes, but services have also decreased. Conversely, job security has declined and basic vacation time ranks among the lowest in the developed world – both public and private employees may have to remain in a position for several years before becoming eligible for a third week of holiday.

Roughly 17 million Canadians are actively involved in the labour force, in contrast to nearly 31 million people in the UK. As in all developed economies, the service industry employs the largest share of the workforce and manufacturing, in all its forms, creates the most wealth. Resources hold a place of particular importance, although their economic impact can be exaggerated.

Southern Ontario and the vast prairies of the Canadian west are extremely productive and farming takes place in almost all regions of the country, yet agriculture employs less than 3 per cent of the national workforce. Farming seems to be an industry in continuous crisis and the most agriculturally based province, Saskatchewan, is losing population. Obviously, the statistic of actual numbers of agricultural workers does not reveal the whole story. Behind the farmers, and just as affected by the state of the agricultural industry, are a myriad services – from equipment sales and production to marketing, transport and education. When drought strikes or when Europe and the USA impose restrictions on aspects of the industry, the shockwaves affect the whole economy.

In a similar vein, geopolitics has had a positive impact on other elements of Canada's resource industries. War in the Middle East and the state of the world economy have driven oil prices to levels not seen since the Gulf War and, as luck would have it, the Alberta tar sands (see p.96) contain the largest single oil reserve so far found on earth. While the oil is very expensive to extract, high prices have led to the investment of astronomical sums in that province and the development of a diverse and sophisticated workforce. Alberta's oil industry makes up over 20 per cent of the province's economy and Calgary has attracted so many head offices that it now comes second only to Toronto. Many of the internal migrants left their home provinces because of weakness in other resource industries. The uncertain nature of prairie agriculture has long prompted farmers' children to move to the cities, but the most dramatic labour shift arose out of the collapse of the Atlantic fishery. Newfoundland, in particular, is gradually emerging from a serious economic depression and the prospect of offshore oil revenues, as well as tourism, may stem the outflow.

Foreign workers and trade are extremely important to Canada's economic well-being. Over 20 per cent of Canada's workforce is foreign-born, and imports and exports make up a huge percentage of the economy. New Canadians have been very successful in diversifying the Canadian economy and opening new markets. The country's small population means that internal consumption simply cannot match production and, with the world's largest economy directly to the south, Canadians spend much of their time selling products, resources and services to the United States. The wealth generated by living next to the last superpower can have some negative impacts, particularly with regard to trade disputes. US tariffs or trade restrictions (whether merited or not) have an immediate impact on the Canadian economy, as does the value of Canada's currency in relation to the US greenback.

While Canadian business is not totally integrated with that in the USA, there is a clear dependence on the US market. Many Canadians end up working in the United States, particularly at a professional level, and nationally the labour market is often compared to the USA, despite significant differences. Much talk circulates around the so-called 'brain drain' from Canada to the USA. The medical industry has suffered from this exodus, as high wages lure Canadian doctors and other medical professionals south to the private US system. More Canadian move south than Americans move north, although this trend may be changing. Canada attracts many professionals from other countries and will continue to need immigrants as the indigenous labour pool ages.

Nationally, the unemployment rate is around 6 per cent. A further breakdown of this percentage reveals that unemployment rates are lowest in the west and highest in Atlantic Canada. An internal system of wealth redistribution, called transfer payments, generates much talk in Canada about 'have' and 'have-not' provinces. Currently, the two main 'have' provinces are Alberta and Ontario. Those two provinces contribute more to Canada than they take out. Albertans pay the most into the country per capita but in gross terms Ontario stands out as the largest contributor. British Columbia has traditionally occupied the spot of third donor province but over the last decade has spent some time in the 'have-not' category. The Olympic-driven construction boom in Vancouver has recently heated the economy there. In the east, Nova Scotia's economy has shown a steady improvement and it may become the first Atlantic province in many years to join the ranks of net contributors to the federal coffers.

The heart of Canadian manufacturing is found in southern Ontario's Golden Horseshoe, around Toronto and in parts of Quebec. The importance of the automobile industry in Ontario and heavy transport production in Quebec cannot be overstated. A couple of Canadian companies produce home-grown brands of buses but no distinct Canadian car exists. Nevertheless, the industry is huge. Canadians produce the second largest number of motor vehicles in the world and the highest number of light-commercial vehicles per capita.

Canadians living outside the central manufacturing areas may be only vaguely aware of how much automobile manufacturing contributes to the Canadian economy. Indeed, most Canadians would claim that resource extraction forms the largest component of the national economy. It is this sector that will most feel the effect of recession in the United States, and the 'R' word has been used to describe the Ontario economy in 2008.

Industry-specific manufacturing tends to locate in areas close to their markets. Edmonton, for example, produces much of the equipment used in oil extraction, and Halifax has a ship-building industry. Pulp and paper mills are found throughout British Columbia and in the forested areas of New Brunswick and Quebec. The comparative isolation of Canadian cities tends to make them self-contained in terms of services.

An important by-product of the Ontario automobile industry has been the labour union movement, although membership, as a percentage of the workforce, is higher in other provinces. The largest single union is the Canadian Union of Public Employees (CUPE), which represents government workers. In terms of the overall labour market, slightly over 30 per cent of the Canadian workforce belongs to unions, with work stoppages in British Columbia and Quebec making the news most often. Without question, unionised employees enjoy higher wages and greater benefits than non-union workers performing similar duties. Depending on their individual allegiances and personal ideologies, Canadians are probably as divided as the British when it comes to issues of organised labour, but strikes tend to be regional rather than national.

Government, in its many manifestations, is a major employer. The many levels of government (and therefore bureaucracy) mean that public employees may work for cities, provinces or the federal government. At the federal level, the civil service employs a disproportionate number of Francophones, partly due to bilingual requirements and also proximity. Located beside the Quebec border, Ottawa encompasses a sizeable Franco-Ontarian population. New Brunswick is the only fully bilingual province and some language requirements apply for employment in its government services – including policing.

During the budget-balancing period of the 1990s, government cut back spending in all ways imaginable and removed some of the traditional security associated with the civil service, although government bureaucracy appears on the increase once again. With more money but a clear deficit in some service areas, governments are scrambling to re-establish service (such as dealing with the immigration backlog). Many services are contracted out, and this has increased the number of people engaged in contracting and consultancy work.

This trend underlines a shift, occurring in much of the developed world, away from lifelong careers. While some people remain in the same position or with the same employer from the time they leave school until they retire, more and more change jobs every few years and often move into private consulting or contracting work as retirement approaches. An improved quality of life and higher financial rewards offset the lack of security.

Overall, the Canadian labour market is fluid and highly skilled, with a very small segment occupied by the informal economy. High levels of education and limited regional opportunities have led to significant movements of people within Canada and abroad. Variances in taxation also have an impact on business and, therefore, regional labour markets. Canada's large cities display an economic vibrancy that comes from their embrace of banking and finance, as well as all things technological. Smaller centres remain either resource- or manufacturing-based and struggle to adapt to a changing global market.

The country's dependence on exports and foreign investment has created a high level of sophistication within the labour market. Low-paying service jobs sometimes result in a corresponding low level of service. The economy's strong growth in recent years has led to some labour shortages at the lower end of the pay scales – which is partly why so many holidaymakers find seasonal work.

Job Ideas

Finding a job in order to pay the rent is not difficult in many parts of Canada, although securing that dream job can take much longer. If you are skilled with your hands, there are thousands of opportunities. The western provinces are desperately short of construction workers and trades are in short supply. It may be hard for electricians to transfer their skills due to the different infrastructure, but carpenters, tilers and the like can find work in the booming housing industry, providing you can pass the Canadian or professional exams.

Construction companies are bringing workers from abroad and colleges cannot train people fast enough for the workforce. If you are interested in making a life in Canada and do not already come with a skill, pursuing in-country training in a specific trade is a real option. This also applies in the medical fields and in policing. In fact the latest Canadian census confirms that the country will remain dependent on immigrants to compensate for low birth rates and an ageing workforce. A worldwide recession will obviously impact the Canadian working environment, but currently many areas suffer from labour shortages.

When looking for work, British and Irish citizens enjoy a small degree of celebrity as a result of their accents. English-speaking Canadians, particularly those with a British or Irish heritage, feel well-disposed towards visitors from the 'old' countries. Canadians view working holidays as a reciprocal arrangement and enjoy the fact that people from the Commonwealth visit their country. Of course an accent will not land a high-paying professional job, but it certainly helps in the service industry and in getting settled.

In ski towns such as Banff and Whistler one could easily come away with the belief that half of all Canadians were born in Australia or Britain. Ski hills actively target **working holidaymakers** – potential employees who do not seek permanent positions and who will work for minimum wages. The logic is obvious. Why not hire an educated and friendly Irish person, rather than try and attract Canadians to jobs that may be good fun but offer little future?

The working holiday culture is similar the world over and a high percentage of those who choose Canada for a year are happy to survive on basic wages and the promise of a ski pass, beautiful views and an active party culture. Moreover, what at first appears to be a shockingly low wage can, in fact, improve with gratuities. A charming smile and a good story can go a long way towards earning an extra C$100 or more a night behind the bar.

Those looking for temporary work to finance their stay in Canada have several interesting options. While **bar or restaurant work** is popular, it can be more difficult to find than one might expect. Gratuities mean a server in Canada can earn a reasonable living and not be overburdened with professional requirements, or even taxes. As a result, better restaurants usually implement a training process that may entail several months of hosting, cooking or cleaning before the employee moves to the profitable serving shifts. Nevertheless, given the size of the restaurant industry in Canada, a bit of perseverance should result in a job.

Hotels are always looking for workers, but make sure the hotel is in a place where you really want to be, because the job itself can be punishing. Non-unionised frontline hotel staff are poorly paid, do not receive gratuities, but do bear the brunt of complaints. Unionised positions become available less frequently and do not usually apply to temporary positions. Second-language skills help when it comes to finding hotel work, and resort hotels may offer some form of accommodation.

Retail industry employers pay little more than minimum wages, but work is always available. If you have any specific product knowledge (shoes, computers, and so on), try those outlets first and you should find a job easily. Some outlets operate on commission and most will have some sort of bonus system for employees, in addition to giving them a discount on products. At the risk of overwhelming the company with applications, try the Mountain Equipment Co-op chain website at **www.mec.ca**. The company has outlets in many major cities and is popular with outdoor enthusiasts. As a co-operative, it offers a reasonable pay base and employees gain access to goods and outdoor courses.

Continuing on with the outdoor-lifestyle theme, **tourism centres** are always on the lookout for people with acceptable driving permits to shuttle and guide tourists. For a different winter experience in the summer, check out the jobs at the Columbia Icefields, located between Banff and Jasper in the Rocky Mountains on **www.brewster.ca/Columbia_Icefield/Icefield.asp**. Working as a **ski instructor** is popular and jobs are not hard to secure if you have the proper qualifications, but the pay is average at best. Working in any role at a ski resort generally results in a free ski pass. Once you start working at a resort location – and there are many in BC, Alberta and Quebec – it should not be hard also to find off-season employment through local connections.

Beyond the predictable job market, those not looking to pursue a career will find many other, more typically Canadian job opportunities. Every summer in British Columbia and other forestry-driven regions, thousands of young Canadians go **tree-planting**. Usually paid per tree, planters live in the great outdoors and replace felled timber with saplings. Healthy, invigorating and reasonably well paid, tree-planting jobs match the industry; so good years for timber mean more trees to plant. The easiest way to find tree-planting work is to visit employment centres at universities and in lumber-based towns. As a general example, try **www.yerc.ca/lmi_forestry.html**, an employment website for the alternative and beautiful town of Nelson in British Columbia's interior.

At various times, the **fruit- and wine-producing** areas of British Columbia and southern Ontario need casual workers, and with a little more experience you may be able to find a few weeks of work during harvest on the prairies.

Outside the very well-beaten path through the Rockies and British Columbia mountains, many other interesting employment opportunities do crop up in other parts of Canada. If you plan to work for only a season or a single year, why not opt for a destination that is very different from where you would want to live permanently? The Yukon is magic and the north has almost no darkness through the summer. The tourist season is short, but it is relatively easy to find work from May to September in Dawson City. While the job would probably involve working in a shop or hotel, you could, while there, stake a claim and pan for gold – several hundred people still prospect up there, and high gold prices encourage mining. For more information contact the Yukon government at **www.gov.yk.ca/services**.

Other northern areas offer a variety of opportunities. The polar bear season in Churchill, Manitoba is short, but some sort of service job in that community of 800 will provide you with a unique experience. The town has a few hotels and restaurants, as well as the usual associated tourist services.

Both the Pacific and Atlantic coasts have beautiful communities and fun environments, but the depressed state of the fishing industry means that hopping on a trawler would be quite difficult. Vancouver Island's economy is in reasonable shape and the mild climate keeps golf courses open year-round. The fact that many Canadians, including young and retired, drift out to the Island increases the competition for jobs in some sectors, but service jobs are available.

Finding a short-term job in the Maritimes will take longer, but the welcome offered by the people makes the effort worth it. Halifax, the largest centre, enjoys the lowest unemployment rate, so for short-term work that city may provide the best option. While knowledge of the French language may not be an absolute necessity in some areas of Quebec, French is the functioning language everywhere except the English-speaking parts of Montreal. And in the same way that people from the Commonwealth choose to work in the western mountains, many Quebecers go west to ski and improve their English. If you would like to find work in Quebec, ask around – you may find some short-term agricultural work tapping for maple syrup.

A move from the working-holiday route to the **professional environment** presents some challenges. Immigration Canada requires a medical clearance for those planning to work in certain professions (teaching, medical) and, once over the first hurdle, provincial standards and rules face the newcomer. Nevertheless, beyond all the bureaucracy, work opportunities do abound.

Many parts of the country experience severe shortages of **medical staff**, particularly doctors and nurses, so finding a position should not be difficult. For an added challenge (and reward), try working in one of the isolated northern communities. Public employees in the north receive an extra allowance and exposure to a truly unique culture. Both hospitals and clinics frequently advertise vacant positions and medical professionals can find work in Atlantic Canada, where wages are a little lower, but so is the cost of living.

After providing proof of training, British and Irish **teachers** should find that local school boards accept their qualifications. Work as a supply teacher (substitute teacher) provides a way to look around for a more permanent position while getting paid.

Academics can sometimes organise a temporary lecturer position at a Canadian university or college. Some positions are set up as exchanges, whereas others may lead to tenure. Universities can be slow in responding and the environment political, but in many respects they do not differ markedly from institutions in the UK. The next few years will see an increasing number of Canadian academics retire, which is likely to create a window of opportunity for a new group of instructors and lecturers. With tertiary education so widespread in Canada, colleges frequently look for people with particular skills to teach more vocational subjects.

As in Britain, experience matters, so your working background at home will have an impact on the sort of employment you qualify for. Some of the work opportunities in this vast, young country will be very different from those in the UK, but the general employment landscape will be quite similar. Banking and finance take place in the large centres, resource work happens on site and construction, in all its forms, follows economic growth – and sometimes drives it. In order to obtain a higher-paying private-sector position, you will need skills, plus a degree of networking. It can take a long time to generate clients for consultancy work, so as much direct experience as possible in a particular industry will help.

When looking for subsistence employment, feel free to approach an employer with your **curriculum vitae** or résumé (*see* p.230). For specific professional jobs, such as those in the medical field, you can find vacant positions online or by calling the **human resources** (HR) departments at hospitals. **Placement agencies** do work in the high-end business sectors but the process of finding a good job can be quite lengthy. Some skills, such as information technology training, transfer fairly easily, but legal training, for example, may not transfer at all. If you are interested in a particular field, contact a few employers and set up some meetings before you move over lock, stock and barrel.

Finding a Job

Canadians generally possess a good, honest work ethic and the country sits in the middle of the pack in terms of economic freedom, several places below the UK. Different regions of the country may claim to have more industrious workers than other areas. Public service employment plays a dominant role in government cities, while the free market is alive and well in others.

Looking for Work

You will have more luck finding a job if you have something specific in mind. Professionals considering a move to Canada should look at the websites of different employers or professional associations to find out, relatively quickly, information about available positions – this is all usually online. Even more importantly, however, you need to determine whether Canada will accept your **qualifications**. If you have qualifications in a specific profession, contact its provincial governing body to see if you may transfer your credentials and what such a process entails. Medical professionals trained in Commonwealth countries do not generally experience too many problems (beyond fees, exams and time), but some engineering training is not recognised. This will also apply to legal and financial trades and academic sectors.

Many of the larger multinational companies have offices and divisions in Canada, so it is always worth looking into a transfer or work exchange. In Canada itself, both the federal government and provincial governments maintain job offices. Not everything available is listed, but you can get some idea of what is out there. A very useful website run by the government of Canada is at **JobsEtc (www.jobsetc.ca)**. JobsEtc provides advice on résumé writing and public and private sector employment and has links to many of the major online employment resource companies such as **Monster (www. monster.ca)**. You could also look on **Workopolis (www.workopolis.ca)**. While it remains relatively rare to obtain a job directly from a website, you will find it offers a good first step and is the easiest option from abroad. Many departments within government and other public sector agencies have embraced online advertising of positions. Most sites include the disclaimer: 'Only applicants selected for an interview will be contacted.' An excellent site dedicated to many fields of public sector employment is **www.jobs.gc.ca**. Provincial government websites also provide links to career opportunities.

Private employment agencies have offices in all major cities and they may be a good option. Not all employers use such services and, as a general rule, the agencies fill needs at the upper and lower ends of the economic spectrum. Temp agencies, although less widespread than in the UK, provide an option for short-term work. Executive head-hunting agencies charge employers impressive finder's fees and often deal with specific industries and skills. All that said, if registering your résumé does not involve a fee (as sometimes it does), it may be worth sending it off to some of these agencies.

Applying for employment 'virtually' has some positives and negatives. The length of time between the date of job postings and the close of applications is usually quite short, and opportunities for communication are limited. The public and even the private sector may advertise positions where a successful candidate has already been identified but the job still has to be openly contested, even though the result may be a foregone conclusion. It can be demoralising to apply for hopeless positions and, even if you are the ideal choice, union or in-house rules may require management to hire within the organisation. Moreover, sending a résumé off into space is not particularly rewarding when it generates no response.

A number of factors govern the time-frame for finding good employment. Qualified professionals may search for six months or more before finding a specific opening in their field. Once established, the process becomes easier as you make contacts while working and gaining experience. Some business-orientated schools and programmes emphasise networking and contacts, whereas others focus more on skills. Depending on your particular field, you should know which is more important.

CVs

Canadian business and administration has moved online and it is perfectly acceptable to use e-mail for contact purposes. Many jobs encourage online applications and much communication takes place virtually. Despite this, the telephone remains the easiest way to speak with someone and it is not inappropriate to call prospective clients or employers.

In Canada CVs are called résumés; though there is no set rule to a résumé's format, it should not exceed two pages in length, except for industry-specific reasons. The one-page résumé style of the USA is used in Canada, but not as a fixed rule. The purpose of a résumé is to present someone's application so well that it is moved on to the interview stage, therefore the document should be designed to be scanned in 30 seconds. There are many sorts of résumé – some in technical professions may just list qualifications on theirs. Follow standard guidelines if you are creating or revising your CV.

A résumé is almost always sent with a covering letter, which should include your contact details, but should not simply repeat everything listed on the résumé. In writing a covering letter, refer directly to the position being applied for and, if possible, address a specific person using his or her correct title.

Experience matters in the Canadian job market and, as so many new graduates already know, you cannot gain experience without a job. **Education** is another vital component, and most of your competitors will be as educated as you are. Where you went to school has much less importance than what you have done and what you can do. All things being equal, British or Irish nationality may give you a slight advantage when it comes to looking for employment in Canada. At the upper-management level, place of origin does not count for much, but in terms of making initial connections Canadians are generally well-disposed towards people from the other side of the Atlantic.

Networking events take place in different cities. You should also check out the local Chamber of Commerce, government-run employment offices and even the local newspaper – all good places to start gathering information. Provided you have a large enough economic reserve, you should be able to dedicate the time needed to find a solid position.

For service and temporary jobs, the process takes less time. Once you have your work permit and SIN card (*see* **Red Tape**, p.149), you can literally wander into different businesses and ask to speak with the manager.

Applying for Work

For specific professions, the application and interview process should fill in any blanks about the applicant's set of skills. However, brain surgeons will generally find work doing brain surgery, regardless of how personable they are. As an 'equal opportunities' country, Canadian employers are somewhat restricted in what they may ask. This fact alone may increase the appeal of the online application process, because human error and prejudgment can be a little more controlled. Employers are not, for example, permitted to ask your age, but they may ask if you are of a legal age to handle alcohol, if that is relevant to the job. If you feel that, despite being qualified for a position, you have been discriminated against by reason of age, gender, ethnicity, or some other rights issue, you do have some legal recourse, but only in more extreme situations. Job descriptions usually include some vague language about disposition or a preference for hard-working team players and employers may invoke such clauses when they choose another candidate.

The interview process for service jobs is often quick and friendly. Give your résumé to the local manager, who can tell you almost immediately if an opening exists. Hiring someone in a basic position presents little risk, and a basic position may lead to opportunities for promotion to better positions (for instance, from dishwasher to kitchen help).

The application and interview process at the professional level takes much longer and is certainly more competitive. In larger organisations, the HR department will screen résumés, so, as a first step, you must make it through that process or else circumvent it by contacting a manager directly. If your résumé does make it through, you can expect to be called in for an interview.

Interviews for managers usually involve a panel of peers, a panel of employees and perhaps a third relevant group. While the time frames for such procedures may drag on, keep in mind that the job was advertised because of a need. It is perfectly acceptable to apply for several positions simultaneously, and it may be worth mentioning other job offers as a negotiating tactic.

In the trades, you may be offered work almost immediately and then evaluated on the basis of performance. During strong economic periods, countless small companies have more work than they know what to do with, and crews are flown across the country in order to meet deadlines. Basic labouring jobs can be just as easy to find; however, as with trades, when the work dries up, everyone is out of a job.

Interviews can be quite formal and surprisingly long. Good interviewers will be polite and friendly, but will ask relevant and pointed questions – without ever crossing legal lines. In this regard, Canada's employment economy is as modern as that in Britain and performance matters. Hiring can be an expensive proposition, so employers take the interview process seriously. Be prepared to give concrete examples and make sure you can back up everything you say.

Pregnant women do not need to disclose that fact to would-be employers – although at some point it becomes obvious! Employers cannot refuse to hire you because of a pregnancy although, if it is well advanced, they may look to other candidates.

You should also provide at least three references as part of a job application. Traditionally, citing overseas referees presented a problem, but e-mail can solve the long-distance issue. You should also provide your referees with an outline of the position applied for so they may address relevant questions clearly. These are not reference letters – prospective employers will phone or at least write.

Being Employed

Employment Contracts

When everything comes together and you receive a job offer, remember that you will be placed on some sort of probation for three months to a year and will have to wait some period of time before any benefits kick in. Negotiating is not uncommon and jobs are often posted with salary and benefit ranges that depend on experience. Contracts will outline working hours, salaries, vacation days, sick leave, pensions and benefits. Some industry contracts (and those contracts drawn up when you sell a business) may include a non-competition clause. This prevents you from establishing a competing business as soon as you leave a position. From a knowledge perspective, such clauses apply particularly within the IT market, as companies spend great sums training specialists who may then leave and try to contract out their services privately.

The contract is between you and your employer and it may involve joining a union (which in most cases happens automatically). Some contracts commit you to a set length of time for the employment, and may include a bonus if fulfilled. Seasonal-work employers (such as at ski hills) often adopt this approach, but make sure you understand the specifics about receiving the bonus. Confirm, for example, that the bonus will be paid even if weather, or other issues not related to you, should force an early closure to the season.

A bonus system is also common in the private sector. Bonuses may double the wages of bankers and executives during good times. Obviously, a bonus is just that, but many accept large bonuses as a regular part of their income. Bonuses paid as a lump sum incur a rather significant tax penalty and, in redundancy cases, the bonus may not be included.

Employment contracts are important and both parties should honour them. The contracts of unionised workers generally contain clauses that set out hours of work and responsibilities. Negotiating unions may ask their members to 'work to rule', which means workers perform only those tasks set out in the contract. Interestingly, this tactic may not always benefit workers, because managers can demand higher productivity during periods of work.

Wages

Wages basically fall into five categories: a true salary; hourly pay; commissions; a combination of commissions (or bonuses) and salary; and contracts. **Salaried** employees receive a wage for a specific number of hours of work. At the very least, they should be available for that time. Salaries would not necessarily prevent the awarding of overtime or bank holiday pay, but that would be written into the contract. School teachers make up one of the largest groups of salaried employees, while politicians form another group.

The pay for an enormous number of Canadians is calculated **by the hour**. Within this group are medical professionals (managers are salaried), most secretaries, fast-food cooks, and almost anyone belonging to a union. The pay stubs of workers with set schedules, such as nurses, will indicate an hourly wage, but the pay they receive amounts to a salary. Depending on union rules and contracts, some workers can earn significantly more money by working overtime, although collective agreements may prevent this.

The regular working week in Canada is 37½–40 hours. Salaried workers and those paid by the hour should receive extra compensation for any additional time worked. Such time would include statutory holidays and overtime. Some employers and collective agreements honour this requirement with time-in-lieu or extra pay (1½–2 times the regular hourly wage). While workers might think these rules sound attractive, the employer may be able to avoid paying for additional labour. When a collective agreement prevents overtime, workers simply have to work their hours – and the conscientious often end up putting in time for free.

People working on **commission** are found in many parts of the business world. Commissions may be called profits or fees, but are calculated on some percentage of a cost or product. This form of payment also occurs in the UK, but anyone entering commission-based employment should understand all aspects of it. Ideally, it is comforting to receive some sort of wage in addition to commissions or bonuses, but in high-earning industries such as stockbroking, up to 100 per cent of earnings may come from commissions. In those instances, as with real-estate sales, the professional will share some percentage of the commission with the employer.

Like commissioned employees, **contract workers** do not necessarily have to adhere to a set number of hours of work, but they do have clear deliverables. A contract writer with a set project fee, for example, will earn proportionately more by finishing the manuscript more quickly. Contract work almost always extends over a pre-determined period of time and, while contract wages can be quite high, employers do not have to pay benefits.

Pay scales change for all types of employees, and, depending on the type of employment, at different rates. Each province has established its own minimum wage and adjusts it from time to time. Salaried employees working for larger companies usually receive a pay increase that at least matches the inflation rate for that year. Commissioned workers may benefit from a rising commission scale, or will simply earn more by selling more – as do servers in restaurants and bars, who make the bulk of their income from tips.

Taxes and Deductions for Employees

All employees (except for some on contract) have taxes and other deductions removed directly from their pay. Wages are generally paid either bi-weekly or monthly, but the amount deposited into your account rarely resembles your gross wage. Taxes are quite high in Canada and vary between regions. A typical employee on a more-or-less fixed salary (plus perhaps a little overtime) has to pay federal and provincial taxes, employment insurance (EI; *see* p.201), Canada (or Quebec) Pension Plan (CPP/QPP, *see* pp.204–205), private or corporate pension contributions, benefit contributions and perhaps union dues.

Healthcare fees (where applicable), city taxes and the dreaded sales taxes are paid separately, but deductions and other costs for someone earning a reasonably high salary can amount to 50 per cent of gross earnings. In fairness to Canadian governments, this figure is often exaggerated. As in the UK, the Canadian tax system is progressive, taking a larger percentage from higher-income groups than from low-income groups; *see* the **Canada Revenue Agency** website, **www.cra-arc.gc.ca**, for up-to-date information on rates and much more. Taxes have dropped slightly at both the federal and provincial levels and, depending on which statistic you consult, the overall tax burden in Canada is similar to that in Britain.

The tax year runs from January to December and most people in Canada have to file their tax return by the end of April. Your employer issues form T4 at the end of the year, which you have to complete and submit. Federal and provincial taxes are filed together everywhere except in Quebec. Regular employees do not find filing terribly difficult and do it online or with the help of an accountant or tax agency. Potential tax deductions include charity donations, Registered Retirement Income Plan contributions, moving costs (between cities), professional dues, education expenses, etc. The self-employed and corporate tax systems are more complicated, but permit many more deductions.

Revenue Canada deducts taxes from pay cheques by extrapolating amounts over 12 months, or perhaps 26 pay periods. Employees on commission or those who receive large bonuses may increase their basic deduction in order to avoid receiving a large bill after filing.

Vacation, Sick Leave and Maternity Leave

As mentioned elsewhere, one of the clear disincentives about moving to Canada is the embarrassingly short **holidays**. New, professional employees manage only about two weeks (10 days) annually and often have to put in several years before reaching a more civilised four. Vacation time is either written into a contract, or accumulated during time worked (essentially the same thing) and in some jobs is paid as a percentage during each pay period. Those wishing to take a longer period away from the office can sometimes apply for a leave of absence (LOA), which will not give you any money, but may protect your job.

Sick leave accrues at fairly generous rates and an inordinate number of employees fall ill just before long weekends and around Christmas. Sick leave covers short- and medium-term illness. In the event of long-term disabilities, people unable to work will eventually move on to a federal government programme. You are permitted to leave work for up to two hours in order to attend an appointment with a doctor or dentist.

In order to qualify for full **maternity benefits**, a woman must have worked at least 600 employment insurance (EI) hours within the previous 52 weeks. The maternity benefit is set at 55 per cent of average insured earnings, up to a maximum of C$413 per week of taxable income. Benefits last a maximum of 50 weeks. In addition to this federal programme (which most people pay into), many employers top up the government payment for a period of three months to a year.

Losing Your Job

Sometimes things just don't work out, and being fired or made redundant (laid off) is rarely enjoyable. If it appears that the writing is on the wall, you have two choices. You could quit and find a friendly person in the organisation willing to act as a referee, or ask to be laid off, which makes it easier to receive unemployment benefits. You should then go to the nearest government office and fill out the paperwork. If you feel you have been fired for unacceptable reasons, it is possible to file an unfair dismissal claim.

Several factors govern the process of removing employees. During the probationary period, an employer can let you go for almost no reason, but once the probationary period is over they must adhere to a process of warnings and documentation. Within the union environment even stricter procedures apply, and workers are rarely dismissed just for average performance. A few absolutes, such as stealing and, in modern times, misuse of the Internet, can result in immediate dismissal.

Freelancing, Contract or Part-time Work

Increasing numbers (up to 25 per cent) of Canadians work on short contracts or part-time. The appeal of freelance work lies in the freedom and flexibility it brings, as well as the potential to make very good money. Individuals in freelance positions are essentially self-employed and therefore are responsible for their own taxes and social security contributions. Part-time employment, on the other hand, depends on the employer.

The term '**freelance**', while understood, is not used all that often. Applied most often to journalists and writers, it also, in the broader sense, includes many workers in the arts, graphic design and IT. Non-writers or artists may call themselves **consultants** or register as an official company with one employee. The retrenchment by the major Canadian company Nortel Networks, combined with deflation of the tech bubble, 'encouraged' many IT specialists to move into private contracting. Workers in Canada's large film industry ply their trades in an even more unusual manner. They are essentially freelance or self-employed, but union regulations protect them on site. When there is work they receive excellent compensation, but then work might dry up for months.

Benefits for **part-time workers** sometimes match those of full-time employees. However, at the lower end such as restaurant work, part-time employees are paid by the hour and, with fewer hours on their pay cheque, they have proportionately fewer deductions and benefits such as vacation pay. In the professional environment, a part-time position may be classified as a fraction of a whole position (for instance, 0.7 or 0.5) and the pay and deductions for those workers is pro-rated in the same manner. New mothers will often return to work part-time while their children are small. These part-time workers earn less than full-time employees but their benefits remain more or less intact.

The **'casual' worker** category comes below part-time status. Although casual workers do not receive the benefits of a fully employed person, taxes should still be deducted directly from their pay. Any wages earned will go into their gross income and may result in other sources of income being taxed back.

Tax and Social Security

As a general rule, the self-employed find themselves in a reasonably comfortable tax situation but a limited benefits position. A freelance or contract worker can 'write-off' almost every expense. While business executives must dress appropriately at their own expense, a freelancer is entitled to claim an extensive range of deductions against income. The home office, lunch, clothing (in some cases), vehicle expenses, telephone and so forth may all be part of the cost of doing business for someone who is self-employed. As a result, many freelance workers end up paying very little in the way of taxes. For those taxes that are due, a quarterly pay scale or a deduction system gets around the problem of receiving a large tax bill once a year.

Whether or not the self-employed person must charge and pay GST and/or PST (the various types of VAT) will depend on the product offered. Unincorporated individuals doing contract work generally do not have to collect this tax. Small businesses do, so it is important to work out these details thoroughly.

Self-employed people are also responsible for paying their own Canada Pension Plan or Quebec Pension Plan contributions, as well as making EI contributions. If the taxable income is quite low, these costs are not insurmountable – although most contract workers will never qualify for employment insurance benefits. In addition to these costs, freelancers pay their own healthcare premiums (where applicable) and may want to acquire some sort of coverage for dental and perhaps prescription costs.

Additional Income and Capital Gains

If you are employed in a regular paying job *and* pursue contracts or additional opportunities on the side, all of your earnings will be combined with your gross income for taxation purposes. For example, as in the UK, Canadians have taken to purchasing rental properties. Any revenue generated from such investments is taxable, but the investment or business entitles you to claim all sorts of legitimate deductions.

Profits from the sale of your principal residence are tax-free, but a profit from the sale of an additional property will incur **capital gains tax**. As a general guideline, the capital gains tax will amount to 25 per cent or 50 per cent of the actual capital gain. Capital gains made from trades in the stock market and other investments are taxed at around 25 per cent. You may write off gains against losses, but that is only because you have less net gain. Restrictions may be placed on how long you can carry losses forward – for such taxation issues it is well worth contacting an accountant.

Worldwide Income and Double Dipping

Canada maintains tax agreements with other countries so that workers do not have to pay tax on the same income twice. If Canada is your primary residence – as determined by home ownership, healthcare premiums and other factors – you must declare your entire worldwide income to Revenue Canada. If you have already paid tax elsewhere on that income, you may be eligible for a credit against the taxation you owe in Canada. In such situations it is well worth obtaining the services of an accountant.

Since 9/11 a general tightening of financial flows has taken place. You must declare all monies over C$10,000 when entering Canada (this should be taken seriously) and, if you do not have a track record with a bank, any large cash deposits may arouse suspicion.

The Audit

While the ability to deduct every last thing may sound appealing, Revenue Canada takes tax evasion extremely seriously. Self-employed individuals should avoid the temptation to conceal income and to write off every last penny, because at some point the government will wonder how you can afford to live. Computerisation of many financial records also makes hiding income sources more difficult. Once Revenue Canada has you in its sights, it may repeat the audit process every few years, and that is no fun whatsoever.

If working for yourself, you should keep all receipts for at least five years and be able to prove that you can afford your lifestyle. The system is complicated but not unfair and, with so many legitimate deductions, it is worth playing by the rules.

For a basic understanding of the Canadian taxation system, visit **Revenue Canada**'s website at **www.cra-arc.gc.ca**. This site will also link you through to a series of free telephone numbers and, with a little patience, you should be able to talk to an actual person.

Starting Your Own Business

After a period of self-employment, you may feel ready to start your own business. Many self-employed people pursue this step, which involves two essential elements. First, you must set up the framework and develop a viable business plan; second, you must put in hundreds of hours of hard work. The term 'business' covers everything from a one-person show right through to an international corporation. Without doubt, small business remains one of the largest employers in Canada.

For many reasons, immigrants to Canada are heavily represented in the small business environment. They run shops and restaurants and provide any manner of services. Often, experienced professionals from other countries will open up very marginal businesses simply because Canada does not accept their qualifications. Other migrants arrive with funds specifically for the purpose of starting a business. Immigration Canada and most of the provinces have established provisions for those migrants who intend to invest in Canada (*see* p.146) and, for some, the investment route offers the easiest way.

Immigration Canada may require proof of a business plan and funds, but even if not, it is essential that you prepare a business plan. As repeated often throughout this book, raw economic data provides only a vague clue to the size and diversity of Canada. Few small or even medium businesses have access to all 32 million Canadians, so any business plan needs to start with a realistic view of the market. On the positive side, provincial governments and the federal government actively encourage business investment. Even municipalities are on-side as they try to support new business and urban renewal.

Specific regulations apply to some businesses, but the basic process of registering and maintaining a business is not too arduous. **Registration** is the first step. If you plan to run a business under your own name, with nothing added to that name, then you do not have to register the company – you will simply be self-employed for tax purposes. To take the business a step further, you can register the name at the municipal level, but protection of the name requires that you register it either provincially or federally.

To register a business name, you will need to find a licensing office – sometimes the same place where you obtained your driver's licence. The next steps include a name search and filing the registration. Some jurisdictions perform name searches online and provide a response within one day, or two weeks by post. You may choose to simply register as a trade and sole proprietor, or establish your business as a corporation. Larger and more complicated businesses may require the assistance of an accountant or lawyer, but operators of small businesses can undertake the procedure on their own.

Search and registry costs vary, but the whole process can cost as little as C$32 for an unprotected trade name. Other options include registration as a limited or incorporated company. Once you have registered a name, you should then organise **licensing** through the local municipality. If you take this step first, and find out that someone else holds your proposed business name, the municipality will charge a fee for a name change. Licensing costs also vary according to the municipality and the type of business, but the process for small-scale enterprises may cost as little as C$150 and take less than an hour to organise. When warehousing and construction form part of the business plan, municipal zoning regulations come into play and the proposal must receive planning and zoning approval.

Provincial authorities control the process of registering a business and therefore you may have to repeat it in each province as your business grows. For a comprehensive **list of municipalities**, visit the Canadian Government website: **www.canada.gc.ca**. Although it takes a bit of time, you can find links to every municipality in the country and obtain contact information. The business-licensing process can be completed online, but it is probably worth visiting the local office. Numerous websites provide business start-up information and municipal pages include many of their names.

The national Canadian Business Services Centres page, **www.canadabusiness. gc.ca**, is an excellent central site for entrepreneurs. This site also provides information about registering **trademarks** nationally. Trademarks, which must be renewed every 15 years, fall under the Trade-Marks Act.

As long as the business conforms to the municipality's zoning regulations, you may choose to either lease or buy a property – or even work from home. Some businesses also lease vehicles, and owners of small-scale limited companies will regularly run most expenses through the company and simply pay themselves a small wage, or take a yearly dividend. Equipment devaluation can be deducted from taxes.

Most businesses must collect **provincial and federal sales taxes** (PST/GST or HST in Atlantic Canada). Individuals with strong backgrounds in book-keeping or accounting may choose to negotiate this tax quagmire on their own, but it can be fairly complicated. Although these taxes are collected on all services or goods provided, the equivalent taxes paid on operating expenses can be deducted, so taxes are not paid twice. Profits will incur business and corporate taxes, as well as municipal rates. Royalties, payable to the provincial and/or federal governments, may apply to resource-based industries.

Case Study: Richard Derham, Business Owner

Originally from Cheshire, and now in his mid-40s, Richard moved to Toronto in 2000. Richard's training as a lawyer took his professional life to London and Paris. After extensive travel and a general disenchantment with life in England, he decided it was time to make a permanent move abroad. Initially Richard was particularly drawn to New Zealand, but was concerned about the distance from his family, particularly because his mother was in poor health. After visiting most major centres in Canada, Richard chose Toronto for its quality of life and the fact that England is only six hours away. As with New Zealand, he was particularly drawn to Canada's mix of large city sophistication and low population density.

How did you organise to work in Toronto?

When I decided to emigrate I went back to school in Paris to study for an MBA. Fortunately I applied for jobs in Toronto from Europe and was offered a position with a management consultancy firm in Toronto and they organised the visa. Immigrating was relatively easy for me once working here, although I have heard numerous horror stories about the time it can take to receive landed immigrant status – and that is only half the process. Again and again people are permitted to move to Canada, yet do not have their professional qualifications accepted. Unless Canada does something to sort this process out, we will be losing good immigrants to other countries.

You now run your own business in Toronto...

After working with the management company for 13 months, a downturn in the market saw several of us made redundant. Instead of carrying on in the same field I decided to branch out and try something entirely new. The courier business is quite extensive in large Canadian cities, so with profitability and

If you are considering starting a business in Canada, the national economy will be grateful for every **employee** you take on. Finding qualified employees may present a challenge, and as an employer you have numerous obligations. It is important to understand provincial working standards and minimum wages, benefits such as CPP payments and other associated costs. For a general outline of human resource issues, refer back to: **www.canadabusiness.gc.ca**, a good HR reference site for small and medium businesses.

While business rules and standards are industry-specific, most governments at all levels in Canada want to encourage investment and entrepreneurship. Business contains inherent risks, but it also offers freedom and potential. Successful small- and medium-sized Canadian businesses often become very involved in local communities. Public-private partnerships have gained popularity as a model for attracting new investment and large events, such as the Olympics. Even regions where the government is decidedly left-wing have seen government regulation replace government ownership. An understanding social responsibility in mind I created a new company in 2002. TurnAround Couriers is an entirely private business venture that employs youth in risky situations and pays market wages, thereby allowing them to enter the workforce and afford unsubsidised housing.

Was it relatively straightforward to start the business?

There really is no need to pay large fees in order to set up a corporation. Most of the process can be done online and it is not too arduous. The challenge, as elsewhere, is to research and develop a viable business model.

Working with younger adults, how do you find Toronto's youth?

They really are not much different from those in England, although notably less aggressive. Ice hockey is the big sport here, but there isn't the hooliganism or violence in the same way as there is football hassle in England. There is no need to cross the street at night (at least downtown) when you encounter a group of well-watered lads.

What are your impressions of Toronto's diversity?

Toronto's multiculturalism was the big draw for me. There is nothing like it in England, not even London. Tolerance is widespread and the ethnic areas are celebrations, not ghettos, and outsiders feel at ease. My wife came to Canada from mainland China, so we are living the modern Toronto reality where over 50 per cent of the population was born outside Canada.

Do you have any advice for anyone considering a move to Toronto?

Don't dilly-dally; it's a great city. Toronto's weather is better than England's, as Is the lifestyle all around. Getting qualified to work in your profession in Canada is difficult and time-consuming, so make sure to have that process clear, or at least be aware that this huge obstacle exists before simply arriving.

of the local market ranks in importance alongside an understanding of macro-economics, and it is well worth gaining some experience in Canada before launching into a major business venture.

Volunteering

In 2001 the Canadian Mint released a commemorative 10-cent coin (dime) that celebrated the International Year of the Volunteer. Canada and particularly the prairie regions continue to maintain a great volunteering tradition, so it may come as a surprise that free labour is not always easy to give away. Many situations arise where volunteers should be able to lend a hand, and with a little effort this is indeed the case, but increased security and safety concerns, as well as competition, have slowed the process. Moreover, non-profit organisations and event organisers do in fact incur expenses with volunteers, so they still have to watch the bottom line, despite not paying wages.

Various shocking revelations about child-abuse issues have led to a tightening of regulations that apply to volunteers working with youth. Disturbingly, several recent high-profile cases have involved adult volunteers in positions of authority who abused children in their care. Accusations have surfaced around hockey coaches, foster families and even within the Scout movement. The organisations continue to function, but volunteers now must undergo a more rigorous screening process, which involves a police check. Fortunately, the check can be done in minutes at the local RCMP office and costs less than C$30.

Volunteers offer their time and help in all sorts of fields and activities. When you land at an airport in Alberta, you will be greeted by friendly, Stetson-wearing volunteers who are happy to help out. Thousands on thousands of Calgarians dedicated their time to make the 1988 Winter Olympics a great success and volunteers form the backbone of numerous events and festivals held across the country annually. Vancouver is currently recruiting volunteers for its 2010 Winter Olympics – see **www.workopolis.com**.

At the social service level, volunteers work for local shelters and food banks and are very involved in church activities. Shelters and outreach organisations receive more than enough support around Christmas, but often have to hunt for help in February. Schools almost always appreciate the support and help of local parents, and junior sports teams could not exist without volunteers. Volunteers support and buoy the political party that represents most closely their vision for the future of the country.

Professionally, new graduates will commonly volunteer in order to make contacts and gain experience. During weaker times in the economy, it can be mildly depressing to witness numerous applicants for one *volunteer* position. Many students will volunteer for all sorts of activities to gain experience and to become connected.

As a newcomer to Canada you may consider volunteering at any number of organisations. Business and social clubs, some connected to those in Britain, exist in many areas, and Canada's multicultural flavour has given rise to many ethnic associations, including Irish, Welsh, Scottish and English societies. Such organisations often undertake fundraising for their own support and to help out in the community.

It is worth doing an Internet search for volunteer opportunities that are relevant to specific areas and fields of service. Even internationally, the **Canadian International Development Agency (CIDA)** supports volunteer programmes – although what this agency considers a volunteer could be called a paid worker by developing-world standards.

References

Canada at a Glance

Capital city: Ottawa

Type of government: Constitutional monarchy, federalist parliamentary democracy, appointed senate

Head of state: Queen Elizabeth II, represented by Governor-General the Right Honourable Michaëlle Jean

Head of government: Prime Minister Stephen Harper (Conservative Party), since 23 Jan 2006; he currently heads a minority government; four political parties are currently represented federally

Administrative divisions: 10 provinces, three territories; each division has a parliamentary government led by a premier

Independence (Confederation): 1 July 1867 (four provinces: Ontario, Quebec, Nova Scotia, New Brunswick)

Area: total: 9,984,670 sq km; land: 9,093,507 sq km; water: 891,163 sq km; second largest country on earth

Coastline: 202,080km

Westernmost major city: Victoria, British Columbia (much of the Yukon Territory is technically further west)

Easternmost major city: Saint John's, Newfoundland

Northernmost city: Iqaluit, Nunavut (over 6,000 inhabitants), above 63 degrees north; Edmonton, Alberta, at 53 degrees north, is the most northerly major city

Geographic highlights: Mild southern climate extending north to the frozen Arctic; huge quantities of fresh water, much frozen; dramatic mountains in the west, central plains; Canadian Shield is the largest physical feature

Bordering countries: United States (only land border), France (Islands of St Pierre and Miquelon), Greenland

Population: 33 million (2008 estimate)

Languages: English (official), French (official), Inuit and aboriginal languages (official within certain territories and districts), Chinese, Hindi, Italian, German, Ukrainian, many more

Religion: Catholic 46 per cent, Protestant 36 per cent, other (including many non-religious) 18 per cent

Legal system: Common Law, Civil Code in Quebec

GDP (2007): US$1.4 trillion

GDP per capita (2007): US$38,200

GDP growth (2007): 2.7 per cent (and falling)

Unemployment: 6 per cent

Life expectancy: 77 male, 83.8 female

The New Face of Canada
   Over five million Canadians, or 16 per cent of the population, consider themselves to be a 'visible minority'. This represents a 27 per cent increase between
2001 and 2006 and has occurred primarily due to immigration and a lower
domestic birth rate. In 2006 nearly 84 per cent of immigrants arrived from non-
European countries. The Chinese community has long been the largest visible
minority but has recently been surpassed by South Asians in population. Other
significant minorities include Blacks, Filipinos and an ever-increasing Latin
American population.

Public Holidays and Celebrations

Public holidays for which employees are to be paid are called statutory
holidays. People having to work on statutory days are either paid extra or given
time in lieu. There are ten national statutory holidays, with most provinces
including one or two more. Christmas Day is probably the quietest of all the
holidays, with the majority of shops and services closing. Perhaps as a response
to the rest, Boxing Day is the most manic shopping day of the year. Special
additional holidays are celebrated under exceptional situations.

Official Public Holidays

1 Jan: New Year's Day; a day of hangovers and polar bear swims – events that
   involve jumping into freezing water.

Good Friday

Easter Monday

Mon before 25 May: Victoria Day (Patriot's Day in Quebec); dating back to 1845,
   Victoria Day was designed to celebrate that sovereign's birthday; now
   formalised in law, Victoria Day serves to celebrate the current monarch's reign;
   the 'May long weekend' is popular for camping and welcoming spring.

1 July: Canada Day, the national celebration of confederation; when the first falls
   on a Sunday the holiday is officially moved to 2 July.

First Mon in Sept: Labour Day; the Labour Day weekend signals the end of
   summer break for students and is popular for watching Canadian Football.

Second Mon in Oct: Thanksgiving – timed for the end of harvest, this truly
   American holiday is celebrated later in the US because of the later harvest.

11 November: Remembrance Day; still taken seriously in Canada – poppies are
   worn; ski resorts in the Rockies try to open for 11 Nov.

25 Dec: Christmas Day – depending on family and ethnic tradition, Christmas is
   sometimes celebrated on the night of 24 Dec.

26 Dec: Boxing Day – taken from the British tradition; massive retail discounts.

Provincial Holidays

Alberta: Alberta Family Day (third Mon of Feb); Heritage Day (first Mon of Aug); Stampede Parade (half-day in Calgary, first Fri in July).

British Columbia: British Columbia Day (first Mon of Aug).

Quebec: Bank Holiday (Jan 2); National Day (24 June, otherwise known St Jean Baptiste Day, named for the patron saint of French Canada.

Manitoba: Louis Real Day (third Mon of Feb); Civic Holiday (first Mon of Aug).

New Brunswick: New Brunswick Day (first Mon of Aug).

Newfoundland: Celebrated on nearest Mon to St Patrick's Day (17 Mar); St George's Day (23 April); Discovery Day (24 June); Memorial Day (1 July) – Canada Day elsewhere in the country; Orangemen's Day (12 July); Regatta Day/Civic Holiday (fixed by municipal council orders, only in Saint John's).

Northwest Territories: National Aboriginal Day (June 21); Civic Holiday (first Mon of Aug).

Nova Scotia: Natal Day (first Mon of Aug).

Nunavut: Nunavut Day (9 July, but may be changed to 1 April).

Ontario: Family Day (third Mon of Feb); Civic Holiday (first Mon of Aug).

Prince Edward Island: Natal Day (by proclamation, usually on first Mon of Aug).

Saskatchewan: Family Day (third Mon of Feb); Civic Holiday (first Mon of Aug).

Yukon: Heritage Discovery Day (third Mon of Aug).

Regional Climate

Averages are at best just that, and extreme weather can be experienced in many parts of the country. Night-time low temperatures in the winter can plummet and wind chill will make moderate temperatures feel much colder. On the up-side, dry weather in the coldest parts of the country makes freezing temperatures more bearable, whereas humidity exaggerates summer heat – in central Canada the 'humidex' is calculated along with temperatures.

Precipitation rates during winter months almost always fall as snow, except on the west coast. In parts of the country where temperatures remain below freezing for long periods, relatively small amounts of snow can accumulate to what appear to be impressive quantities.

Weather Data for the Main Centres

Calgary
January high: −3.6°C; July high: 23.2°C
Average precipitation including rain and snow: 399mm; snow: 135.4cm
Wet days: 111

Charlottetown
January high: −3.4°C; July high: 23.1°C
Average precipitation including rain and snow: 1,201mm; snow: 338.7cm
Wet days: 177

Edmonton
January high: −8.2°C; July high: 23°C
Average precipitation including rain and snow: 461mm; snow: 129.6cm
Wet days: 123

Fredericton
January high: −4°C; July high: 25.6°C
Average precipitation including rain and snow: 1,331mm; snow: 294.5cm
Wet days: 156

Halifax
January high: −1.5°C; July high: 23.4°C
Average precipitation including rain and snow: 1,474mm; snow: 261.4cm
Wet days: 170

Montreal
January high: −5.8°C; July high: 26.2°C
Average precipitation including rain and snow: 940mm; snow: 214.2 cm
Wet days: 162

Ottawa
January high: −6.3°C; July high: 26.4°C
Average precipitation including rain and snow: 911mm; snow: 221.5cm
Wet days: 159

Regina
January high: −11°C; July high: 26.3°C
Average precipitation including rain and snow: 364mm; snow: 107.4cm
Wet days: 109

Saint John's
January high: −1.7°C; July high: 20.2°C
Average precipitation including rain and snow: 1,482mm; snow: 322.1cm
Wet days: 217

Toronto
January high: −1.3°C; July high: 26.5°C
Average precipitation including rain and snow: 819mm; snow: 135cm
Wet days: 139

Vancouver
January high: 5.7°C; July high: 21.7°C
Average precipitation including rain and snow: 1,167mm; snow: 54.9cm
Wet days: 164

Victoria
January high: 6.5°C; July high: 21.8°C
Average precipitation including rain and snow: 858mm; snow: 46.9cm
Wet days: 153

Whitehorse
January high: −14.4°C; July high: 20.3°C
Average precipitation including rain and snow: 269mm; snow: 145.2cm
Wet days: 122

Winnipeg
January high: −13.2°C; July high: 26.1°C
Average precipitation including rain and snow: 504mm; snow: 114.8cm
Wet days: 119

Yellowknife
January high: −23.9°C; July high: 20.8°C
Average precipitation including rain and snow: 267mm; snow: 143.9cm
Wet days: 118

Source: Environment Canada

Canadian Calling Codes

All telephone numbers in Canada comprise seven digits. In more populated areas the three-digit area code is also required, whereas in other jurisdictions only the seven-digit phone number is required. In small communities all local numbers may share the first three numbers, so, while they must be dialled, people may only quote their last four numbers when giving their phone number – 'my number is 1710'.

Long-distance calls require a '1' at the beginning, and calls to points outside North America begin with 011 + country code. A call to the UK therefore begins with 011-44 (and drops the 'zero' from the local British area code).

Local codes are listed below.

Alberta
403 (Calgary and southern Alberta)
780 (Edmonton and northern Alberta)

British Columbia
250 (British Columbia except Vancouver area)
604 (Vancouver area)
778 (Vancouver area)

Manitoba
204

New Brunswick
506

Newfoundland and Labrador
709

Northwest Territories
867

Nova Scotia
902

Nunavut
867

Ontario
807 (northern Ontario)
705 (central Ontario)
613 (Ottawa and southeastern Ontario)
519 (southwestern Ontario)
416 (central Toronto area)
647, 289, 905 (Greater Toronto area)

Prince Edward Island
902

Quebec
418 (Quebec City and eastern Quebec)
450 (southern Quebec excluding Montreal)
514 (Montreal)
819 (western Quebec)

Saskatchewan
306

Yukon
867

Dictionary of Useful and Technical Terms

English Canadian

The majority of Canadians speak English as their first language and English is the language of business, even in parts of Quebec, therefore British and Irish migrants have little trouble making themselves understood. In the far north and other aboriginal-dominant regions, indigenous languages continue to be used and any effort to learn those idioms will be very well received. The Inuit language that is spoken by a majority in Nunavut even uses its own, phonetic-based alphabet and the language is considered extremely difficult to learn.

In this section there is a list of words and phrases used in English that are specific to Canada. There is also a section geared specifically to French Canadian. For a more discussion of accents and the origin of Canada's languages *see*

'Language', pp.26–30. Note that across Canada there will be regional names and expressions assigned to everything from shoes to drinks.

Clothing

balaclava a one-piece face and neck protector, popular with bank robbers

gloves can be more formal and separate the fingers, but simply are not warm enough in really cold weather

long johns thermal underwear

mittens (mitts) for covering the hands, these are traditionally made of knitted material; the fingers are not separated

sweater jumper, pullover

tank top singlet

track pants tracksuit, jogging or sweat pants

tuque or toque (rhymes with 'spook') the commonly used named for a hat worn in winter and usually made from knitted material; ski hill toques are often colourful and artistic

turtle neck warm shirt or undershirt with a high neck

Items Related to Cold Weather

block heater inserted into a vehicle's engine, the heater should be plugged in, to stop the engine from freezing; you will notice plugs hanging out of the front of automobiles and even public parking lots have sockets; block heaters do not warm the insides of cars

plus 15s or ***plus 10s*** above-ground, enclosed walkways joining buildings; along with tunnels, most major city centres are navigable without facing the elements

winterise to prepare anything (from your garden hose to lakeside cabin) for winter

zamboni a unique machine designed to polish ice for hockey and skating

Food

alcool pure grain alcohol sold in Quebec

all dressed with all the toppings; used for potato chips (crisps), pizza, burgers

back bacon Canadian bacon; sometimes rolled in peameal (like cornmeal, only it's made from peas); more like ham than rasher bacon

beavertail deep-fried wheat pastry, resembling a beaver's tail, which can be finished with sweet or savoury fillings or even used for wrapping hotdogs

Bloody Caesar a Calgary tradition, similar to a Bloody Mary, except it's made with vodka and clamato (clam and tomato) juice instead of plain tomato juice

butter tart a very small (single-serving) pie; they taste like pecan pies without the pecans

double double a coffee with double milk and two sugars; the term was popularised by the doughnut chain Tim Horton's

eggplant aubergine

green pepper capsicum

Kraft dinner, or ***KD*** Kraft macaroni cheese

Nanaimo bar a sweet slice, named after the town of Nanaimo on Vancouver Island in British Columbia; it resembles a brownie but usually contains coconut and is topped with a layer of white butter-cream icing and another of solid chocolate

perogy Ukrainian-Russian pasta-like dough pocket that is stuffed with potato-based fillings and then boiled or fried; commonly eaten with breakfast

rye a grain, and the principal ingredient in Canadian whiskey

screech Newfoundland rum, not a subtle flavour

smoked meat Montreal Jewish speciality, similar to corned beef

tortière a savoury meat pie usually made of pork and seasoned with cloves, popular in Quebec; *tortière* is the traditional Québécois Christmas Eve meal

Units of Money and Other Financial Matters

buck this American term is also used in Canadian vernacular for money: 'Did that really cost a hundred bucks?'

dime 10 cents

loonie 1 dollar coin – received its name from the loon depicted on one side

nickel 5 cents

penny, cent 1 cent

quarter 25 cents

twoonie 2-dollar coin depicting polar bears (the coin could be called a 'moonie' because it's 'the Queen with a bear behind')

ABM automatic banking machines, cashpoints

ATM automatic teller machines, cashpoints

CPP Canada Pension Plan

EI employment insurance, government programme for the unemployed; the programme was formally called unemployment insurance and the term 'UI' or 'UIC' is still sometimes heard

GST goods and services tax, 5 per cent that goes on top of just about every purchase (in addition to the provincial sales taxes); the previous prime minister, Jean Chrétien, got elected partly because he promised to get rid of this tax, but he never did

Interac debit machines used to pay with your bank card, not a credit card

PST provincial sales tax

QPP Quebec Pension Plan

RESP registered education savings plan

RRSP (RSP) registered retirement savings plan

Other Terms

Alberta clipper area of low pressure that forms in winter over the province of Alberta in the lee of the Rocky Mountains

allophone someone whose first language is neither English or French

Anglophone someone who speaks English as a first language

canadarm robotic arm (made in Canada) on the US Space Shuttle

Canuck a Canadian

cell phone mobile telephone

the Charter the Canadian Charter of Rights and Freedoms

Chesterfield couch or sofa

Cowtown nickname for Calgary, Alberta

CPR Canadian Pacific Railway

CSIS (pronounced 'SEE-sis') Canadian Security Intelligence Service

deke to move rapidly or with agility; a hockey term for faking out an opponent

dépanneur a corner or convenience store in Quebec

dick all doing nothing

dipsy-doodle a tactic designed to confuse, evade, or outwit opponents or competitors

drug store chemist; the term pharmacy is also used, in fact the pharmacy is found inside the drug store; true to its name, drug stores also sell cigarettes, sweets (candies) and many other items including, in some cases, electronics

duplex single building divided in half with two sets of inhabitants

eh? the quintessential Canadianism, a little more common in rural areas, but heard throughout as a finish to a sentence

elastic rubber band

First Nations or *aboriginal people* traditionally known as Indians

flyers pamphlets or leaflets used for advertising; mail boxes are often filled with them

for sure definitely

Francophone someone who speaks French as a first language

Genie Awards national film and television awards

ghost car unmarked police car

the Habs nickname for the Montreal Canadiens Hockey Team

hang up the skates to retire

hoser unsophisticated person

housecoat dressing gown, robe, bathrobe

Hogtown Toronto (also the Big T.O.)

Joual a Quebec working-class dialect that's a striking mix of English and French; varies from region to region; sometimes called 'Frenglish'

Juno Awards Canada's national music awards

keener an enthusiastic or very keen individual; usually trying to get into someone's good books

klick or click kilometre or kilometres per hour, for example, the speed limit is 110 klicks

lineup line of people waiting, usually for service; 'there was a really long lineup at the bank'; Canadians sometimes also use the British term 'queue'

Lotus Land nickname for Vancouver, British Columbia

lucked out this means you had good luck

Meech Lake a 1980s failed attempt to bring Quebec into the constitution; still discussed

Métis of mixed aboriginal and European heritage; the term is specific to a series of cultures that have some legal recognition in western Canada

mickey 13 ounces of liquor in a flat, curved bottle, supposed to fit in your pocket and favoured by drunks; **mini-mickey**: 6.5 ounces of alcohol

midnight sun long hours of daylight in the far north during summer

molson muscle the beer- or pot-belly acquired by drinking too much beer

Mountie member of the Royal Canadian Mounted Police

North of 60 either used to describe the High Arctic or a television series of the same name

parkade a public car park, usually with covered parking stalls

pogey (un)employment benefits; 'I'm getting pogey' means, as the British would say, 'I'm on the dole'

RCMP (Mounties) Royal Canadian Mounted Police; rarely seen in their classic red serge outfits, the RCMP are the national police; provincial police services exist in some provinces, whereas in other jurisdictions cities run a local service; the RCMP operates as the primary policing force where a provincial or city service does not exist

reserve, or **rez** a parcel of land allotted for Native Canadians

runners athletic or running shoes

RV or **motor home** caravan; these are larger than in the UK and very popular throughout the continent

scads many or lots

shinney or **shinny** an early form of hockey; now means a pick-up hockey game where people just show up and play; played recreationally all over Canada, on ice skates, inline skates, or in shoes

shit disturber an instigator, particularly one who for no good reason turns stones better left unturned

sixty-pounder a bottle of alcohol containing 66 fluid ounces

Ski-doo snowmobile; the word 'Ski-doo' is the brand name for snowmobiles made by a large Quebecois company called Bombardier (pronounced 'bom-BAR-dee-AY'); in Canada, 'ski-doo' is one of those brand names that have evolved into generic terms

Snowbirds when the snow falls, they fly; retired Canadians who void winter by going south are known as snowbirds, also the élite flying squadron of the Canadian air force are called the Snowbirds

Sovereigntists the term used for separatists in Quebec; rather than outright separation, they want sovereignty (independence)

stogie a cigar; the term 'fag' is not applied to cigarettes

the Rock nickname for the Island of Newfoundland

trash an American word for garbage, sometimes used in Canada; 'rubbish' is rarely heard

VLT video lottery machines, common in many pubs and apparently highly addictive to some people; sometimes referred to as 'vidiot' machines.

French Canadian

Even if you are a French-speaker it may take a little while to become accustomed to the nasal Canadian accent. Fortunately, the French is not all that different from what is spoken in France, with the exception of some very old constructions and unique expressions.

Listening to French Canadians talk, you will quickly notice an inflection that represents a Zed sound (more pronounced in Montreal) as well as the common use of 'le' (rhyming with the English 'the') at the end of sentences. Even in speeches politicians inflect the 'le', in much the same way as English Canadians use 'eh'.

The formal *'vous'* and familiar *'tu'* continue to be used and in a business setting it is always safer to rely on the 'vous'.

These are a few of the most common words and phrases:

bonjour/salut/'allô hello

au revoir/salut/ 'bye' goodbye; most notable, *bonjour* is also used for 'goodbye' in the English sense of the word.

bonsoir/bonne nuit good evening/goodnight

s'il vous plaît? please (this is even used for the familiar 'tu' form)

bienvenue welcome

Je m'excuse Excuse me

pardon excuse me/I am sorry

Je suis désolé(e) I am sorry

Ce n'est pas grave It doesn't matter

OK OK

oui (also 'Ouais', pronounced 'way') yes

non no

rien nothing

Je ne sais pas (J'sais pas) I don't know

Je ne parle pas français/anglais I don't speak French/English

Parlez-vous anglais? Do you speak English?

Aide-moi Help me

Comment ça va/Comment allez-vous? How are you?

One notable difference between the French spoken in France and that of Canada is the replacement of '*est-ce que*', which roughly translates to 'Do?' in English. Although questions such as '*Est-ce que tu parles français?*' (Do you speak French?) are perfectly understood and may be used, you are more likely to hear the more formal French form of '*Parles-tu français?*'. The familiar '*tu*' is also sometimes doubled up: '*Tu aimes-tu mon auto?*' (Do you like my car?).

The dreaded anglicisms or English words that are so resisted in France have also entered the Canadian vernacular, albeit in an entirely different manner. Many English words (often of Canadian or American origin) are simply translated – 'popcorn' becomes '*maïs soufflé*' while alternative words have been kept. An English 'pullover' is a '*pull*' in France, a 'sweater' in English Canada and '*un chandail*' in Quebec.

Despite claims that the French in France has been more overwhelmed by *les anglais*, there are many English words integrated into French Canadian, although their meanings and usage may differ slightly from the English use. Pronunciation is sometimes incorporated into the French Canadian accent, whereas other words are pronounced in an almost mock American manner. These are just a few; the French equivalent is listed in parentheses.

English Words Now Integrated into French Canadian

all dress (garni) used with food in Canada; an 'all dress jacket potato'

C'est correct, all right, ok (d'accord, correct) that's fine? OK

anlway (de toute façon) so..., well..., therefore..., anyway...

bachelier (célibataire) single person, bachelor

bachelor (studio) one-room apartment (bachelor or studio)

balance (reste, différence) the balance in a transaction – a word of French origin

bargainer (marchander) to bargain

canceller (annuler) to cancel

caucus (réunion) caucus, meeting (political)

Cheddar (fromage canadien) Cheddar cheese (clearly from the English source)

cosy (confortable) cosy

dam! (zut!) damn!

date (rendez-vous) in the romantic sense

dîner (déjeuner) lunch

dumb (stupide) dumb or stupid

fair (juste) fair or just

fancy (élégant) elegant, or fancy in Canada

gambler (joueur de casino) gambler, pronounced almost the same way

game (partie, match) match, game

gang (bande de copains) group of friends

gasoline (essence) petrol, gas or gasoline in Canada

A huge number of English and American technical words have been incorporated into French Canada: helmet, bumper, muffler and so on. You may hear both the English or French terms used and both should be understood.

In addition to the many *anglicismes* incorporated into the language, there are other words that are either lost to the French spoken in France, or were born in Canada. One fun older expression, which may still be understood in parts of southern France, is *'avoir mal aux cheveux'* – literally meaning 'to have painful hair', but referring to a hangover.

Other Common French Canadian Words and Phrases

à c't'heure now
à plan full
chum boyfriend
blonde girlfriend
gars guy, bloke
chu (*je suis*) I am
valise trunk (boot)
Wapiti elk in Canada (similar to caribou), the term Wapiti is aboriginal in origin
une pièce used for a dollar

Many swear words (*gros mots*) are born from the Catholic Church. You will frequently hear versions of *'tabernac'* (from the tabernacle), a classic Québécois word that is used much like 'damn' or 'oh no'. There are several others that you will discover with a little effort.

To pursue studies of French Canadian language and culture, there are numerous immersion courses throughout Quebec and in other parts of Canada. Government bursaries for the study of both official programmes are available, usually to full-time students and teachers.

Films

The Canadian film industry is not well known internationally, although it does enjoy a following in France. Nevertheless, many films are developed, shot and produced in Canada. The following is a short list of some successful Canadian films:

Mon Oncle Antoine (1971)
Les Ordres (1974)
The Apprenticeship of Duddy Kravitz (1974)
Le Déclin de l'empire américain (1986)
Jésus de Montréal (1988)
Thirty-two Short Films about Glenn Gould (1994)
Crash (1996)

The Sweet Hereafter (1997)
Atanarjuat (2002)
Les Invasions barbares (2003)
The Saddest Music in the World (2004)
Shake Hands with the Devil: The Journey of Roméo Dallaire (2004)
C.R.A.Z.Y. (2005)
Bon Cop, Bad Cop (2006)

Other recent Canadian movies well worth viewing include the top 10 list from the 2007 Toronto International Film Festival:

L'Âge des ténèbres (Denys Arcand)
Amal (Richie Mehta)
Continental, un film sans fusil (Stéphane Lafleur)
Eastern Promises (David Cronenberg)
Fugitive Pieces (Jeremy Podeswa)
My Winnipeg (Guy Maddin)
A Promise to the Dead: The Exile Journey of Ariel Dorfman (Peter Raymont)
The Tracey Fragments (Bruce McDonald)
Up the Yangtze (Yung Chang)
Young People Fucking (Martin Gero)

Additional films of life in Canada, including social commentaries and mini-series, can be obtained through the CBC website at **www.cbc.ca**.

Further Reading

Writings about Canada are collectively called 'Canadiana' and can be found in bookstores and libraries. Canada boasts a respectable number of writers and a wide variety of academics. The following lists include a few of the better known titles. Regionally, academics at universities across the country are studying their areas and, although Canada as a country is not nearly as old as Britain, its unique history and mix of cultures make for some interesting reading. Canadian academics and particularly historians have the benefit of drawing from various historiography styles: British, French, American and a home-grown fusion.

A small selection of recommended books includes:

Axworthy, Lloyd, *Navigating A New World: Canada's Global Future* (Vintage Canada, 2004). Axworthy was a prominent left-leaning Liberal member of parliament representing a Winnipeg riding. He is now president of the University of Winnipeg.

Baird, Elizabeth, *Canadian Living Cooks: 185 Show-stopping Recipes from Canada's Favourite Cooks* (Random House Canada, 2003).

Barber, Katherine, *Canadian Oxford Dictionary of Current English* (Oxford

University Press, 2005).

Berton, Pierre, *The Last Great Gold Rush: 1896–1869* (Doubleday, 2001). Raised in the Yukon, Berton is one of Canada's best-known popular historians. Many of his 50 works are recommended. He died in 2004.

Boyden, Joseph, *Three Day Road* (Penguin Canada, 2005). A critically acclaimed novel exploring the First Nations' experience during the First World War.

Duncan, Dorothy, *Nothing More Comforting: Canada's Heritage Food* (Dundurn Press, 2003).

Finkel, Alvin, *Social Policy and Practice in Canada: A History* (Wilfred Lauier University Press, 2006). An excellent history of Canada's alarmingly slow development of social programmes and services.

Ferguson, Ian, *How to Be a Canadian: Even if You Are Already One* (2001).

Gougeon, Gilles, *A History of Quebec Nationalism* (James Lorimer & Co., 1994).

Grescoe, Taras, *Sacré Blues: An Unsentimental Journey Through Quebec* (Macfarlane Walter & Ross, 2001).

Hallowell (editor), *Oxford Companion to Canadian History* (Oxford University Press, 2004).

King, Thomas, *Our Story* (Doubleday Canada, 2004).

Kobalenko, Jerry, *The Horizontal Everest, Extreme Journeys on Ellesmere Island* (Soho Press, 2003). An outstanding visit to Canada's north.

Makra, Kevin, *The Internet Job Search in Canada* (2005).

An Essential Guide to Finding a Job Using the Internet (Sentor Media Inc., 2004).

Reed, Kevin, *Aboriginal Peoples* (Oxford University Press, 1998).

Richler, Mordecai, *Oh Canada Oh Quebec* (Penguin Books of Canada Ltd, 1992). Richler, who died in 2001, was one of Canada's literary superstars. Many of his novels are well worth reading and capture life in 20th-century Montreal. His Jewish background features prominently, and his writing is entertaining and irreverent. This particular book is a very political and challenging look at Quebec's history.

Santin, Aldo, *The First Canadians: A Profile of Canada's Native People Today* (James Lorimer and Co., 1995).

Other well-known Canadian authors include:

Atwood, Margaret: *The Handmaid's Tale*

Cohen, Leonard, poet and songwriter: *Suzanne*

Coupland, Douglas: *Generation X*

Laurence, Margaret: *The Diviners*

Mitchell, W.O. : *Who Has Seen the Wind*

Montgomery, Lucy Maud: *Anne of Green Gables*

Mowet, Farley: *Never Cry Wolf*

Ondaatje, Michael: *The English Patient*

Shields, Carole: *The Stone Diaries*

Chronology

10,000–25,000 years ago	First Canadians arrived from Siberia
9,000–10,000 years ago	Clovis culture spread through Canada
AD 1000	The Icelandic Leif Ericsson sails to Vinland (probably Newfoundland)
1497	John Cabot, an Englishman, is the first to lay claim to 'new-found-land'
1534	Jacques Cartier, a Frenchman, sails into the Gulf of St Lawrence and trades with the Mi'kmaq people
16th and 17th centuries	Explorers search for the Northwest Passage to Asia; various settlements are attempted
1608	Samuel de Champlain sails up the St Lawrence and establishes a colony known as 'Quebec', meaning 'narrowing of the river'
1668	The British erect a fort in James Bay and trade with the local Cree
1702–13	During the War of Spanish Succession the French take control of many posts that belonged to the Hudson Bay Company; the 1713 Treaty of Utrecht settles some territorial claims
1755	Governor Lawrence of Nova Scotia expels those who will not swear allegiance to the British king
1759	Fighting between French and British troops in Quebec City
1763	The French cede most of their American holdings at the Treaty of Paris
1774	The Quebec Act is passed by the British Parliament
1783	Peace treaty after American War of Independence
1783	The Northwest Company is formed by Montreal merchants
1793	Alexander Mackenzie crosses the western mountains to reach the Pacific
1793	Captain James Cook sails past Vancouver Island and charts the west coast
1837	Rebellions in Upper and Lower Canada
1867	The Dominion of Canada becomes the first independent country within the Commonwealth
1873	The Mounties are formed
1874	Alexander Graham Bell invents the telephone
By 1914	The population is almost 8 million; there are nine provinces and two territories
1914–18	60,000 Canadians killed during the First World War
1919	Winnipeg General Strike
1929	Stock market crash
1939–45	Many Canadians killed during the Second World War

1950s	Mass immigration
1968–84	Pierre Trudeau governor: transfers constitution from Britain to Canada and enshrines bilingualism and multiculturalism as national institutions
1976	Olympic Games in Montreal; separatist Parti Quebecois elected in Quebec
1988	Winter Olympics in Calgary
1990s	Free Trade Agreement (FTA) signed with USA, followed by NAFTA (North American Free Trade Agreement) which includes Mexico (a broader Free Trade of the Americas still pending)
1993	Liberals under Jean Chrétien take power from the Tories and win three straight elections; Montreal Canadiens are the last Canadian team to win the Stanley Cup (a majority of players on all teams in the league remain Canadian)
1995	Quebec holds second referendum on separation – the 'No' (pro-Canada) side win with 50.4 per cent – many 'no' ballots are also not accepted
2001	The events of Sept 11 result in a limit on trade and border movements to the USA; lower interest rate encourages an already booming housing market; Canadian troops join NATO in Afghanistan
2005	Hung parliament, with Liberal government entangled in a financial scandal
2006	Conservatives, led by Stephen Harper, form a minority government
2007	Canadian dollar reaches parity with the US currency for the first time in decades

Useful Addresses

Embassies and Consulates

Canadian High Commission
Trafalgar Square, Consular and Passport Section,
Canada House, London SW1Y 5BJ
t (020) 7258 6600/7258 6356, **f** (020) 7258 6533
ldn.consular@international.gc.ca
Open Mon–Fri 9–3 (except holidays).
For general passport enquiries/application forms.

Canadian High Commission: Immigration Division
38 Grosvenor Street, London W1K 4AA
Open Mon–Fri 8–11.
For immigration enquiries.
www.cic.gc.ca

Contacting the Immigration Division is best on-line. This is a lengthy process, but the division will not accept phone calls, and all correspondence must be in English or French.

Canadian Embassy in Ireland
7–8 Wilton Terrace, Dublin 2, Ireland
t (01234) 4000, **f** (01) 234 4001
dubln@international.gc.ca

Quebec
The government of Quebec selects its own immigrants in co-operation with the government of Canada. If you wish to settle in Quebec, you must contact the nearest office of the **Québec Immigration Service**. You can get information at **www.immq.gouv.qc.ca** or through **www.canada.org.uk/visa-info**.

Honorary Consulates
Honorary Consuls provide notarial services and emergency assistance, as well as with passport application forms. They do not issue passports or any kind of immigration visas.

Birmingham Consulate of Canada
55 Colmore Row, Birmingham B3 2AS
t (012) 1236 6474, **f** (012) 1214 1099

Belfast Consulate of Canada
Unit 3, Ormeau Business Park
8 Cromac Avenue, Belfast
t/f (0208) 9127 2060

Edinburgh Consulate of Canada
50 Lothian Road, Festival Square, Burness, Edinburgh, EG3 9WJ
t (013) 1473 6320, **f** (013) 1473 6321

Cardiff Consulate of Canada
c/o Airlodge, Port Road, Rhoose, Vale of Glamorgan CF62 3BT
t (014) 4671 9172, **f** (014) 4671 0856

For British and Irish consulates and high commissions in Canada, *see* p.150.

Canadian Banks in the UK
Note: These banks primarily offer business and offshore services and are not directly linked to branches in Canada. Opening an account in Canada is easy and delays in transferring money from the UK are generally generated by British banks. When moving to Canada, **do not** sever ties with your UK bank(s) as, once residency has been severed, it is almost impossible to open an account in Britain.

Bank of Montreal
95 Queen Victoria Street, London EC4V 4H
t (020) 7236 1010, **f** (020) 7664 8161

Bank of Nova Scotia
Scotia House, 33 Finsbury Square, London EC2A 1BB,
t (020) 7638 5644, **f** (020) 7638 8488

Royal Bank of Canada
71 Queen Victoria St, London EC4V 4DE
t (020) 7489 1188, **f** (020) 7329 6144

Immigration and Legal Services

Blake Lapthorn Tarlo Lyons
t (020) 7814 6932
info@bllaw.co.uk, www.bllaw.co.uk

Invest You Can (Immigration and Legal Matters)
3BC Macnaghten Road, Bitterne Park, Southampton, Hampshire SO18 1GL
t (02380) 679070 or **t** 07779 320413
info@investyoucan.com

Immigration Unit
UK **t** 0845 260 6030, from abroad **t** + 44 (0)1784 497 690
info@immigrationunit.com, www.immigrationunit.com

International Removal Companies

British Association of Removers
Tangent House, 62 Exchange Road, Watford, Hertfordshire WD18 0TG
t (01923) 699480
www.removers.org.uk

Anglo Pacific
Units 1 & 2, Bush Industrial Estate, Standard Road, Acton, London NW10 6DF
t 0800 633 5445
info@anglopacific.co.uk, www.anglopacific.co.uk
Also offices in Manchester and Glasgow.

Crown Worldwide Ltd.
19 Stonefield Way, South Ruislip, Middlesex HA4 0BJ
t (020) 8839 8000
london@crownrelo.com, www.crownrelo.com
Also has offices in Birmingham, Glasgow, Leeds, Aberdeen and in Ireland.

Dolphin Movers Ltd.
2 Haslemere Business Centre, Lincoln Way, Enfield, Middlesex EN1 1TE
t 0800 032 9777 (freephone), **t** (020) 8804 7700
sales@dolphinmovers.com, **www.dolphinmovers.com**

Excess International Removals
4 Hannah Close, Great Central Way, London NW10 0UX
t (020) 8324 2000
sales@excess-baggage.com, **www.excess-baggage.com**
Also has offices at airports and railway stations countrywide.

Property Services

Invest You Can (Canadian Property Specialist)
3BC Macnaghten Road, Bitterne Park, Southampton, Hampshire SO18 1GL
t (02380) 679070 or **t** 07779 320413
info@investyoucan.com, **http://investyoucan.com**

Horizon Properties
www.horizonproperties.ca
Free service that matches you with a Canadian estate agent.

Index

Page references to maps are in *italics*.